BUDDHIST AND JAIN PERIOD

BUDDHIST AND JAIN PERIOD

By

Suraj Vashishth

2008

CYBER TECH PUBLICATIONS
4264/3, Ansari Road, Daryaganj, New Delhi-110002 (India)
Ph.: 011-23244078. Fax: 011-23280028
E-Mail: cyberpublicationsdelhi@yahoo.com

BUDDHIST AND JAIN PERIOD

Suraj Vashishth

First Edition 2008

Published by :

G.S. Rawat for **Cyber Tech Publications**
4264/3, Ansari Road, Daryaganj, New Delhi-110002 (India)
Ph.: 011-23244078. Fax: 011-23280028
E-Mail: cyberpublicationsdelhi@yahoo.com

Printed at : **Amit Enterprises**, Maujpur, Delhi, (9810878184)

Preface

The culture of India was moulded throughout various eras of history, all the while absorbing customs, traditions, and ideas from both invaders and immigrants. Many cultural practices, languages, customs, and monuments are examples of this co-mingling over centuries. India was the birth place of religious systems such as Hinduism, Jainism, Buddhism, and Sikhism, each of which have had a strong influence not only over India but also over the rest of the world. Indian philosophy throughout the ages has had a tremendous impact on world thought, especially in the east. Various theistic schools of philosophy, such as the many schools of Buddhism and Jainism, have had huge influences, but also, India produced some of the longest and most influential secular traditions of logic, rationalism, science, mathematics, materialism, atheism, agnosticism, etc. Many of the complex scientific and mathematical concepts such as the idea of zero, found their way to Europe via Arab intermediaries. The most famous school of Indian atheism, is Charvaka, considered by some to be the oldest materialistic school of thought in the world, composed around the same time as the Hindu Upanishads, as well as the philosophy of Buddhism and Jainism.

Every dharmic religion originated in India, including Hinduism, Buddhism, Sikhism, Jainism and other schools of language. Today, Hinduism and Buddhism are the world's third and fourth largest religions respectively, with a collective 1.4 billion followers, despite being free of any evangelistic traditions. Sikhism,Buddhism and Jainism are systems that are strong and influential not only in India but across the world.

The undersigned is confident enough that this work of him would be beneficial to all students and readers. This book presents cultural origin and development of both Jainism and Buddhism in the world.

—Author

Contents

1

Introduction

EARLY MEDIEVAL INDIA

Many historians, Indian and British, have tended to look at South Asian history from the point of view of the north, and defined the medieval period mainly in terms of the Muslim conquests and Islamic institutions. These did not play a major role, however, until the 13th century. Until the last 25 years, those that bothered to talk about the previous seven hundred years between the fall of the Gupta Emperors and 1200 A.D. saw these centuries as a sort of preparation for the Islamic governments which followed. So these years of the early medieval period have been characterized as witnessing the degradation of the culture of the classical Gupta period and its political order. This northern-centered view dismisses the parts of the subcontinent in the south where Islamic states never established stable governments. But this view was oriented in the end more toward justifying or condemning British Rule than it was in exploring the actual historical experience of South Asia between 500 A.D. and 1200 A.D.

The focus here is on two major characteristics of the early medieval period, the structure and scale of the political forms which evolved and the gradual development of regional cultures and economies.

Some authors divide the subcontinent up into four major regions, or megaregions: south, east, central and north India.

Medievalist Burton Stein has pointed to the existence of six major regions, the south, the west (containing Maharashtra and Gujarat), the east, the north, the central and the northwest (containing Punjab, Sind, and Baluchistan). These divisions are relevant toStein's discussion of the kinds of states which appeared between 500 AD and 1700. He figured that about 20 kingdoms succeeded in extending their sovereignty beyond a single megaregion, if we count the megaregions as six in number. Two thirds of these were ruled by Hindu dynasties, but the most durable of these imperial states was the Muslim Mughal empire, from about the middle of Akbar's reign, around 1580, to the reign of Muhammad Shah in 1730. Dominance in more than one region by almost all of these states was usually the accomplishment of a single ruler, a great conquering warrior like Pulakesin II of the seventh century Chalukyan kingdom or the mid-tenth century Krisna II of the Rashtrakutas, both of the Deccan.

Besides these20 kingdoms which for a time at least spanned two or more large regions, there were numerous others the scale of whose authority was far more limited, but whose duration could nevertheless be considerable. From inscriptions and literary sources we get information on over 40 royal dynasties who endured for a period in the megaregions. The chronicles of temples, royal genealogical texts, and oral traditions tell of both wealthy kings and local chiefs who attempted to achieve royal status.

The existence of so many rulers tells us that the early medieval period witnessed the emergence of new state forms, compared to the late Vedic and classical periods. There is, however, little agreement among historians about the character of these states and their form. However, the kingdom of Harsha is often taken as the typical state when scholars talk of Indian feudalism.

Harsha ruled a realm nearly as large as the Gupta kingdom during the first half of the seventh century. His capital was Kanauj, modern Kanpur, in the fertile plain between the Ganges and the Yamuna rivers, the doab. The capital had originally been at the old Mauryan capital of Patalipurtra in the eastern Gangetic basin. Here there was rich agricultural potential and the revenues from trade which entered the Gangetic Plain at this point. However, with a shift to the west came improved defence of the entire plain from the Hun tribesmen who had preyed upon the Guptas.

A set of inscribed copper-plates of 632 AD provides insight into the structure of Harsha's state. This inscription recorded a gift of land to two Brahmins by a military officer in Harsha's service.. Among the protectors of the gift were a set of political personnages in whose hands major elements of state power appeared to be vested. Some were 'great neighbors' of King Harsha, his mahasamantas. Others were 'great kings' (maharajas) who acknowlegded Harsha's overlordship. Still others served the chakravartin, as he styled himself, in various capacities, including as soldiers. Lowest among the guarantors of permanence of the gift were the local community, the 'janapada', where the gifted lands were located.

Donations to Brahmins, Buddhists and Jainas before the time of Harsha had usually come from a royal prince or a provincial governor. In these copper-plates, however, the first of the dignitaries to be mentioned was the Mahasamanta who ruled a territory adjoining the core tract of the king around Kanauj. This, even though the donor of the land was a military servant of Harsha and the executor of the grant was an accountant in the king's service. Mahasamantas, or as they often also called themselves, mahasamantaraja, were independent rulers of realms near the core tracts of an overlord and might have paid tribute to the latter as well as providing military service. In most cases they were territorial magnates in their own rights, either by inheritance or conquest. Among them would also have been some who served kings like Harsha and were given lands to support their official duties in a manner similar to a feudal grant in Europe.

Titles and land grants were the means that higher lords expressed ties to lesser rulers in a massing of followerships. The great kingships of early medieval India were constituted by such followings. Rulers of this time spoke of their samantachakra, their circle of subordinates: the large the circle, the greater the lord. A lord gained a high royal rank with a large following of minor rulers who served him in some fashion and honored him in political ritual. Both superior and inferior lords enhanced their security by such arrangements. Whether Harsha's kingdom was actually less centralized than the Guptas is uncertain, but the pattern of political agreements was different.

What is clearly different between the polity of Harsha and that of the Guptas is that the Guptas had few formidable opponents within northern India and, until quite late in the dynasty, not very formidable enemies without. The contrast with Harsha could not have been greater. He was humbled by the Chalukyan king Pulakeshin II when he sought to extend his authority southward into the Deccan. Harsha's successor was immediately crushed by the king of Bengal. This opened an era of incessant conflict covering several centuries and centering on Kanauj and Harsha's rich patrimony there. During that time warlords from every direction--from Bengal, from the Deccan, from Rajasthan in the west and from Kashmir in the north--strove to hold Kanauj. Central Asian Muslims finally ended their conflicts by imposing their rule over the whole of the Gangetic region.

Elsewhere in India the centralization of the Mauryan and Gupta regimes is wholly absent. There is no question but that the states in Deccan and the south did not have administrations as describe in the arthasastra. First notice of these states came in Ashoka's edict speaking of the kingdoms to which he sent Buddhist missionaries. Here the kings of the Cholas and the Pandyans in the far south are mentioned, along with kings of Syra, Macedonia, Epirus on the Ionian coast and Cyrene in north Africa. By the early centuries of the first millenium, next to the ancient Cholas and Pandyas were the Chera kings of the south-west coast of Kerala, the Satavahanas over the entire Deccan plateau, and the Chedi rulers of Kalinga on the north-east coast of modern Orissa. Some of the minor ruling houses of the fourth century were to attain very considerably greater sovereignty by 500 AD when Guptas still ruled their core Gangetic territory: Pallava and Kadamba kings ruled over eastern and western Deccan tracts, Vakatakas over the central and northern Deccan and a set of small kingdoms were found along the Orissan coast: eastern Gangas, Nalas, Mahakantaras. By the early seventh century, when Harsha's kingdom flourished in the central Ganges, the far south had come under Pallava kings of Kanchipuram and much of the central and eastern Deccan was under the Chalukyas of Badami, Pulakesin's line.

Where did these peninsular kingdoms come from? We have mentioned the impact of the Mauryan Empire on state formation--here we will elaborate on that.

The earliest peninsular kingdoms date from around the turn of the present era and appear to contain some Mauryan institutions which had emerged in two peripheral parts of Ashoka's realm. A king Kharavela established an extensive state centered on Kalinga.

This you may remember as the area which Ashoka had brought into his empire with a military campaign that was so bloody that he announced that he would renounce violence. Kharavela was a Jain and though he should accordingly, it seems, have adopted the non-violence principle of that faith (ahimsa), he proved to be a masterful soldier. His conquests to the north and south brought him enormous wealth. Trade also added to the wealth of his state, whose coast was mentioned by Pliny the Elder, a Roman writer, in his work Natural History.

Evidence suggests, in fact, that Buddhist and Jaina monasteries consituted nodal points on a far-flung trade system linking coastal Kalinga to the interior. Kharavela had no successor, so that kingdom ceased with his death, but further south the Satavahana kingdom sprawled across the whole of the peninsula, connecting the interior centres of trade and metal production (which had emerged during the period of Ashoka) with both trade coasts. The Saravahanas proved a longer-lived kingdom owing partly to a series of able rulers and also to the offer of more political scope to local magnates than seemed available under the Mauryas, who had appointed governors to these distant places. Trade between both of the coasts of the realm remained important according to the first century writings of the Greco-Egyptian geographer Ptolemy. And, as in the case of Kalinga earlier, Buddhist and Jaina monastic establishments were supported by royal endowments even though its rulers were Hindu. These attracted crowds of pilgrim-consumers making these institutions nodes in an extensive trade network. Trade, then, was an important basis of penninsula kingdoms and that in close association with Jaina and Buddhist institutions.

These enjoyed high prestige and prominent positions in many parts of India during the early centuries of the first millenium, but no where so much as in the Pala kingdom of Bengal during the ninth century. Hinduism had experience a comeback and further development in the emerging centers of regional culture in south India, in the Deccan and in many parts of northern India, but not in Bengal. Its Pala kings gave massive support to Buddhists of the Mahayana sect, giving it the flavor of the Tantric tradition of Bengali religious practice. From Bengal this variant was carried by missionaries to Tibet where it shaped the Buddhism there. The Bengali city Nalanda was the major centre of Buddhist learning in the eastern Gangetic region, and its educative functions were supported by income from hundreds of villages granted by Pala rulers. Buddhist scholars from South-east Asia were drawn there for instruction in Mahayana doctrines and practices. Nalanda and the contemporary center of high learning at Taxila, on the opposite side of the subcontinent, trained many of the monks that served Buddhist institutions in and beyond India. Thus, these monastaries along with Jain monastaries, were involved in state and community formation and the major commercial develoopments that were taking place in the last half of the first millenium AD. The repressions of Jains and Buddhists in the early medieval period may have resulted partly from the deep involvement of both sects in secular activities. By 1000 AD both sects had been rendered marginal by the Hindu sects which were expanding in the new regional cultures of the subcontinent.

As mentioned earlier, a major characteristic of the early medieval period was the development of regional societies. The regional kingdoms had fluid boundaries. They were polities defined less by administration and alliance than by language, sectarian affiliations and temples. Within the limited regions defined by the distribution of any king's shifting suzerainty, new political, linguistic and literary and social histories took a shape that remain recognizable even in contemporary modern India. Religion was at the heart of this regionalizing process: gods, temples, inspired poets and philosophers. Expanding trade may have set off political processes with new patterns of competition, but religious doctrinal and institutional developments affected patterns of state formation and the political institutions which emerged.

Buddhism and Jainism were displaced from their towering positions after Mauryan times with considerable difficulty in some places. Only with the Islamic conquests of the 12th century, when Muslims destroyed many of their sacred places, were Buddhists in Bengal overwhelmed, as Bengalis either converted to Islam or were recruited to the worship of the Hindu god, Vishnu.

More characteristic in some ways was the experience of the Tamil Country, which proved the model for the southern penninsula. It was the Tamil variant of Hindu culture which spread as well to South-east Asia.

Religious change inevitably merged in a variety of ways with both linguistic and political development: all shaped the regionalisation process. Driving the Tamil cultural process was a deadly struggle between a new sort of Hindu worship and the religious hegemony of Buddhists and Jains, their doctrines, and the political support they had from some rulers of TAmils around the sixth century. Little is known about these kings.

We have mostly hostile commentators who describe them as 'evil', but they may have been hill chiefs that extended political control over the plains of Tamil Country and patronized Buddhist and Jain institutions and teachers. Even when these so-called 'usurpers' were driven off by kings such as the Pallavas, the latter followed and supported Jainism until persuaded otherwise by teachers of a new devotional faith. The Pallava Mahendravarman (d. 630 AD) renounced his Jain affiliation and became a worshipper of Shiva, turning against and prosecuting Jains. Other Tamil rulers did the same then and later as the Shiva cult armed itself with a power theology to compete against that of Buddhist and Jains.

A major formulator of that Hindu theology was a Brahmin named Shankara (788-820 AD), who combined philosophical thinking with impressive administrative skill. To defeat the Jains and Buddhists and to brand them as heterodoxies, Shankara returned to the ancient Upanishads from which the Buddhist doctrines had evolved. Shankara offered newe explanations of salvation and of knowledge equal to those of the powerful non-Hindu sects of his time. Besides incorporating and surpassing Buddhism's doctrines, Shankara copied their institutions by establishing monastaries in many places. Four which were famous as missionary centres became especially important and their leaders became known as Shankaracharyas.

Thus, Shankara's influence was not wholly intellectual. In addition to incorporating Buddhist and Jain models for faith and organization, he also incorporated popular worship of lord Shiva, particularly songs of praise. These hymns of devotion-of overwhelming love for Shiva or Visnu-became the foundation for the new and popular cult of Hinduism that has endured until the present throughout India. Called bhakti, this form of religious devotionalism began in Tamil country during the sixth century. There had been earlier forms of devotionalism, in particular that found in the Bhagavadgita, devotional poetry to the god Krishna. This had been composed abourt the first century AD and was incorporated into the Mahabharatha about a century prior to Shankara.

Further developments of bhakti religion among Tamils were the work of poet devotees and other theologians. Between the sixth and tenth century 63 Shiva and 12 Vishnu-worshipping poets created a large corpus of Tamil devotional songs and all are revered as saints by Tamils. Theological works of doctrines for worship of both Siva and and Vishnu followed shortly as Brahmins took advantage of the intellectual base which Shankara had provided. This work protected Brahminical leadership role in religious affairs.

Here are examples of some bhakti devotional songs from this period in the Tamil Country. By the poet Nammalvar, referring to Vishnu in his incarnation as Krishna as a mischievous child:

For his devoted servants

he's easy to reach,

but for everyone else

he's a mysterious sage:

our elusive lord,

who kindled passion in the goddess born from a lotus,

was caught in the act

stealing butter from the churn.
How could he bear his shame
when they bound his waist
and tied him fast to a mortar?

A poem to Shiva by Shaivite Manikkavacakar:

Dog that I am,
I turned all my thoughts to you,
I filled my eyes with the image
of your feet, bright as flowers
and bowed before them,
I surrendered my voice to your bell-like words,
then you came to me,
and all my five senses rejoiced,
O wonder-worker who comes inside of me
and rule me,
great ocean of nectar,
lord tall as the mountains
with body bright as a red-lotus forest,
you gave yourself
to this lonely man
who has no place in this world
or in any other.

Here is a song to Shiva by the woman, Karaikkal Ammaiyar:

She has shriveled breasts
and bulging veins,
in place of white teeth
empty cavitires gape.
With ruddy hair on her belly,

a pair of fangs, knobby andles and long shins

the demon-woman wails at the desolate cremation ground

where our lord

whose hanging matted hair

blows in all eight directions,

dances among the flames

and refeshes his limbs.

His home is Alankatu.

This popular religious development spurred the development of first Tamil and then other languages between 1000 and 1300 AD. In the 12th century bhakti hymns were composed in Bengal by the saint Jayadev, and in Mathura by Nimbarka. The latter was a south Indian Brahmin whose devotion of the god Krishna led to a missionary call that helped to make Mathura the center of the Krishna cult. Literary works along with such technical aids as grammars and dictionaries could be found in Marathi, Bengali, and several other languages. Two other literary projects were expecially important besides the bhakti songs. One genre preserved or invented temple myths about the gods sheltered in temples, gods who were the objects of bhakti songs and devotional theology. Temples gave institutional focus to this reformed Hinduism. The other stimulous to the literature of the early medeival age were chronicles of ruling families of the period.

Temples and kings were decisive shapers of regional cultures; both institutions had the further effect of stimulating urbanization. Looking to Tamil Country for examples, we find that the Shiva temples of the sacred places of Chidambaram and Madurai became the chapel shrines of the Chola and Pandya kings respectively. Both ruling families lavished treasure for adorning the dieties and attracted a large permanent population of priests at each temples and throngs of pilgrims whose needs created the foundations for substantial urban centres. We know this from documents inscribed on the stone basements and walls of both temples and from the chronicles (mahatmya) praising the god in each. These inscriptions show how each diety was transformed from being a local protecting divinity by stories which assimilated them to Shiva legends found in Sanskrit puranas or earlier literature.

This process is sometimes called Sanskritization and illustrates one way the values and symbols of the Gangetic Plain spread throughout the subcontinent. Former territorial spirits were redefined to be great gods with cosmic powers. At the same time as Sanskritization was going on, however, royalization was also taking place. Chiefs who wanted the power and status of kings found that one way to legitimize their claims as chakravartins was to transform their guardian divinities into Shiva or Vishnu, deities worthy of the adoration and devotion of would-be emperors.

It is important to point out that Shiva and Vishnu were seen also as kings, as ruling gods. The human king in a region ruled on their behalf. As Kulke and Rothermund relate, the divine gods held court surrounded in their temples by sub-regional gods. These were the family gods of the human king's samantas. The sub-regional gods again rallied the village gods around them during festivals, just as headmen were occasionally invited to attend the court of a prince. The legitimacy of a human ruler was enhanced in this way. The more "royal" the cult of the territorial god, the more legitimate the claim of a king to rule that territory on behalf of the god. The bhakti cults contributed to this devotion to gods and kings in medieval India.

Temples played a major role in royal politics not only because the ruling aspect of the diety was emphasised, but because of the nature of temple ritual. Temple administrators, acting for the god, honored the men and women who endowed worships at a temple, giving gifts of land, produce or jewels.

The greater the gift, the greater the honor which was given/ shown as part of the ritual of worship.

The major texts outlining the ritual of temple worship are called the Agamas, the oldest of which were written in Sanskrit between the 3th and 7th centuries. Worship, called puja, was to be performed three to six times a day. It was done daily, but there were special pujas for special occasions and for the expiation of sins to aleviate a great problem. These rites were rites of adoration of the diety during which food was offered to him or her. Arccanai were rituals done just for the beneit of the worshipper. Puja was costly, involving washing the icon in special substances like milk and clarified butter, giving food, providing dancing to entertain the diety, dressing the icon in flowers, cloth and jewels, offering incense and making a sacrifice. The honors could be costly as well, ranging from giving a donor the food and water left over from the puja to the silk turban worn by the diety when he went in procession.

Not just kings, but all donors received honors in the court of the god. Thus they came to share the god's sovereignty in the same way as did those men who took part in rituals organized in the courts of human kings. Donors competed for these honors in temples, as they did for honors in the courts of princes. Thus we can see how the expansion of temple worship implied also the expansion of royal values, or royal ideologies.

In the early medieval times, the kings' temples were also palaces where royal business was conducted and royal ritual enacted. The word for temple in Tamil, for example, also means palace. Royal capitals thus became or were temple-centers. Many of these capitals became the major temples of the time. Each was not only a sacred place for the royal deity, but also the place where the kings lived. Both god and king attracted subjects and devotees in large number. The care of both kinds of pilgrims and the objects of their adoration, human and divine, made each capital city an economic centre as well. To that spur to urbanization was added the imitations of the subordinates of kings, those magnates to whom the title samanta applied, who maintained smaller courts in the scores of kingdoms of the early medieval age. During this time, then another of India's historic urban phases took place, the third urbanization, after the first of the Indus Valley and the second of the Gangetic Plain in pre-Mauryan times.

Rich and powerful associations of urban-based corporate trade bodies in south India conducted their commerce over the whole of the peninsula and beyond to South-east Asia. The most famous of them took its name from a capital of one of the earliest of the medieval kingdoms, the Chalukyas. During the heyday of their rule over the Deccan in the seventh and eighth centuries Chalukyan kings had capitals at several places in Karnataka, including Ayyavole (modern Aihole). Taking as their name 'the 500 svamis (lords) of Ayyavole' in hundreds of stone inscriptions, partly in Sanskrit, partly in one of the southern languages, these prestigious traveling traders flourished from the ninth to the fourteenth centuries. Their inscriptions dot the entire southern peninsula, tracing an inter-regional and international trade nexus of merchants. These trade groups provided one of the conduits for translating Dravidian culture from India to South-east Asia, a spill-over and extension beyond the subcontinent of early medieval urbanization.

That the formation of cultures and states in South-east Asia was deeply influenced by India has long been recognized. Different theories give founding roles to the conquests of Indian warriors or to missionary activities of Brahmin scholars or to the penetration of Indian merchants. Each of these explanations can be supported by some evidence, but the most likely major shaper of contact between southeastern India and south-eastern Asia were the efforts of South-east Asian rulers. They discovered in India the means for creating great kingships of their own, as a result of contacts with

Indian soldiers, merchants and Brahmins. The major source of this Indian modelling was Tamil country, along with others from south-eastern India. There are several indications of this. The script adopted for the earliest of inscriptions in insular and peninsular south-east Asia was the sort that prevailed in Pallava inscriptions. The sculptural tradition of south-east Asian Buddhists was adopted from Amaravati in coastal Andhra during the fifth century AD. The temple architecture in Java and Cambodia was drawn from Pallava and Chola prototypes. Later south-east Asians took models of excellence from north-east India, during trips to Nalanda. South-east Asian monks visiting Bengal induced Bengali Buddhists, like the monk Kumara Ghose, to travel to the courts of South-east Asian kings.

Not all of the culture contact between south and south-east Asia was peaceful. The Chola king Rajendra claims in some of his inscriptions to have made conquests in the Malayan peninsula. Some historians have suggested that he was attempting to establish commercial dominance. The later introduction of Islam into Malaya, Java and Sumatra came also from south-east India.

Muslims were present in India from the time of the founding of Islam. India's west coast knew Muslims and others from western Asia as part of the commercial expansion of the early medieval period. Arab and Jewish merchants not only journeyed along this coast on the Arabian Sea, but some were granted special protection for their religions and were even freed of tax obligations. This is known from inscriptions such a one of the eighth century on copper-plates granted to the Jewish merchant-elder Joseph Rabin, at the port of Cochin. A small Jewish community continues still to live there. At about the same time another sort of Muslim presence is recorded in the form of an Arab army which conquered Sind, the ancient heartland of the Indus cities, and parts of Punjab to the east. India's Islamic period might have begun at this early time rather that in 1200 AD, except for the resistence to Arab invaders by the various kings of Kanauj such as Yasovaram around 736 and later Rajput chiefs and kings like the Gujara-Pratiharas who held Kanuauj and most of northern India until around 950 AD. Not long after that however, in the year 1000 AD, incursions began from other Muslim fighters who were not Arabs but steppe-fighters from Central Asia.

Looking b.-k over the period 500 to 1200 we are able to see only dimly the heritage of the Gupta golden age. The early medieval period was a distinct departure in many ways and it was the pattern for future development. The regionalization of culture, of religion and of politics was the critically significant process of the early medieval age. This involved two sorts of subordinate processes. One was the extension and transformation of Sanskritic forms dating from Gupta times. Many forms, however, were adapted to local values and were brought into localized culture through modification.

Simultaneously as well, local and even folk cultural elements were given Sankritic meanings. An instance of this was the 'marriage' of the protecting goddess Minakshi at Madurai in Tamil Country to Shiva. She was in a sense turned into Siva's Sanskritic wife Parvati in a temple ritual sponsored by the Pandyan kings.

This sort of synthesizing of political, religious and cultural elements was a central feature of the regional process and assured that whatever unity is assumed about the classical Gupta age was forever dissolved in later times. As to which of the components of the regionalizing processes may have been the more important, or determining--political or religious or cultural--that is very difficult to decide.

One can say that the ambition of local chiefs to become kings gave a boost to the royalisation of the gods and construction of temples. But if a powerful desire to worship the gods had not existed--in the bhakti movement--poeple would not have attended temple worship. We can say, too, that expanded trade and Jain and Buddhist religious activities during and after the Mauryan period gave impulses to state formation. Taxing trade gave chiefs and kings extra income.

Ambitious chiefs tried to legitimize their enlarged claims through their utilization of Jain, Buddhist, and Hindu ritual. This utilization became a process of regionalisation in that it was necessary tc mix northern symbols of divinity with local ones, since the gods of the Hindu pantheon were distant from the experience of ordinary people.

At the same time, Buddhist values supported impulses among Hindus of devotion toward dieties who were brought into the everyday life of ordinary people.

The north Indian Shiva and Vishnu were joined by a relative recent addition to the Sanskritic pantheon, Krishna, and all three became the object of devotion of people who were part of the culture of the immanence of the divine. Influence from the indigenous culture of South Asia, the pre-Vedic culture, contributed to the religious change which saw the great gods inhabiting stone and metal idols in temples, making them more accessible. The worship of these idols through song and myth contributed to the popularity of literature in regional languages and to the growth of regional languages. The association of royal establishments with these temples enhanced the status of both gods and human rulers.

This period of political and cultural creativity coincided with the rapid development of commodity production, the manufacturing by hand of goods which made India's reputation in these early times as a land of fabulous wealth and elegance. This reputation attracted people to the subcontinent, feeding further the vitality of commerce within and beyond South Asia.

It is often observed that Jain and Buddhist ideologies lingered so long in India because they provided a moral coloration to the practical values of merchants and moneyed men. They may also have provided an institutional framework that linked Buddhist and Jain monasteries with the high commerce of the age.

Hindu temples would eventually assume that role. Another aspect of the political and cultural development of the age was the widespread acceptance of caste as a way to incorporate disparate groups into the new states and the new links between urbanization, commerce and manufacturing. Elites in areas of fertile agriculture patronized Brahmin families, granting them rich villages and lands, in return for priestly services which would legitimize the elite, landed status.

Brahmins were not only necessary to would-be kings over expanded domains; they were also interesting to the lords of villages as a way of strengthening their authority over the low status laborers who worked their rice fields. In dry land areas, where hunters and pastoralist and dry land agriculturalists held sway, Brahminical influence was not so powerful and caste had a milder impact on social formations.

Though Buddhist and Jain institutions were ultimately made marginal by first, devotional Hinduism and then by iconoclastic Islam, much in their ideologies and many of their institutions enjoyed a long life in parts of the subcontinent--as Buddhism did in Bengal and Jainism in Karnataka. The heritage of their principles lived on the reformed Hinduism of Shankara's teachings. But more impressively, Buddhism experienced a full rebirth outside of India--in Tibet and China and in South-east Asia--as a result of the work of missionaries from India, as well as the interest of travelers at the Buddhist universities at Takshisilla and Nalanda.

States and their formation in this era remains a problem because of differences among historians about whether the pre-Islamic era was, like that of Europe, feudal. How are these monarchies to be characterized? There is wide spread agreement now that none of these monarchies were centralized. There is also some agreement among historians that the samanta was an important identifying institution of politics. Samantas are first known in the fifth century AD Gupta kingdom of Samudragupta. Here they were military, possibly tribute-paying subordinates who, nevertheless, were also independent rulers of tracts adjoining the often modest core realm of a 'world-conquoring' chakravartin. Later the same term was extended to include military servants of kings who attained a high degree of independence on lands granted for their services, hence a kind of feudalization.

If the exact characterization of the state is elusive, there are other aspects of early medieval politics about which there is more certainty. One has to do with the extent and importance of urbanizatioin. This was another of the intensive urban phases in India's development. And it gives reason to be sceptical of speaking about an Indian feudalism. Nowhere is this clearer than in the way that the city of Kanauj in the western Gangetic plain was the focus of north Indian politics for several centuries during which competing conquerors from the north, south, east and west strove to seize and hold it, because the city had become the emblem of the chakravartin.

But, all over the subcontinent other cities were created as the centres of other lordships. We have evidence in, among other sources, impressive and large ruins. The study of these remains has made historical archaeology a major intellectual enterprise in modern India.

The pronounced urban character of the early medieval age--produced by a combination of religious and political causes--accounts in part for the attraction of India as a permanent homeland for the Turkic steppe fighters. Cities could be dominated so as to provide the means to sustain the new institutions of Islam and a new elite of Muslim fighters and rulers.

Of the new medieval epoch that begins around 1200 AD modern Indian historians continue in the main to insist that the establishment of permanent Muslim rule over the Gangetic plain was as violent a change as the founding of British sovereighty during the middle of the eighteenth century. This interpretation, however, stems more from a focus on the modern era and its problems, than an unprejudiced look at historical sources.

The medieval age which began about 1200 AD was made possible by the sheer multiplicity of states in the subcontinent. Each was centered upon a city to be conquered and hinterlands to be ruled by Muslim horsemen of central Asia. However, even if political forms in South Asia made such conquests possible, the forces which provoked the invasions lay outside the subcontinent. It was contradictions in the wider world of Islam itself that changed the course of the Indian middle age.

2

Buddhism and Jainism

Introduction

Buddhism is a philosophy and/or religion based on the teachings of the Buddha, Siddhartha Gautama (Sanskrit; in Pali, Siddhattha Gotama), who lived between approximately 563 and 483 BCE. Originating in India, Buddhism gradually spread throughout Asia to Central Asia, Tibet, Sri Lanka, Southeast Asia, as well as the East Asian countries of China, Mongolia, Korea, and Japan.

The aim of Buddhist practices is to become free of suffering (dukkha). Some schools emphasize awakening the practitioner to the realization of anatta (egolessness, the absence of a permanent or substantial self) and achieve enlightenment and Nirvana. Other Buddhist scriptures (the "Tathagatagarbha" sutras) encourage the practitioner to cleanse him/herself of the mental and moral defilements of the "worldly self" and thereby penetrate through to a perception of the indwelling "Buddha-Principle" ("Buddha-nature"), also termed the "True Self" (see "Mahayana Mahaparinirvana Sutra"), and thus become transformed into a Buddha. Some other schools appeal to bodhisattvas for a favourable rebirth. Some others do none of these things. Most, if not all, Buddhist schools also teach followers to perform good and wholesome actions, to avoid bad and harmful actions. There can be very large differences between different Buddhist schools of thought.

Buddhist morality is underpinned by the principles of harmlessness and moderation. Mental training focuses on moral discipline (sila), meditative concentration (samadhi), and wisdom (praja).

Buddhism, per se, neither confirms nor denies the existence of the supernatural (gods, demons, heavens, hells, etc.). Some Buddhist schools do employ deities and celestial protectors in their practices, but these are generally considered to be emanations of the meditator's own mind and thus not fundamentally real.

Meaning of Buddha?

Buddha is a word in the ancient Indian languages Pali and Sanskrit which means "one who has become awake". It is derived from the verbal root "?budh", meaning "to awaken or be enlightend." The word "Buddha" denotes not just a single religious teacher who lived in a particular epoch, but a type of person, of which there have been many instances in the course of cosmic time. (As an analogy, the term "American President" refers not just to one man, but to everyone who has ever held the office of the American presidency.) The Buddha Siddhartha Gautama, then, is simply one member in the spiritual lineage of Buddhas, which stretches back into the dim recesses of the past and forward into the distant horizons of the future.

Gautama did not claim any divine status for himself, nor did he assert that he was inspired by a god or gods. He claimed not to be a personal saviour, but a teacher to guide those who choose to listen. A Buddha is any human being who has fully awakened to the true nature of existence, whose insight has totally transformed him or her beyond birth, death, and subsequent rebirth, and who is enabled to help others achieve the same enlightenment.

The principles by which a person can be led to enlightenment are known as the Buddhadharma, or simply the Dharma. Dharma in this sense of the rather complex term means, "law, doctrine, or truth." Anyone can attain what the Buddha attained regardless of age, gender, or caste. Indeed, Buddhists believe there have been many solitary buddhas (Pali pacceka-buddha; Sanskrit: pratyekabuddha) who achieved enlightenment on their own but did not go on to teach others. According to one of the stories in the Sutta Nipata, the Buddha, too, was wondering about to teach humans because he despaired of their limited capacity for understanding. The Vedic (early Hindu) god Indra, however, interceded, and requested that he teach despite this. That the historical Buddha did so is thus a mark of special compassion.

Origin of Buddhism

Legend has it that the Buddha to be, Siddhartha Gautama, was born around the 6th century BCE. His birthplace is said to be Lumbini in the kingdom of Magadha, in what is now Nepal. His father was a king, and Siddhartha lived in luxury, being spared all hardship.

The legends say that a seer predicted that Siddhartha would become either a great king or a great holy man; because of this, the king tried to make sure that Siddhartha never had any cause for dissatisfaction with his life, as that might drive him toward a spiritual path. Nevertheless, at the age of 29, while being escorted by his attendant Channa, he came across what has become known as the Four Passing Sights: an old crippled man, a sick man, a decaying corpse, and finally a wandering holy man. These four sights, as they are called, led him to the realization that birth, old age, sickness and death came to everyone, not only once but repeated for life after life in succession for uncounted aeons. He decided to abandon his worldly life, leaving behind his wife and child, his privilege, rank, caste, and to take up the life of a wandering holy man in search of the answer to the problem of birth, old age, sickness, and death. It is said that he stole out of the house in the dead of night, pausing for one last look at his family, and did not return there for a very long time.

Indian holy men (sadhus), in those days just as today, engaged in a variety of ascetic practices designed to "mortify" the flesh. It was thought that by enduring pain and suffering, the atman (Sanskrit; Pali: atta) or "soul" became free from the round of rebirth into pain and sorrow. Siddhartha proved adept at these practices, and was able to surpass his teachers. However, he found no answer to his problem and, leaving behind his teachers, he and a small group of companions set out to take their austerities even further. He became a skeleton covered with skin, surviving on a single grain of rice per day, and practiced holding his breath. After nearly starving himself to death with no success (some sources claim that he nearly drowned), Siddhartha began to reconsider his path. Then he remembered a moment in childhood in which he had been watching his father start the season's plowing, and he had fallen into a naturally concentrated and focused state in which time seemed to stand still, and which was blissful and refreshing. Perhaps this would provide an alternative to the dead end of self-mortification?

Taking a little buttermilk from a passing goatherd, he found a large tree (now called the Bodhi tree) under which he would be shaded from the heat of the mid-summer sun, and set to meditating. This new way of practicing began to bear fruit. His mind became concentrated and pure, and then, six years after he began his quest, he attained Enlightenment, and became a Buddha.

Historically speaking, there are questions about this story. First, there are other narrative versions of his life that do not exactly match-one has it that the Buddha leaves home in the "prime of his youth", his parents weeping and wailing all the while. Second, we know from other sources that the country of Magadha, where he was born, was an oligarchic republic at that time, so there was no royal family of which to speak. However, regardless of the details of his early life, the evidence strongly indicates that the Buddha was indeed a historical person living in approximately the same time and place in which he is traditionally placed.

It has also been advanced that the pervasive influence of Jain culture and philosophy in ancient Bihar gave rise to Buddhism.

The Buddhists always maintained that by the time Buddha and Mahavira were alive, Jainism was already an ancient and deeply entrenched faith and culture in the region. Buddhist scriptures record philosophical dialogues between the wandering seeker Buddha and Jain teachers such as Udaka Ramaputta. Early Buddhists posited the existence of 24 previous Buddhas (Buddhas who walked the earth prior to Gautama Siddhartha) many of whose names are identical to those of the 24 Jain Tirthankaras and other traditional Jain figures. Buddhist scriptures attest that many of the first Buddhists were in fact Jains (Nirgranthas as they were then called, meaning "the unbonded ones"), whom Buddha encouraged to maintain their Jain identity and practices such as giving alms to Jain monks and nuns. The famous ancient parable of the blind men and the elephant illustrates the Jain science of Anekantavada, and is found in the Buddhist Pali text called Udana. Like most splinter groups generally, writers of the Pali texts clearly rejoiced in criticizing (and at times ridiculing) the Jains and celebrating the conversion of another Jain to Buddha's path. The texts show that Buddha vigorously appealed to the Nirgranthas that his path was nothing different from that with which they were already familiar, simply better.

The Buddhist formulation of the "Middle Way" was a post-Buddha response by the Buddhist monastic community to criticism by the Jains (as seen in Jain texts such as the Sutrakritanga Sutra and Acharanga Sutra) that the Buddhist Bhikkhus (mendicants) were lax and not living the rigorous life of a true ascetic or Shramana (Samana in Prakrit). In defining the Middle Way, Buddhist scholars branded their faith with a unique identity that distanced itself from Jain tradition by providing an alternative to "extreme asceticism" (i.e., Jainism) on one hand and Buddha's own princely hedonism on the other.

In describing Buddha's six-years of spiritual searching after leaving his family, Buddhist scriptures from the early post-Buddha period detail certain fasts, penances and austerities which Buddha undertook whose descriptions are elsewhere found only in the Jain tradition (for example, the penance by five fires and the consumption of food using only one's cupped hands). To this day, many Buddhist teachings, principles and terms remain identical to Jain ones. In short, a large body of evidence suggests that Buddhism is, in large measure, an offshoot of Jainism.

JAINISM

The oldest continuous monastic tradition in India is Jainism, the path of the Jinas, or victors. This tradition is traced to Var-dhamana Mahavira (The Great Hero; ca. 599-527 B.C.), the twenty-fourth and last of the Tirthankaras (Sanskrit for fordmakers). According to legend, Mahavira was born to a ruling family in the town of Vaishali, located in the modern state of Bihar.

At the age of thirty, he renounced his wealthy life and devoted himself to fasting and self-mortification in order to purify his consciousness and discover the meaning of existence. He never again dwelt in a house, owned property, or wore clothing of any sort.

Following the example of the teacher Parshvanatha (ninth century B.C.), he attained enlightenment and spent the rest of his life meditating and teaching a dedicated group of disciples who formed a monastic order following rules he laid down. His life's work complete, he entered a final fast and deliberately died of starvation.

Faiths in Jainism

The ancient belief system of the Jains rests on a concrete understanding of the working of karma, its effects on the living soul (jiva), and the conditions for extinguishing action and the soul's release. According to the Jain view, the soul is a living substance that combines with various kinds of nonliving matter and through action accumulates particles of matter that adhere to it and determine its fate. Most of the matter perceptible to human senses, including all animals and plants, is attached in various degrees to living souls and is in this sense alive. Any action has consequences that necessarily follow the embodied soul, but the worst accumulations of matter come from violence against other living beings.

The ultimate Jain discipline, therefore, rests on complete inactivity and absolute nonviolence (ahimsa) against any living beings. Some Jain monks and nuns wear face masks to avoid accidentally inhaling small organisms, and all practicing believers try to remain vegetarians. Extreme renunciation, including the refusal of all food, lies at the heart of a discipline that purges the mind and body of all desires and actions and, in the process, burns off the consequences of actions performed in the past. In this sense, Jain renunciants may recognize or revere deities, but they do not view the Vedas as sacred texts and instead concentrate on the atheistic, individual quest for purification and removal of karma. The final goal is the extinguishing of self, a "blowing out" (nirvana) of the individual self.

History

By the first century A.D., the Jain community evolved into two main divisions based on monastic discipline: the Digambara or "sky-clad" monks who wear no clothes, own nothing, and collect donated food in their hands; and the Svetambara or "white-clad" monks and nuns who wear white robes and carry bowls for donated food. The Digambara do not accept the possibility of women achieving liberation, while the Svetambara do. Western and southern India have been Jain strongholds for many centuries; laypersons have typically formed minority communities concentrated primarily in urban areas and in mercantile occupations. In the mid-1990s, there were about 7 million Jains, the majority of whom live in the states of Maharashtra (mostly the city of Bombay, or Mumbai in Marathi), Rajasthan, and Gujarat. Karnataka, traditionally a stronghold of Digambaras, has a sizable Jain community.

Ritual Activities

The Jain laity engage in a number of ritual activities that resemble those of the Hindus around them. Special shrines in residences or in public temples include images of the Tirthankaras, who are not worshiped but remembered and revered; other shrines house the gods who are more properly invoked to intercede with worldly problems. Daily rituals may include meditation and bathing; bathing the images; offering food, flowers, and lighted lamps for the images; and reciting mantras in Ardhamagadhi, an ancient language of northeast India related to Sanskrit.

Many Jain laity engage in sacramental ceremonies during life-cycle rituals, such as the first taking of solid food, marriage, and death, resembling those enacted by Hindus. Jains may also worship local gods and participate in local Hindu or Muslim celebrations without compromising their fundamental devotion to the path of the Jinas. The most important festivals of Jainism celebrate the five major events in the life of Mahavira: conception, birth, renunciation, enlightenment, and final release at death.

Jain Pilgrimages

At a number of pilgrimage sites associated with great teachers of Jainism, the gifts of wealthy donors made possible the building of architectural wonders. Shatrunjaya Hills

(Siddhagiri) in Gujarat is a major Svetambara site, an entire city of about 3,500 temples. Mount Abu in Rajasthan, with one Digambara and five Svetambara temples, is the site of some of India's greatest architecture, dating from the eleventh through thirteenth centuries A.D. In Karnataka, on the hill of Sravana Belgola, stands the monolithic seventeen-meter-high statue of the naked Bhagwan Bahubali (Gomateshvara), the first person in the world believed by the faithful to have attained enlightenment, so deep in meditation that vines are growing around his legs.

At this site every twelve years, a major concourse of Jain ascetics and laity participate in a purification ceremony in which the statue is anointed from head to toe. Carved in 981, the statue is considered the holiest Jain shrine. In addition to its lavish patronage of shrines, the Jain community, with its long scriptural tradition and wealth gained from trade, has always been known for its philanthropy and especially for its support of education and learning. Prestigious Jain schools are located in most major cities. The largest concentrations of Jains are in Maharashtra (more than 965,000) and Rajasthan (nearly 563,000), with sizable numbers also in Gujarat and Madhya Pradesh.

PHILOSOPHICAL DEVELOPMENT FROM UPANISHADIC METAPHYSICS TO SCIENTIFIC REALISM

Upanishadic Philosophy: Preparing the Ground for Rationalism

Although the Upanishadic texts (like some of the earlier Vedic texts) are primarily concerned with acquiring knowledge of the "soul", "spirit" and "god"-there are aspects of Vedic and Upanishadic literature that also point to an intuitive understanding of nature and natural processes. In addition, many of the ideas are presented in a philosophical and exploratory manner-rather than as strict definitions of inviolable truth.

Although the Upanishadic texts goaded the Upanishadic student to concentrate on comprehending the inner spirit, rational investigation of the world by other scholars was not entirely squelched, and eventually, the Upanishadic period gave way to an era which was not inimical to the development of rational ideas, even encouraging scientific observation and advanced study in the fields of logic, mathematics and the physical sciences.

Following an era when rituals and superstitions had begun to proliferate, in some ways the Upanishadic texts helped to clear the ground for greater rationalism in society. Brahmin orthodoxy and ideas of ritual purity were superseded by a spiritual perspective that eschewed sectarianism and could be practised universally, unfettered by an individual's social standing. Much of the emphasis was on discovering "spiritual truths" for oneself as opposed to mechanically accepting the testimony of established religious leaders. Although there is a thematic commonality to the Upanishadic discourses, different commentators offered subtly varying perspectives and insights. The concept of god in Upanishadic (and even earlier Vedic) thinking was quite different from the more common definition of god as creator and dispenser of reward and punishment. The Upanishadic concept of god was more abstract and philosophical. Different texts postulated the doctrine of a universal soul that embraced all physical beings. All life emanated from this universal soul and death simply caused individual manifestations of the soul to merge or mingle back with the universal soul. The concept of a universal soul was illustrated through analogies from natural phenomenon.

> *"As the bees make honey by collecting the juices of distant trees, and reduce the juice into one form. And as these juices have no discrimination, so that they might say, I am the juice of this tree or that, in the same manner, all these creatures, when they have become merged in the True, know not that they are merged in the True...."*

> *"These rivers run, the eastern (like the Ganges) towards the east, the western (like the Indus) towards the west. They go from sea to sea (i.e., the clouds lift up the water from the sea to the sky and send it back as rain to the sea). They become indeed sea. And as those rivers, when they are in the sea, do not know, I am this or that river, in the same manner, all these creatures, proceeding from the True, know not that they have proceeded from the True...."*

In another story, the "wise" father, expounder of the Upanishadic concept of god, asks his son to dissolve salt in water, and asked him to taste it from the surface, from the middle and from the bottom. In each case, the son finds the taste to be salty. To this his father replies that the 'universal being' though invisible resides in all of us, just as the salt, though invisible is completely dissolved in the water. (Chanddogya, VI)

As a corollary to this theory emerged the notion that even as individual beings might refer to this universal soul-i.e. god in varied ways-by using different names and different methods of worship-all living beings were nevertheless related to each other and to the universal god, and capable of merging with the universal god. This approach thus laid the foundation for egalitarian and non-discriminatory philosophies such as Buddhism and Jainism (as well as non-sectarian streams of Hinduism) that followed the Upanishadic period. As is evident, such an approach was not incompatible with secular society, and permitted different faiths and sub-faiths to coexist in relative peace and harmony.

In the course of defining their philosophy, the scholars of the Upanishad period raised several questions that challenged mechanical theism (as was also done in some hymns from the Rig Veda and Atharva Veda). If god existed as the unique creator of the world, they wondered who created this unique creator. The logical pursuit of such a line of questioning could either lead to an infinite series of creators, or to the rejection or abandonment of this line of questioning. The common theist solution to this philosophical dilemma was to simply reject logic and demand unquestioning faith on the part of the believer. A few theists attempted to use this contradiction to their own advantage by positing that god existed precisely because "He" was indescribable by mere mortals. But, by and large, this contradiction was taken very seriously by the philosophers of the Upanishadic period. The Upanishadic philosophers attempted to resolve this contradiction by defining god as an entity that extended infinitely in all dimensions covering both space and time. This was a philosophical advance in that it attempted to come to terms with at least the most obvious challenges to the notion of god as a human-like creator and did not require the complete rejection of logic.

Another philosophical advance of the Upanishadic period was that religion was transformed from the realm of bookish parroting of scriptures to the realm of advanced intellectual debate and polemics. The Upanishadic philosophers did not lay down their conclusions as rigid doctrines or inviolable laws but as seductive parables-sometimes displaying remarkable worldly insight and analytical skill. By attempting to win over their followers through analogies from nature, and by employing the methods of abstract reasoning and debate, they created an environment where dialectical thinking and intellectual exchanges could later flourish.

In the very process of their questioning, (and albeit speculative reasoning about god), they had opened the door for rationalists and even outright atheists who took their tentative questioning about the role and the character of god as "creator" to conclusions that rejected theism entirely. But in either case, many rationalist and/or naturalist philosophical streams emerged from this initial foundation. Some were nominally theistic (but in the abstract Upanishadic vein), others were agnostic (as the early Jains), while the early

Buddhists and the Lokayatas were atheists. Thus even though the Upanishads contained much that should rightly be dismissed as abstruse intellectual jugglery and philosophical mumbo-jumbo, the Upanishadic philosophers had levelled the ground for the seeds of rationalism to flourish in Indian soil.

The Vaisheshika School

The Vaisheshika school (considered to be founded by Kanada, author of the Vaisesika Sutra) was an early realistic school whose main achievement lay in it's attempt at classifying nature into like and unlike groups. It also posited that all matter was made up of tiny and indestructible particles-i.e. atoms that aggregated in different ways to form new compounds that formed the variety of matter that existed on the earth.

Their philosophy was described through the enumeration of the following concepts: Dravya (Substance), Guna (Quality), Karma (Action), Samanya (Generality), Visesa (Particularity), Samavaya (Inherence) and abhava (non-existence).

Dravya (or substance) was understood as the specific result of a particular aggregate effect-i.e. the combination of atoms in a unique way. Substances were repositories for qualities and actions. Guna or quality was that which resided in a dravya. Qualities did not however contain qualities themselves. 24 qualities were enumerated, such as-color, form, smell, touch, sound, number, magnitude, distinctions, conjunction, disjunction, nearness, remoteness, heaviness, fluidity and viscosity. (As was typical of the times, psychological attributes such as pleasure, pain, desire, aversion, effort, tendency, cognition, impression, and ethical attributes such as merit and demerit were also included in the list, *i.e.*-qualities that were inapplicable to inanimate objects were not treated separately)

Action or Karma represented physical movement. Unlike quality which was passive, Karma was dynamic. Action was the determinant of conjuction and disjunction. Five types of action were noted: throwing upwards or downwards, contraction, expansion and locomotion.

Satta or physical existence was viewed as being the common attribute of substance, quality and action-i.e. only existing (as opposed to imaginary) entities could have substance, qualities and be capable of action.

Samanyata or 'generality' was seen as a mental construct to create common classes of substances, qualities or actions while Visesata (particularity) was used to identify and separate individual items from their general classes. Samavaya or inherence was a relation that existed in those things that could not be separated without destroying them.

Four categories of Abhava as negation or non-existance were listed: pragabhava or prior non-existance, referring to the absence of an object before it's creation; dhvamsabhava or posterior negation, as the absence of an object after it had been destroyed; anyonyabhava or mutual non-existance, refering to an object being distinct and different from the other; atyantabhava or absolute non-existence, indicating non-existence in the past, present and future, citing the example of air as permanently lacking in smell-(which was presumably true in a period where air pollution must have been uncommon!).

An important contribution of the Vaisheshika school was a careful study of the time-relation in a chain of causes and effects. In a very rudimentary way, the school (along with other such schools) anticipated the theory of time calculus which could also be extended to space calculus.

The Vaisheshika school thus served as an important step in the study of science by enumerating concepts that could further the study of physics and chemistry. In addition, the the study of medical science (including veterinary science) received considerable impetus from such attempts at methodical observation and classification.

The Nyaya and Related Schools

The Nyaya schools complemented and built on the Vaisheshika school by elaborating on the process of accumulating valid scientific knowledge through accurate perception and generating valid inferences.

The school articulated four means of acquiring valid knowledge: pratyaksha or perception through one of the senses; anumana or inference; upamana or comparison with a well-known object; or shabda-verbal testimony.

The conditions of perception, and it's range and limits were carefully studied. Trasarenu-the minima sensibile (i.e. the minimum visible), anubhuta-rupa-the infra-sensible, abhibhuta-the obscured perception, and anubhuta-vriti-potential perception, were recognized as different types of perception.

A general methodology of ascertaining the truth (tattva) was described which consisted of describing a proposition (uddesa), the ascertainment of essential facts obtained through perception, inference or induction (laksan or uppa-laksana), and finally examination and verification (pariksa and nirnaya). This process could involve examples (drishtanta), logical arguments (avayava), reasoning (tarka) and discussion (vada)-, intellectual exchange, or interplay of two opposing sides in the process of arriving at a decisive conclusion. A successful application of this method could result in a siddhanta-i.e. established principle-(or in the case of mathematics-a theorem or theory) elucidated through proofs (pramana). Alternatively, it could lead to a rejection of the initial proposition.

The Nyaya school identified various types of arguments that hindered or obstructed the path of genuine scientific pursuit, suggesting perhaps, that there may have been considerable practical resistance to their unstinting devotion to truth-seeking and scientific accuracy. They list the term jalpa-an argument not for the sake of arriving at the truth but for the sake of seeking victory (this term was coined perhaps to distinguish exaggerated and rhetorical arguments, or hyperbole from genuine arguments); vitanda (or cavil) to identify arguments that were specious or frivolous, or intended to divert attention from the substance of the debate, that were put-downs intended to lower the dignity or credibility of the opponent; and chal-equivocation or ruse to confuse the argument. Three types of chal are listed: vakchala-or verbal equivocation where the words of the opponent are deliberately misused to mean or suggest something different than what was intended; samanyachala or false generalization, where the opponents arguments are deliberately and incorrectly generalized in a way to suggest that the original arguments were ridiculous or absurd; uparachala-misinterpreting a word which is used figuratively by taking it literally. Also mentioned is jati, a type of fallacious argument where an inapplicable similiarity is cited to reject an argument, or conversely an irrelevant dissimiliarity is cited to reject an argument.

The Nyaya school also recognized that intelligent and meaningful debates were not possible if certain fundamental principles and basic definitions and concepts were not mutually accepted. Nigrahasthana was the term used to identify disagreements based on absence of mutually acceptable first principles. An example might be a debate between a theist who rejected logic, and a non-theist who rejected faith.

The Nyaya school also listed five classes of logical fallacies (hetvabhasa): savyabhichara or the inconclusive type which employed reasoning from which more than one conclusion could be drawn but was used to insist on a single specific conclusion; viruddha or contradictory, where the reasoning used actually contradicted the proposition to be established; kalatita-where the elapse of time had made the argument invalid; sadhyasama, the unproven type, where the reasoning employed rested on arguments or principles that had not been proven and require proofs themselves-*i.e.* this was the type of fallacy where one unproven result was merely converted into another unproven result.; and finally prakaranasama-where the reasoning employed provoked the very question it was designed to answer-i.e. a recursive fallacy.

In this manner, the Nyaya school defined a very sophisticated school of rational philosophy where the process of scientific epistemology was analyzed threadbare and all the dangers of unscientific reasoning and propaganda ploys were skillfully exposed.

CAUSALITY

Buddhist and Jain scholars, as well as later Hindu scholars offered their own approaches to scientific reasoning. Virtually all the rational schools were concerned with describing causality and causal relationships, and recognized that effects may not have single causes but may require a group or conjunction of causes to occur.

Buddhist scholars emphasized that cause and effect need not have a linear effect but that desired effects may also require the right conditions for their fruition. (That is to say that for a plant to grow successfully, it would not only need the right seed, but that it would also need the right type of soil, fertilization, sunlight and water.)

Both the Jains and the Buddhists correctly speculated that a potential for the desired effect must also be present in the cause or causal agent. (For instance, only a mango seed could produce a mango tree because only the mango seed incorporated the potential of developing into a mango tree.) As another example, one could note that something with brittle properties such as glass might break upon impact whereas something strong such as steel would survive. Thus a physical impact on substances of different properties would have different results.

The Nyaya school also recognized co-effects-i.e a series of antecedants could cause a series of effects-either successive and staggered in time, or near simultaneous. Nyaya texts on causality indicate that there was an awareness that light travelled at a very high speed but the transmission of light was not instantaneous.

BUDDHIST AND JAIN ATOMIC THEORIES

The Buddhist and Jain philosophers also proposed their own variations of the atomic theory. Like the Vaisheshikas, atoms were perceived as infinitely small by the Jainas. But the Jainas went a step further by positing that the union of atoms required opposite qualities in the combining atoms-as is true in the case of electrovalent bonding. However, they erred in thinking that covalent bonding (which does not require opposite polarities in the combining atoms) could not occur. But their intuition that opposite polarities created mutual attraction and facilitated chemical reactions was correct. In the Buddhist view, matter was in fact an aggregate of rapidly recurring forces or energy waves. Their theory was illustrated with examples drawn from natural phenomenon involved with light emission. An atom was perceived as a momentary flash of light combining and separating from other atoms according to strict and definite laws of causality. Physical matter was thus seen as a denser and more concentrated form of light. Although at odds with other atomic theories of the time, their approach fit in with their general view that all things in nature were temporal, that there was constant change in nature-that degradation and renewal were continuous processes.

THE SYADVADA SYSTEM OF JAIN LOGIC

Jain philosophers also made certain important contributions to the science of epistemology by proposing that the truth of a concept or observation could not only be true or false but indeterminate-and combinations of the above-such as true under some conditions (or true at a particular time or place-or true based on the validity of certain inferences) and false under other conditions, or true under some conditions but indeterminate under others, and so on. This led to a matrix of seven possible states of the truth (true, false, true or false, indeterminate, true or indeterminate, false or indeterminate, true or false or indeterminate).

Jaina rationalists also studied the relationship between the universal and the particular and made important points concerning generalities and individual peculiarities. They also noted that objects in the real world exist in a network of relationships with each other-and have specific attributes that mark them temporally and spatially: "Every real is thus hedged round by a network of relations and attributes, which we propose to call its system or context or universe of discourse, which demarcates it from others." Jaina philosophers also successfully synthesized earlier debates on change and permanence by positing that all objects (or parts of objects) passed through phases of "existence, persistence, and cessation" and that reality was therefore a complex combination of things relatively permanent yet also relatively changing.

These ideas thus formed the foundations of Indian science and contributed to the gradual elaboration of mathematics and astronomy, as well as agricultural and meteorological sciences. Developments in metallurgy and civil engineering also followed. Medicine and surgery perhaps received the greatest and the earliest impetus from these developments. Developments in philosophy also led to concomitant developments in the realm of art and culture.

Yet. to a considerable extent, knowledge about the progress of science and reason in Indian history is often scarce. These (and other such) historical contributions were either denied or demeaned during the process of colonization, and are only now beginning to be re-acknowledged within

India and abroad. But in A. D 1068, Indian contributions to the mainstream of science were held in great esteem and readily acknowledged in some parts of the world:

Here is what Said Al-Andalusi, an 11th C Spanish scholar, court historian and chronicler wrote then: "Among the nations, during the course of centuries and throughout the passage of time, India was known as the mine of wisdom and the fountainhead of justice and good government and the Indians were credited with excellent intellects, exalted ideas, universal maxims, rare inventions and wonderful talents... They have studied arithmetic and geometry. They have also acquired copious and abundant knowledge of the movements of the stars, the secrets of the celestial sphere and all other kinds of mathematical sciences. Moreover, of all the peoples they are the most learned in the science of medicine and thoroughly informed about the properties of drugs, the nature of composite elements and peculiarities of the existing things." (Abu'l-Qasim's comments on India in Tabaqat al-Umam (Categories of Nations))

Development of Philosophical Thought and Scientific Method in Ancient India

Contrary to the popular perception that Indian civilization has been largely concerned with the affairs of the spirit and "after-life", India's historical record suggests that some of the greatest Indian minds were much more concerned with developing philosophical paradigms that were grounded in reality. The premise that Indian philosophy is founded solely on mysticism and renunciation emanates from a colonial and orientalist world view that seeks to obfuscate a rich tradition of scientific thought and analysis in India.

Much of the evidence for how India's ancient logicians and scientists developed their theories lies buried in polemical texts that are not normally thought of as scientific texts. While some of the treatises on mathematics, logic, grammar, and medicine have survived as such-many philosophical texts enunciating a rational and scientific world view can only be constructed from extended references found in philosophical texts and commentaries by Buddhist and Jain monks or Hindu scholars (usually Brahmins).

Although these documents are usually considered to lie within the domain of religious studies, it should be pointed out that many of these are in the form of extended polemics that are quite unlike the holy books of Christianity or Islam. These texts attempt to debate the value of the real-world versus the spiritual-world. They attempt to counter the theories of the atheists and other skeptics. But in their attempts to prove the primacy of a mystical soul or "Atman"- they often go to great lengths in describing competing rationalist and worldly philosophies rooted in a more realistic and more scientific perception of the world. Their extensive commentaries illustrate the popular methods of debate, of developing a hypothesis, cf extending and elaborating theory, of furnishing proofs and counter-proofs.

It is also important to note that originally, the Buddhist world view was an essentially atheistic world view. The ancient Jains were agnostics, and within the broad stream of Hinduism-there were several heterodox currents that asserted a predominantly atheistic view. In that sense, these were not religions as we think of today since the modern understanding of religion presumes faith or belief in a super-natural entity.

That so many scholars from each of these philosophical schools felt the imperative to prove their extra-worldly theories using rationalist tools of deductive and inductive logic suggests that faith in a super-natural being could not have been taken for granted. This is borne out by the memoirs of Hieun Tsang (the Chinese chronicler who traveled extensively in India during the 7th C. AD) who describes the merchants of Benaras as being mostly "unbelievers"! He also wrote of intense polemics and debates amongst followers of different Buddhist sects.

Similiarly, there is other evidence that suggests that amongst the intellectuals of ancient India, atheism and skepticism must have been very powerful currents that required repeated and vigorous attempts at persuasion and change. Nevertheless, over centuries, the intellectual discords between the believers and non-believers became more and more muted. The advocates of mystic idealism prevailed over the skeptics, so that eventually, (at the popular level) each of these philosophies functioned as traditional religions with their pantheon of gods and goddesses enticing and lulling most into an intellectual stupor. But at no point were the advocates of "pure faith" ever powerful enough to completely extinguish the rationalist current that had so imbued Indian philosophy.

EARLY RATIONALIST SCHOOLS

One of the most ancient of India's rationalist traditions is the "Lokayata". Maligned and discredited by the evangelicals of mystical Buddhism and Vedantic Hinduism, their world view was sharply atheistic and scientific for their time. Unlike those who believed in reincarnation or an after-life, and in the indestructibility of the human soul-they refused to make artificial distinctions between body and mind.

They saw the human mind as part and parcel of the human body-not as some separate entity that could have an independent existence from the human body. They acknowledged nothing but the material human body and the material universe around it. They rejected sacrificial gifts and offerings for the after-life as was common amongst followers of Brahmanical Hinduism during the time of Medhatithi in A.D 900 (a commentator on the writings of Manu who acknowledges that the Lokayatas were atheists or non-believers.)

For instance, they ridiculed the Brahmanical rituals of animal sacrifice: "If a beast slain in the Jyotistoma rite itself goes to heaven, Why then does not the sacrificer also offer his father?"

> *"If beings in heaven are gratified by our offerings made here, Then why not give the food down below to those who stand on the housetop?"*
>
> *"If offerings produce gratification to beings who are dead, why make provisions for travellers when they start on a journey?"*
>
> *"If he who departs from the body goes to another world, How is it that he comes not back again, restless for love of his kindred?"*

The Lokayatas dismissed the Vedic priests and their Vedic mantras as nothing but a means of livelihood for those lacking in genuine physical or mental abilities. Instead, they gave primacy to human sense-perception, and through the application of the inferential process-they developed their theories of how the world worked.

One of the most notable aspects of the Lokayata belief system was their intuitive understanding of dialectics in nature.

Many argued the mind-body separation as follows: Since the body is made up of things lacking consciousness-but the mind is a conscious entity-mind and body must necessarily be different-and consciousness must imply the existence of something else akin to the "soul". The Lokayatas countered this by citing the example of fermentation-how an intoxicating drink could be produced from something that was not itself an intoxicant.

In essence they had discovered the principle that the whole was greater than the sum of it's parts. That physical and chemical processes could lead to dramatic changes in the properties of the substances combined. They were able to understand how special transformations could produce new qualities that were not evident in the constituent elements of the newly-created entity.

As keen observers of nature, they were probably amongst the first to understand the nature of different plants and herbs and their utility to human well-being. As such, it is likely that Indian medicine gradually evolved from the early scientific knowledge and understanding of the Lokayatas. Since the Lokayatas believed that consciousness emerged from the living human body, and ended with it's death-it is more than likely that the widely prevalent Indian custom of cremating the dead also originated amongst them.

This is not to say that the Lokayatas' understanding of the world was as elaborate and precise as that provided by today's science. By the standards of the 20th century, some of their formulations could be considered primitive and inadequate. That is only to be expected. Knowledge of science has expanded considerably since their times. But what is more important is that their world view was driven by a rational and scientific approach.

For instance, some later philosophical schools countered the Lokayata arguments concerning mind-body unity by bringing up the evidence of memory. Nyaya-Vaisesika philosophers like Jayanta and Udayana pointed out that the process of daily eating meant that the human body was constantly changing. The process of ageing also pointed to how the human body was ever-changing. Yet, an old person could remember in detail an incident from childhood. In other words-they tried to argue that memory was evidence of a human soul that existed beyond the mere physical body. Yet, we know today that memory is but a combination of proteins that can survive the length of human existence. There is both continuity and change in nature. The Lokayata world view howsoever sketchy and incomplete was not in contradiction with modern science.

If some of their characterizations required later revisions or refinement, or even corrections, it didn't take away from their fundamentally scientific approach. Their inadequacies were a consequence of incomplete knowledge and the understandable inability to see all the complexities of nature that we are now able (through advanced scientific instruments and centuries of accumulated knowledge). Their errors did not, however, stem from stubborn faith or deliberate rejection of reality and real-world phenomenon.

In practice, (according to some historians) India's ancient Tantric followers may have also had a largely rational world view, which sprang from a practical mindset and was impaired only by the limited amount of scientific knowledge available to humanity at that time. Critics of the tantrics dismissed them as sexually obsessed hedonists. But they failed to acknowledge that the early tantrics had an intuitive scientific streak and their understanding of sexual reproduction is probably what may have also impelled them to develop basic agricultural tools and other implements. In that sense, they were India's early technologists.

THE AGE OF SCIENCE AND REASON

But even amongst those Indian philosophers who accepted the separation of mind and body and argued for the existence of the soul, there was considerable dedication to the scientific method and to developing the principles of deductive and inductive logic. From 1000 B.C to the 4th C A.D (also described as India's rationalistic period) treatises in astronomy, mathematics, logic, medicine and linguistics were produced. The philosophers of the Sankhya school, the Nyaya-Vaisesika schools and early Jain and Buddhist scholars made substantial contributions to the growth of science and learning. Advances in the applied sciences like metallurgy, textile production and dyeing were also made.

In particular, the rational period produced some of the most fascinating series of debates on what constitutes the "scientific method": How does one separate our sensory perceptions from dreams and hallucinations? When does an observation of reality become accepted as fact, and as scientific truth? How should the principles of inductive and deductive logic be developed and applied? How does one evaluate a hypothesis for it's scientific merit? What is a valid inference? What constitutes a scientific proof?

These and other questions were attacked with an unexpected intellectual vigour. As keen observers of nature and the human body, India's early scientist/philosophers studied human sensory organs, analyzed dreams, memory and consciousness. The best of them understood dialectics in nature-they understood change, both in quantitative and qualitative terms-they even posited a proto-type of the modern atomic theory. It was this rational foundation that led to the flowering of Indian civilization.

This is borne out by the testaments of important Greek scientists and philosophers of that period. Pythagoras-the Greek mathematician and philosopher who lived in the 6th C B.C was familiar with the Upanishads and learnt his basic geometry from the Sulva Sutras. (The famous Pythagoras theorem is actually a restatement of a result already known and recorded by earlier Indian mathematicians). Later, Herodotus (father of Greek history) was to write that the Indians were the greatest nation of the age. Megasthenes-who travelled extensively through India in the 4th C. B.C also left extensive accounts that paint India in highly favorable light (for that period).

Intellectual contacts between ancient Greece and India were not insignificant. Scientific exchanges between Greece and India were mutually beneficial and helped in the development of the sciences in both nations. By the 6th C. A.D, with the help of ancient Greek and Indian texts, and through their own ingenuity, Indian astronomers made significant discoveries about planetary motion. An Indian astronomer-Aryabhata, was to become the first to describe the earth as a sphere that rotated on it's own axis. He further postulated that it was the earth that rotated around the sun and correctly described how solar and lunar eclipses occurred.

Because astronomy required extremely complicated mathematical equations, ancient Indians also made significant advances in mathematics. Differential equations-the basis of modern calculus were in all likelihood an Indian invention (something essential in modeling planetary motions). Indian mathematicians were also the first to invent the concept of abstract infinite numbers-numbers that can only be represented through abstract mathematical formulations such as infinite series-geometric or arithmetic. They also seemed to be familiar with polynomial equations (again essential in advanced astronomy) and were the inventors of the modern numeral system (referred to as the Arabic numeral system in Europe).

The use of the decimal system and the concept of zero was essential in facilitating large astronomical calculation and allowed such 7th C mathematicians as Brahmagupta to estimate the earth's circumferance at about 23,000 miles-(not too far off from the current calculation). It also enabled Indian astronomers to provide fairly accurate longitudes of important places in India. The science of Ayurveda-(the ancient Indian system of healing) blossomed in this period. Medical practitioners took up the dissection of corpses, practised surgery, developed popular nutritional guides, and wrote out codes for medical procedures and patient care and diagnosis. Chemical processes associated with the dying of textiles and extraction of metals were studied and documented. The use of mordants (in dyeing) and catalysts (in metal-extraction/purification) was discovered.

The scientific ethos also had it's impact on the arts and literature. Painting and sculpture flourished even as there were advances in social infrastructure. Universities were set up with dormitories and meeting halls. In addition, according to the Chinese traveller, Hieun Tsang, roads were built with well-marked signposts. Shade trees were planted. Inns and hospitals dotted national highways so as to facilitate travel and trade.

India's rational age was thus a period of tremendous intellectual ferment and vitality. It was a period of scientific discovery and technological innovation. Accompanied by challenges to caste discrimination and rigidity and religious obscurantism-it was also a period of great social upheaval that eventually led to society becoming more democratic, allowing greater social interaction between members of different castes and expanding opportunities for social mobility amongst the population. Social ethics drew considerable attention in this period. Rules of engagement during war were constructed so as to eliminate non-military casualties and destruction of pasture-land, crop-land or orchards. The notion of chivalry in war was popularized-it meant not attacking fleeing or injured soldiers. It also required warring armies to provide safe passage to women, children, the elderly and other non-combatants.

The rational period thus saw progress on several fronts. Not only did it create an enduring foundation for India's civilization to develop and mature-it has also had it's impact on the growth of other civilizations. In fact, India's rational period served as a vital link in the long and varied chain of human progress. Although colonial history has attempted to usurp this collective heritage of the planet and make it exclusively euro-centric, it is important to note that fundamental and important discoveries in science and innovations in technology have come from many different parts of the globe, albeit at different times and stages of world civilization. India made significant contributions in this regard. If India is to fully recover from the depredations of colonial rule, it is imperative that we don't forget the achievements of this inspiring epoch.

3

Buddhist Ethics and Social Criticism

Buddhism arose in India during a period of intense intellectual and social ferment. It was a period during which the authority of the Vedas had been placed in doubt, the concept of god as a supreme being and creator was in question, the hereditary restrictions on caste mobility were under attack, and the efficacy of Brahminical rituals was being challenged. The authors of the Upanishads had opened the door for various heterodox currents to emerge in society, and amongst the most significant of these were the Lokayatas who polemicized against religious charlatans, and the Nyayavadis whose rational epistemology created the foundation for intense philosophical debate and encouraged the investigation of the real world based on reason and logic, freed from the burden of superstition and irrational adherence to burdensome rituals. Various ideological sects competed for the attention and acceptance of the ruling elites and the public. The most important amongst these were the Jains and the Buddhists. Although each of the various sects made original and interesting contributions to philosophy, it was the early Buddhists who attempted to provide a unified philosophical system where ethical conduct and social criticism lay at the very core of their ideological system.

Although today, Buddhism is viewed as a religion by many of its followers, the early Buddhists sects were either strongly atheistic or agnostic. The atheists believed that rather than "God having created man in his own image" it was man who had created "God" in his image. In their view, the liberation of humanity was contingent upon humanity shedding the delusion that "God" existed.

Other parables from surviving Buddhist texts indicate agnosticism. For instance, there is a suggestion that Buddhist followers ought not to waste their time on unsolvable metaphysical questions such as "does god exist". The search to identify the "one true god" or to speculate on the nature of god was seen as an exercise in futility.

But the most frequently cited argument against god by the Buddhists was that if an omnipotent and omniscient being such as "God" truly existed, and who was also all good, there could not be the kind of dukkha (suffering) that was so widespread in the real world.

These shlokas (verses) from the Bhûridatta Jataka illustrates this point:

If the creator of the entire world they call "God" be the lord of every being, why does he order such misfortune, and not create concord?

If the creator of the entire world they call "God" be the lord of every being, why let prevail deceit, lies and ignorance, why create such inequity and injustice?

If the creator of the entire world they call "God" be the lord of every being, then an evil master is he, knowing what's right did let wrong prevail!

Unlike religions that ascribed earthly miseries to human sinfulness that brought upon the wrath of a vengeful god who needed to be feared, Buddhism saw the root of human suffering in ignorance that could only be ended through the acquisition of wisdom. Rather than expect some supernatural entity to end human suffering, the Buddhists argued that it was in human hands to end their sorrows through conduct and action driven by knowledge and correct understanding of human nature and the physical world. Hence, the aspiration for knowledge (jigyasa) was seen as the answer to blind faith. Although the Buddhists were not alone in developing this view, the elaboration of this point of view became pivotal to early Buddhist philosophy.

Central to Buddhist philosophy was an understanding of human nature and what caused dukkha-i.e. human suffering. They saw human personality as constituting five attributes, i.e. body, feeling, perception, disposition and consciousness, and used this framework to develop their understanding of human suffering. Citing examples of conditions that led to human suffering, such as aging, sickness and death, or association with the unpleasant, (or separation from the pleasant), or the inability to get what one wished-they concluded that suffering was a condition of stress and conflict inherent within human existence and interaction with the world.

They also connected suffering to the very impermanence of things. They observed how people lamented over the loss of a loved one, or experienced sorrow when something or someone that had once given them happiness became separated from them.

They noted that even human pleasures were not immune from suffering because they didn't last forever, and the loss of pleasure inevitably left people feeling deprived. Seeing as how clinging to things (that were necessarily impermanent) was one of the primary causes of dukkha, they cautioned against excessive attachment. At the same time, they recognized a recurring and more general type of existential unease and anxiety (aniccha) that arises from the very transience of life, and our inability to control or comprehend all worldly phenomenon, which they characterized as viparinama-dukkha.

But the Buddhists did not see dukkha only emanating from the difficulties of an individual. They also saw suffering emerge on a much larger scale from hostile social conditions such as poverty, war, and social oppression which they described as dukkha-dukkha.

As a formula (char-mulya) for addressing these different types of suffering, the Buddhists advocated a four-fold scheme of a) recognizing the problem i.e. suffering (dukkha); b) identifying the cause of the suffering-such as craving stemming from ignorance (samudaya); c) establishing the goal of ending the problem (nirodha)-i.e. the cessation of suffering (nirvana); d) conducting life in a manner that was consistent with the cessation of suffering-following the right path or engaging in the right practice (marga).

Followers were thus goaded into developing both a sense of personal ethics and a social conscience:

> *"He who has understanding and great wisdom does not think of harming himself or another, nor of harming both alike. He rather thinks of his own welfare, of that of others, of that of both, and of the welfare of the whole world. In that way one shows understanding and great wisdom." Anguttara Nikaya-(Gradual Sayings)*
>
> *"By protecting oneself (e.g., morally), one protects others; by protecting others, one protects oneself." Samyukta Nikaya (Kindred Sayings)*

Human actions (kamma, kaama, or karma) in the Buddhist framework were to be judged based on both the intention or motive (chetanaa) and the consequences (vipaaka) of the action. Altruistic actions which helped in the establishment and promotion of a just society were encouraged in the dharmaniyama (moral duty code).

{The discourses, or suttas in the Digha Nikaya, illustrate how there was deep concern with the creation of social conditions favorable to the cultivation of Buddhist values and the expansion of social equity and justice. These views undoubtedly influenced the creation of a "welfare state" during the reign of emperor, Ashoka (B.C. 274-236)}

In their theories of causality Buddhists challenged the view that human destiny was unaffected by the ethics or morality of human actions. They countered the doctrine of amoral causation (akriyavaada) whose adherents argued that there was no merit in doing good and no demerit for doing evil. (An extreme expression of such thinking was seen in philosophers who denied all morality and saw no crime in the killing of any person.)

Realizing that such a world-view could lead to the rejection of moral distinctions and personal responsibility for ones actions, they argued strenuously against such beliefs. They also argued against the theory of Makkali Ghosha (or Ghoshala) who believed that human fate was predetermined, and therefore denied that human actions had any bearing on the results of things (ahetuvaada) and maintained that human intention and effort were essentially powerless in changing human destiny, and therefore advocated fatalism (niyati).

They also countered philosophers from the school of "absolute skepticism" who doubted everything and never committed themselves to any specific position in doctrinal debates. Philosophers from this school such as Sanjaya Belarthaputra (who was known as a theorist of endless equivocation or an equivocationist (amraavikkhepavaadin)) were criticized in the Brahmajaala Sutta (or Sutra) as "eel-wrigglers" who were incapable of taking a definitive stance on the vital philosophical questions of the day. Such skepticism was seen as emanating from both the fear of being in error and the lack of knowledge (or inability) to provide reasonable answers to question put forward for discussion. Such all-pervading doubt coupled with a cynical skepticism (vichikicchaa) was viewed as a serious mental hindrance, a fetter in the path to wisdom.

Other theories that contradicted the notion that human actions mattered were theories of accidentalism (ahetu-apachayavaada), theistic determinism (ishvaranimmaana-vaada) and past-action determinism (purvaketavaada or purvekatahetu). All of these were were opposed by the Buddhists. Accidentalism was an indeterminist theory which held that whatever was experienced was uncaused and unconditioned by human intervention. Theistic determinism was a determinist theory, which held that whatever was experienced was due to God's will or by plan of a "Supreme-Being". Past-action determinism was also a determinist theory, but it held the belief that whatever was experienced, whether pleasurable or painful or indifferent was entirely due to ones past actions (from a previous life), and ones present actions had no relevance.

The danger in each of these theories was highlighted in these words: "Thus for those who fall back on these three erroneous views as essential dogma, there is neither the will to do what is ought to be done, or not to do what is ought not to be done, nor necessity to do this deed or abstain from that deed. No moral improvement or intellectual culture can be expected from them." Some of the theories in circulation at that time built on a germ of truth but generalized to the point of absurdity. For instance the accidentalists were correct only to the extent that certain things did indeed appear to happen by random chance or accident. But they failed to recognize that sometimes what may have seemed to be accidental was more due to inadequate understanding or improper or incomplete perception, and that other activities had a clearly discernible cause. To deal with the extreme generalizations of such theorists, they introduced a middle standpoint for their epistemology and ethics.

They thus rejected the theory admitting that everything exists (sabba atthii ti) and in permanence-i.e. the extreme of eternalism (sassatavaada), and its opposite which advocated that nothing actually exists (sabba natthii ti) i.e. nihilism (the denial of all reality in real-world phenomenon) or the extreme of annihilationalism (ucchedavaada). Related to their critique of the eternalist and nihilist philosophies was their rejection of both hedonism and self-mortification (attakilamathaanuyoga) which they viewed as painful, fruitless, unprofitable and ignoble.

Buddhist texts also expressed suspicion about claims by heretical teachers of being constantly "all-knowing" and "all-seeing" and in possession of "all-embracing knowledge-and-vision." Such claims were countered with arguments relating to the actual behaviour of such charlatans in different situations. For instance, they wondered why such "all-knowing" and "all-seeing" spiritual teachers lost their way in an unfamiliar place or why they were unable to escape from trouble while countering a fierce animal such as dog, elephant, horse or bull. Moreover, if they were really omniscient, they wouldn't need to ask for people's names, clans, or the name of a village or market town or make enquiries about anything. That they did such things indicated that their knowledge was evidently limited just like that of any average worldly person (puthujjana).

Unlike religions that were based on revealed truth or the sanctity of every word in a holy textbook, the Buddhist belief system prescribed reasoning based on investigation as the means of determining ones dhamma, (or dharma as in Hindu practise). In a parable in the Kaalaama Sutta, followers of Budhism are advised not to accept any moral codes on the following ten grounds: (1) Vedic authority (anussava), (2) tradition (paramparaa), (3) hearsay or report (itikiraa), (4) textual authority (pittakasampadaa), (5) apparent agreebility of the view (sama o no garu), (6) authority of the holder of the view (takkahetu), (7) apparent logicality of the view (nayahetu), (8) the fact that the view is an accepted standpoint (aakaaraparivitakka), (9) inadequate reflection on reasons (bhabbaruupataa), or (10) the fact that the view agrees with one's own (ditthinijjhaanakkhanti).

In this manner, the Buddhism developed a very sophisticated philosophical system in which social ethics were integrated with rational investigation of human nature, social organization and the physical world. Buddhist ideas and concepts left a powerful impression on other Indian philosophical and religious belief systems, and over time, many commonalities developed amongst the competing ideologies.

However, there were also certain problems with the Buddhist world view which prevented its complete acceptance by intellectuals committed to the scientific method. For instance, although the Buddhists rejected the theory of past action determinism, they did posit the existence of a soul which survived a person's death and carried with it the merits and demerits of a person's past lives. Presumably this concept was essential to the Buddhist goal of encouraging right conduct but it was rejected by those who considered the soul as inseparable from the body and did not believe that the soul survived death. Those who rejected the concept of transmigration of the soul naturally couldn't accept the idea that human destiny had anything to do with merits and demerits accumulated in previous incarnations of the "soul". In their view, morality and ethics were entirely social constructs and had to be dealt with accordingly. The realists (such as the Nyayavadis) who shared the Buddhist concern for morals and ethics in society argued that while morals and ethics ought to be encouraged, they could only be enforced through societal laws and judicial codes.

Another problem facing the Buddhists was that in many ways, their views were too advanced for their times. Society had not yet developed to the point where education was universal, and knowledge of the real world sufficient to prevent superstitions and irrational beliefs from being completely abandoned by the masses. In an era where society had only limited control over nature, it was inevitable that sections of society would continue with beliefs in deities and supernatural phenomenon in the hope that they may be spared from natural disasters or that their crops might withstand attacks from pests and disease. Thus although the Buddhists had a very important and salutatory effect on Indian society, the most advanced Buddhist concepts could be understood and practised by only a minority in society.

Over time, the spirit of inquiry and rational investigation that had spurred the early Buddhist scholars towards dialectical thinking and critical social analysis became more and more replaced by narrow and literalist interpretations of the earlier texts. For instance, advice against accepting something that appeared "logical" without personal verification was taken to mean that logic could be rejected. Advice against wasting ones time on unsolvable metaphysical questions was also taken too literally and many Buddhist scholars remained aloof from the metaphysical debates pursued by other philosophical schools such as those of the Jains and the Nyaya Vaisheshikas. What they didn't anticipate was that some of these debates might lead to useful advances in mathematics or deeper understanding of human thought processes and new insights on human memory and psychology. These led to valuable advances in the interpretation of moods and emotions-thus benefiting Indian art, literature and music.

In addition, later Buddhist monks lapsed into some of the very things that had been attacked by the early Buddhists such as indulgence in unnecessary and elaborate rituals, belief in supra-natural phenomenon, and alienation of the priests from the masses. Activities such as meditation which were encouraged as a means to gaining wisdom became ends in themselves, and were turned into idealistic fetishes. Although Buddhist monks dutifully delivered sermons on right conduct and right action, they often failed to engage in relevant and timely social criticism-and did not always connect the textual suggestions to concrete practice. Intra-Buddhist disputes developed around less significant details, even as some of the most important ideas that had initially shaped the philosophy were pushed into the background. As a result Buddhism as it was practised came to be associated with idealism and inaction. Whereas the early Buddhists saw no merit in worshipping god or its images, later Buddhism developed a pantheon of deities not very different from other Indian religions.

Thus even as Buddhism had spread almost throughout Asia by the 5th-6th C AD, it gradually began to lose its distinct edge and liberating influence on much of Indian society. Within the Indian subcontinent, strains of Buddhism survived in Sri Lanka, Bengal, Bhutan, Sikkim, parts of Bihar and Nepal, and parts of Sindh, Punjab, Kashmir and Afghanistan. In parts of Orissa and adjoining regions (such as Chhattisgarh and Telengana), Tantric (and other) influences reshaped the practice of Buddhism. Yet, Buddhism continued to have an impact outside India and developed pockets of influence as far West as Syria, as well as in much of Central Asia (including what is now Uzbekistan, Tajikistan, Kyrgyzia, Kazakhstan) and Tibet. In the East, its influence was felt on virtually every nation including Burma, Thailand, Malaya and Indonesia, Laos, Cambodia, Vietnam, China, Korea and Japan.

As noted earlier, the vast literature of Buddhism (like much of Hindu or Jain literature) was not a literature of revelation and authority. Its essays on social ethics and moral responsibilities, its treatises on philosophy and science, its art and poetry were but pointers to a path to wisdom. This gave Buddhism both flexibility and adaptability. Owing to its non-hegemonic character and humanist appeal, Buddhism was adopted without coercion or force. It was also successfully fused with Hinduism in many parts of South East Asia just as elements of it had been integrated into Hindu practices in India.

In China, it was integrated with Taoism and Confucian principles; in Japan with Shinto beliefs. For several centuries, within India and outside, several people followed multiple faiths and identified as both Buddhists and Hindus, or as both Buddhists and Tantrics, (or Buddhists and Taoists) and so on. During the Gupta period (and in other reigns), philosophers from various schools of thought received royal patronage and temple grants were conferred for the construction of Buddhist and Hindu monuments alike.

It is also important to recognize that the form of Buddhism that was embraced in each nation was often quite different. For instance, in Western and Central Asia, it was not the philosophical or intellectual aspects of Buddhism that were popularized, but rather, its personal moral codes. Buddhist prosletysers imbued their stories of the Buddha with examples of miraculous healing and super-natural compassion so as to win more followers.

While such tendencies were also to be seen as Buddhism travelled within India or outwards, in Burma, Sri Lanka and Thailand, Buddhism developed organizational structures that appear to have been much more resilient. It was perhaps realized that the development of Buddhist virtue would require leadership and constant interaction with the community. In these nations, Buddhism did not degenerate into the extremes of mysticism or retreatism that became commonplace in certain parts of India (such as in the foothills of the Western Himalayas). Burmese and Thai monks maintained a practical and benevolent connection with the community, and thus retained a measure of respect within the community.

This also appears to be the case in Japan. In Korea, the emphasis on gaining wisdom was taken very seriously, and Buddhist monks took the lead in promoting mass literacy. This propelled the growth of technologies associated with the production of paper, writing instruments, inks, and furniture. And unlike in India, (where due to Upanishadic influences, "inner" wisdom came to be favored over outer wisdom), Buddhist concern for disseminating the writings of the Buddha had significant positive secular impact. In Korean (and other Eastern) Buddhism, there was the correct realization that a Buddhist mindset, or that a Buddhist society could not be constructed overnight. There was thus the emphasis on the (helical) upgradation of individuals and society towards greater "Buddhahood". This philosophical element was perhaps signficant in that it prevented the sort of philosophical stagnation that occurred in India, where followers too often sought immediate succuor, and thus not only became divorced from reality, but also lost sight of the strategic potential of the philosophy.

In addition, it ought to be noted that Buddhism in India also had to contend with strongly anarchic and ultra-democratic tendencies. Precisely because its philosophical structure emphasized the relative and changing nature of truth, different tendencies under the Buddhist mantle competed for leadership through argument and debate. Initially, this led to important advances in democratic practices within the Sanghas. But over time, it also led to clashes of egoes, hair-splitting and deadlock. While some Buddhist sects compromised and fused with other tendencies (even alien tendencies), others remained fiercely autonomous. To survive, Buddhism had to confront both the tendency to be co-opted, as well as the tendency to atomize.

However, the catastrophic demise of Buddhism in India was triggered by the onslaught of Islam which first obliterated the remnants of Buddhism in Central Asia, and then later in Afghanistan and India. By and large, Buddhism survived only in those countries that escaped invasions by Islamic conquerors. As a gentle faith that encouraged its followers to abjure violence, it was perhaps unable to protect itself from iconoclasts and proselytizers who intended to enforce a new religio-political order. Accustomed to centuries of peaceful co-existence, India's Buddhists had not anticipated the need to develop viable strategies for self-defence that could have combated the violence of India's Islamic conquerors who virtually obliterated Buddhism from the land of its birth.

Yet, it also appears that (in large part) later Buddhism had deviated considerably from the rational principles outlined in the early texts. Monasteries often became isolated from mainstream society, and monks who focused exclusively on meditative practices and idealistic or esoteric philosophical speculation contributed little to social progress. Some have even argued that the monastic orders had degenerated into sheer parasitism and were becoming a heavy social drain. Consequently, value judgements on the demise of Buddhism and the rise of Islam in India need to be made with a measure of caution.

Nevertheless, it must be acknowledged that the ascent of Islam was concomitant with the eclipse of Buddhism, and since the influence of Buddhism was greatly dependant on the existence of the monastic orders, the destruction of monasteries and their conversion to mosques and institutions of Quranic learning simply lead to mass conversions to Islam.

In the long term, this could have had the effect of stunting India's future intellectual development, since the destruction of important institutions of Buddhist learning also led to a notable decline in the opportunity (and social sanction) to study secular subjects such as logic and epistemology (which were also taught at Buddhist universities-such as Bhagalpur).

It might also be observed that the destruction of Buddhist centers of learning coincided with the destruction of extremely valuable textual materials-which could have been potentially rediscovered, and revived or reinterpreted by future generations of Indians so as to achieve a society that was more thoughtful and learned. Islamic texts did not offer anything comparable in terms of causality or epistemology. Nor did they offer the psychological, sociological, or moral insights that had been developed under the ambit of Buddhism. Nor was there any comparable stress on seeking knowledge or constantly updating ones understanding of nature and human society.

One can, therefore, only speculate as to the full consequences of this profound sociolgical and cultural loss (and discontinuity).

But East of India, Buddhism did survive, and in countries such Korea, Thailand and Burma, it continued to enjoy a loyal popular following. Philosophical innovations also took place, and as noted earlier, Buddhist scholars in China, Korea and Japan offered their own commentaries and somewhat individual interpretations of Buddhist concepts and formulations outlined in later (5-7th C.) Indian texts. And although the sacking of monasteries and centers of learning (such as Nalanda and Vikramshila in Bihar) led to records of the original Buddhist texts being permanently destroyed, it has been possible to reconstruct some of them from translations that survived outside India such as in Thailand and Tibet.

Notwithstanding the virtual erasure of Buddhism in India, it is possible to infer from these reconstructed texts and other archaeological records (and surviving monuments and artifacts) that Buddhism had a very powerful impact in shaping the destiny of India, and in triggering a social and cultural renaissance that would take Indian and other Asian civilizations to a higher level of social, cultural and material development.

4

Buddhism and Jainism in Early Period

INTRODUCTION

One could clearly identify two phases in the early period, namely the pre-Buddhist and the Buddhist period. The technological and cultural connections between South India and Sri Lanka go back to the prehistoric period. There are some very early sites from the middle Stone Age or the Mesolithic period in Sri Lanka dating to around 30,000 B.C. (they have been extensively cross-dated). There are suggestions that this may have been an intrusive community to Sri Lanka from South India, as the technological, cultural and subsistence patterns they reveal is similar to sites in the far South, in Tirunelveli district and elsewhere.

Then comes the period around 1000 B.C., when we have the earliest intrusion of the early Iron Age, what was till recently known as the proto-historic megalithic Black and Red culture. The critical elements for kicking off the beginnings of history-the use of metal and ceramic, the introduction of domesticated varieties of animals and plants (especially Oryza sativa or paddy), and the introduction of the earliest village culture with small crafts like bead-making and pottery making. The most interesting aspect of this culture is, however, the introduction of the burial cult, or what I would call the memorials, popularly known as the megalithic burials, and the associated ceramic ware called the Black and Red ware that bears post-firing graffiti marks.

So this forms the common cultural and technological identity of that time, in a wide sense. This phase goes on into the early historical period, chronologically identified as the 3rd and the 4th century B.C. when north Indian ideologies like Buddhism and Jainism enter Sri Lanka and South India.

The cultural and historical linkages of the period after the 3rd century B.C. is something, interestingly enough, that we have not looked at very seriously in Sri Lanka. This is because in the past, for historiographical reasons, Sri Lankan historical studies often looked both for sources and for inspiration to North India. This has something to do with both the nationalist movement during the colonial period, and the post-colonial period when identities were beginning to be established. In a kind of Indo-centric way, the Sinhala-speaking people often tried to link their identities to North India and to an 'Aryan' connection, and the Tamil-speaking people often looked to South India and a 'Dravidian' identity.

What was the nature of the historical exchange in the two regions between 6th century B.C., the time of the Buddha, and the 3rd century B.C.?

We believe that there were intrusions of the North Indian ideologies to South India prior to the Mauryan period-as archaeological evidence from Amaravathi suggests. Excavations here indicate that luxury items such as the Northern Black Polished Ware moved to the south both through the southern trade route, the Dakshinapatha (mentioned even in the Arthasastra of Kautilya), and also along the east coast looping trade network, the long distance trade network coming from the Gangetic delta to the South and touching even Sri Lanka. Either specialised traders were carrying these items or there was a down-the-line exchange, where items were moving on their own from community to community, or from centre to centre. The chank (conch) shell, a specific luxury item found in the Gulf of Mannar, is found in northern sites. The trade in pearls, again from the Gulf of Mannar, is mentioned in the early texts, the Pali texts. Later the Jatakas mention the long-distance trade network. By the 3rd century, or the Mauryan period, you find inscriptions by Settis, the merchant bankers, in Amaravati.

What perhaps the Mauryan empire did was to become a catalyst and provide a greater fillip for the more organised expansion of the northern social ideologies. For example, monks coming as missionaries, or groups bringing a message, with the clout of the Mauryan empire. The very fact that a chieftain in Sri Lanka in the central province takes the title Devanampiya, the epithet given to Asoka, would suggest this. There are suggestions that some of the Kerala chieftains took titles that would be translated as Devanampiya, or Beloved of the Gods. In the northern areas of Tamil Nadu, you find the inscriptions of the Adiyamans who called themselves Sathyaputra. This is the name given in the Asokan inscriptions to 'southern neighbours'. It is possible that the Mauryan empire may have been sitting there at the back of it with some degree of legitimising force.

So does the Mauryan period then mark any kind of historical watershed?

Not the Mauryan period precisely but certainly the 4th and 3rd century B.C. For instance, the intrusion of northern social ideologies was important. Because they bring not only a doctrine, but also a whole new culture: a new language medium, maybe even a script. Then you have things like lifestyles, food habits, architectural constructions, and technology-the Sangam works mention the Mauryan military technology and prowess. There is the use of coin money. You find the earliest issues of punch-marked coins found in the South-in Kerala and in the southern parts of Tamil Nadu-where this apparently had an influence on the earliest issues of the Pandyan coins in the symbols and the patterns they carry. So there is very definitely what I would call a watershed established in the 4th and 3rd century B.C. and what the Mauryans perhaps did was to consolidate this.

Does the Mauryan empire give political legitimacy to these changes or are these economic changes wrought by Mauryan rule directly?

I think it is interlinked. We definitely see both in Andhra and in Tamil Nadu regions a shift of human settlements from the peripheral hills towards the plains, a shift towards the east and to the river valleys of the Krishna, the Cauvery and the Tamiraparni settlements. Why these people are shifting is something we have never properly tried to look at. They may have wanted greater agricultural production, and/or they were probably coming to the coastal areas where they were probably making contact with traders.

The second thing is, as much as they were moving into these areas, it could not happen within the pre-existing situation. They had to change socially and structurally. Their patterns of subsistence change, their production system changes as they are now producing to a kind of a demand situation, and you suddenly see a kick-off in the specialisation of products in this period. You are finding more sophisticated specialisation coming in.

We see the prelude to the state. Powerful chieftains emerge over petty chieftains, the Perumagans for example. You have them now encroaching into new environmental and geographical regions, establishing their hegemonic control over populations, fertile areas and resource areas especially over raw materials-like gems, iron ore, and so on. In the Mauryan inscriptions at Amaravati, a whole series of clans are mentioned whose members are incorporated into the Mauryan army and given titles of military commanders. This was an excellent strategy followed by the Mauryans as these people are acculturated into the new situation.

So about the watershed, I think this period very definitely had its specific features, and I highlight three factors, namely, changing social hierarchies, political structures getting transformed, and new resource areas being encroached into.

What about the role of Buddhist and Jain monks as carriers of the new ideology?

Well, the external factors were the southern expansion of the Mauryan empire and long-distance trade, which happens before the arrival of northern social ideologies. Then of course the more permanent mark comes with the arrival of the Jains, the Ajivikas and the Buddhist clergy who mingle with the people. It is very interesting; if you map-and we have done this-the pre-existing megalithic Black and Red ware habitation and burial sites and the earliest Buddhist and Jain sites, they overlap. At Amaravati, the Mahastupa sits on a burial site. In Sri Lanka in the southern Deccan and even in Tamil Nadu, almost with all early Buddhist sites, the megalithic site and the Buddhist site are often separated just with a small rock outcrop. The monks moved in various ways to the southern Deccan: through the Dakshinapatha, along the eastern coastal route, and some with merchants. And they obviously were living with these early agricultural communities because the message given by the Ajivikas, Jains or Buddhists would not have had any relevance to a hunting-gathering society. It had to be a settled agricultural society having certain types of social differentiation, one facing some degree of tension, in transition from one cultural phase to another.

What is the significance of the Brahmi inscriptions as a source for this period?

The Brahmi script in the southern Deccan and in Andhra coincides with the Nanda-Maurya period approximately. The language here and in Sri Lanka is Prakrit. It is interesting that in the Sri Lankan and South Indian Brahmi inscriptions, including in Tamil Nadu and Kerala, particular letters or symbols are added for the convenience of local phonetics. Kailasapathy has suggested that Tamil was an elite language. The script was borrowed and the earliest donations are engraved in the Tamil language in Tamil Nadu. In Sri Lanka, it remains Prakrit although there are lots of Dravidian-and

Mundari-sounding personal names. We do not really know why. One of the suggestions I made was that Prakrit was brought through merchants and Buddhist monks and could be established more easily at the upper level, the upper crust of society. What is very interesting in the Sri Lankan inscriptions is that sometimes the letters are written upside down; so obviously the person engraving it did not understand it.

Iravatham Mahadevan suggests that literacy in Tamil appeared to have been far more democratised than elsewhere because the language of the Brahmi inscription was Tamil. He says that this is because the state in Tamil Nadu was relatively independent of Mauryan hegemony whereas this was not the case in Andhra and Karnataka.

He is quite correct because those regions were under the Mauryas. A large segment of the population was probably using Dravidian or proto-Dravidian languages or other regional dialects. But Tamil certainly had developed as a norm of expression for the common people than Prakrit. So I think Tamil played a much stronger role as a medium connecting the rulers to the ruled, whereas in Sri Lanka it did not take such strong root. It is only in subsequent periods that you see that happening.

Buddhism takes very different trajectories in Sri Lanka and south India.

I think that one of the issues we have to seriously look at is the emergence of Mahayanism and the resurgence of Brahminic practices in the south. For instance, Mahayanism is a response to what Theravada Buddhism, or orthodox Buddhism, could not do. The latter had a social appeal at a personal level. But Mahayanism also could not do what Brahminism did, incorporating the pre-existing pre-Buddhist cults and deities into its fold more effectively, particularly during the period of land grants of the feudal period. So you had the rulers, particularly the Satavahanas and the

Ikshvakus, granting Brahmadeyas and so on to the priests, who in effect start the process of land reclamation for agriculture as they move into probably socially backward areas, tribal areas that have all these cult practices. Now Buddhism could not do that because it could not move away from the trade routes. It could not move away from urban centres because their main base was there, and it did not have a philosophy and ideology to market itself outside.

There was also a shift of trade patterns. By about the 3rd and the 4th century A.D. you find a shift of trade to Sri Lanka as an entrepot. There is the decline of the Roman trade even in the South, though trade did not collapse altogether. The traders were the chief patrons of Buddhism, and with more and more rulers opting for a Brahmanic identity, state patronage to Buddhism also collapses. Buddhist monasteries were huge entities, which needed regular income, patronage, maintenance and some degree of security provided by the state. Once state patronage stopped, the plug was pulled. And when the trade pattern shifted, it collapsed altogether.

By contrast, what happened in Sri Lanka?

Sri Lanka did not have such a strong tradition of pre-Buddhist cults and practices, and what existed was incorporated very successfully into Buddhism. Here monks not only went into urban areas but also into very remote areas. They went into remote hills around trade routes. The monasteries, which by the 1st to 3rd centuries A.D. are huge, then incorporated all these areas into their network. The monasteries ran huge establishments; they carried on trade and all sorts of things. So that provided them sustenance and the state became their chief patron.

You have been involved in excavations and restoration of the several of the major archaeological and historical sites in Sri Lanka, including the Jetavana heritage site. Could you tell us something about heritage management in

Sri Lanka, and how you have integrated the requirements of tourism with conservation, and ongoing research?

I actually work at Anuradhapura as the co-Director of the Citadel Archaeological Excavation. Jetavana is a part of the Central Cultural Fund Archaeological Site projects of UNESCO (United Nations Educational, Scientific and Cultural Organisation), established in 1988-89. This has several heritage sites and Jetavana is one of those. The Jetavana is the largest existing brick constructed stupa in the world scaling 400 ft in height and established in about 3rd century A.D.

We are exposing the site for presentation for cultural tourism and also using the funding generated out of the project for training archaeologists through our department in the university for conservation, excavation and archaeological research. We are able to maintain a good balance of future resource persons on the one hand while also generating an income. All these sites are marketed with a dollar ticket for tourists.

After I took over the site in 2000, we have reoriented the whole project with a new research agenda. We have tried to contexualise Jetavana in the larger context of the ancient city of Anuradhapura by trying to understand its urban processes and its support base. Second, we are trying to understand the site in the historical context of the cultural, religious, technological and trade links that Sri Lanka had with the outside world. Third, we are now going in for a new site presentation format. We are to introduce a public participatory interactive museum, where the museum is presented as an integral component of the Anuradhapura site on the one hand, and to the history of Sri Lanka and the outside world on the other. One of the major flaws in our museum presentation (as in an Indian or South Asian museum) is that it is extremely parochial, highlighting probably only one culture, or a majority culture. They often lose out on some of the most important things about material culture. We plan to take the visitor through historical phases to provide an understanding of various aspects of the monastery and monastic life through a one-and-a-half hour walk tour. Our focus is the student body, and our presentations will, for a start, be trilingual.

Today there are enormous pressures on heritage and heritage sites, particularly in heritage-rich Third World countries. There are pressures created by the processes of globalisation and privatisation, something you have been talking about; from fundamentalists who seek to find new political uses for heritage and from war and civil strife as we have seen in Iraq. In Sri Lanka too, you must have faced all or some of these pressures. How have you dealt with them?

There is a direct pressure on heritage from war. Further, archaeology is politicised both by the majority community and also by minority fundamentalism. History is used to legitimise their own political agenda and also to stake claims, for instance, for the homeland theory, or to prove the antiquity of a community.

A second major danger to heritage sites is antique looting. Sri Lanka is now a top spinner in that. One of my biggest worries is that there are many affluent people getting involved in this. The drug-runners and the gun-runners are the primary sources who push the antiques and Sri Lanka has turned out to be an entrepot for looted antiques. When the stock market collapsed in the late 1980s, antiques became a very good source of investment because it they have an appreciative value. We know that some corporate sector people are involved, and also some foreign embassy staff. Despite stringent laws, this goes on.

Third, we are concerned that archaeology in Sri Lanka today has turned out to be a money-spinner. There are some archaeologists who are trying to push an agenda for a larger private sector role in the management of museums and world heritage sites. The priorities of hoteliers and tour operators are totally different and I am not too happy about the integrity of the private sector in Sri Lanka. Archaeologists must be in total control of the heritage sites for many good reasons. I have nothing against private involvement in certain areas, which we have, but strictly under our control.

What about the role of international organisations like the UNESCO in heritage management? I think that even UNESCO has to create a better track record on conservation. One area I have been very critical of is the area of funding. They do not try to ensure that the money be utilised not just for the majority community or one particular group. It was not till very recently that we had a policy for multireligious and multicultural representations through our heritage sites.

What is the future of archaeology education in the context of the privatisation of higher education in your country that you have been concerned about? How will people be attracted to the field if they cannot find jobs after that?

We have to accept certain situations about the globalisation process that is taking place, and the plans to privatise. As archaeologists we have seen this coming and we have tried to reorient ourselves in preparation. We have structured our courses in a very strong marketing way. We are working on sites that are linked to the global market for tourism. On the other hand we are working on 'Archaeology and Sustainability': archaeological research that makes an input to the nation's development grid. We are researching environmental issues, ancient technology, and ethnology, which involves mapping and documenting, peoples' past and present lifestyles. We have done mineral resource studies and are helping the geological department in their mineral prospecting.

Finally, a question on the media and heritage. In your country what has been the role of the media in highlighting heritage preservation and promotion?

Archaeologists and media practitioners both seek facts. We try to be objective, impartial, and independent in our data retrieval and dissemination. Our professions are both problem-oriented and issue-related because we are also social activists. In Sri Lanka the response to the question, "Who owns the past? Who owns heritage?" is often very parochial. I got a student to do a dissertation on media reportage on heritage. The media will do romantic and irrelevant stories, often based on half-truths to kick up their circulation, and to keep alive feelings of nationalism. The television, newspapers and other media have given exaggerated reports that have led to the looting of archaeological sites. It is very dangerous. They may say that golden Buddhist statues are available somewhere for the public to see. Within two months the site is looted. Or they say there are rubies in the eyes of some Buddha in a particular place. We have monitored this. At least two-thirds of the sites reported like that were looted within three months. They even give a road map for antique looters to find the place easily! But some sections of the media have been conscious and responsible in their reportage.

How productive has your visit to Chennai and meeting with Indian researchers been?

We have been talking to academics and researchers here and it has been very productive. We all share the very same issues and problems, and what we are trying to do is to forge closer links and form a consortium of south Indian and Sri Lankan archaeologists. They are many areas-faculty/student exchange, resource person development-where we can help each other. There has been a greatly positive response from the State Department of Archaeology and the University Department of Archaeology in Chennai to these efforts.

5

Hindusim Through the Ages

Hinduism has a long and complex history. It is a blend of ancient legends, beliefs and customs which has adapted, blended with, and spawned numerous creeds and practices.

PREHISTORIC RELIGION: (3000-1000 BCE)

The earliest evidence for elements of the Hindu faith date back as far as 3000 BCE. Archaeological excavations in the Punjab and Indus valleys (right) have revealed the existence of urban cultures at Harappa, the prehistoric capital of the Punjab (located in modern Pakistan); and Mohenjodaro on the banks of the River Indus.

Archaeological work continues on other sites at Kalibangan, Lothal and Surkotada. The excavations have revealed signs of early rituals and worship. In Mohenjodaro, for example, a large bath has been found, with side rooms and statues which could be evidence of early purification rites. Elsewhere, phallic symbols and a large number statues of goddesses have been discovered which could suggest the practice of early fertility rites. This early Indian culture is sometimes called the Indus Valley civilisation.

PRE-CLASSICAL (VEDIC): (2000 BCE-1000)

Some time in the second millennium BCE the Aryan people arrived in north-west India. The Aryans (Aryan means noble) were a nomadic people who may have come to India from the areas around southern Russia and the Baltic. They brought with them their language and their religious traditions. These both influenced and were influenced by the religious practices of the peoples who were already living in India.

Worship

- The Indus valley communities used to gather at rivers for their religious rituals.
- The Aryans gathered around fire for their rituals.
- The Indus valley communities regarded rivers as sacred, and had both male and female gods.
- The Aryan gods represented the forces of nature; the sun, the moon, fire, storm and so on.

Over time, the different religious practices tended to blend together. Sacrifices were made to gods such as Agni, the God of Fire, and Indra, the God of storms.

Writings: Aspects of the Aryan faith began to be written down around 800 BCE in literature known as the Vedas. These developed from their oral and poetic traditions. You can see some of the Vedic tradition in Hindu worship today.

The Caste System

The Aryans also introduced the varna system (varna = estates or classes) to India, which may have contributed to the caste system we see today. Some think that it developed from a simpler two-tier structure consisting of nobles at the top, and everyone else below. Others say that it was established and practised by the priests who divided society into three parts:

- The priests (or Brahmins).
- The warriors (the Kshatriyas).
- The ordinary people.

THE RISE OF JAINISM AND BUDDHISM: (800-600 BCE)

Buddhism and Jainism emerged from India around 800-600 BCE, a period of great cultural, intellectual and spiritual development and both had an enormous influence on Hinduism. Some of the previously accepted truths of the religion were beginning to be questioned and the religious leaders were being asked to defend their views and teachings. Furthermore, the old tribal structure of society was diminishing. The result was an increasing number of breakaway sects, of which Buddhism and Jainism were probably the most successful.

Buddhism: Buddha was born in the sixth century BCE as Gautama Siddhartha. He was a member of the powerful warrior class. He renounced the pleasures and materialism of this world to search for the truth. Through this quest he developed his basic principles for living. Buddhism became the state religion of India in the third century BCE. Buddhism had a great influence on Hinduism, from the way it used parables and stories as a means of religious instruction, to its influence on Indian art, sculpture and education.

Jainism: The founder of the Jains, Mahavira ("the great hero"), was a near contemporary of the Buddha's and he rejected the caste system, along with the Hindu belief in the cycle of births. Mahavira was the twenty fourth of the Tirthankaras, the "Path-makers", or great teachers of Jainism. They developed the concept of three ways, or "jewels"-right faith, right knowledge and right conduct. The Jains were never a numerically large group but their influence was out of all proportion to their size and distribution. Mahatma Gandhi, whilst himself not a Jain, embraced their doctrine of non-violence to living things.

The End of the Era

During the last centuries of the previous era, the Mauryan empire ruled much of India. The most famous ruler, Asoka, although a Buddhist himself, thought that the Brahman religion was worthy of respect. Brahmanism revived with the end of Mauryan rule, and at the same time devotion to individual gods, such as Vishnu and Siva, began to grow. Some of the early Hindu images date from this period.

The Start of the Current Era

The first 400 years CE were a time of upheaval in the Hindu heartland. A variety of invaders ruled the area, bringing injections of their own cultures and beliefs. Hinduism strengthened, and the cults of individual gods grew stronger. Goddesses, too, began to attract followers.

The Rise of "Hinduism"

The years to 1000 CE saw Hinduism gaining strength at the expense of Buddhism. Some Hindu rulers took military action to suppress Buddhism. However it was probably developments in Hinduism itself that helped the faith to grow. Hinduism now included not only the appeal of devotion to a personal god, but had seen the development of its emotional side with the composition and singing of poems and songs. This made Hinduism an intelligible and satisfying road to faith to many ordinary worshippers.

Advent of Islam

Islam arrived in the Ganges basin in the 7th century, but its influence was not really felt until the Turks arrived in the 11th and 12th centuries CE. Islam and Hinduism were in conflict because, although the mystical traditions of both religions had some common ground, Muslim rulers sought to conquer Hindu territories and, from the 17th century, to assert the superiority of Islam.

Islam was established-and flourished-chiefly in areas where Buddhism was in a process of slow decline, that is mainly around modern-day Pakistan, Bangladesh and Kashmir. Hinduism remained strongest in the south of India.

Western Influence

Hinduism as it is known and recognised today has been greatly affected by the influence of western thought and practices. In the 18th and 19th centuries, missionaries from Europe attempted to convert Hindus to Christianity with varying degrees of success. This challenged Hindu leaders to reform many practices and in some cases, revive old practices. This period has been recognised as a period of Hindu revivalism.

Rammohan Roy

An early leader in this field was Rammohan Roy (1772-1833), a scholar who spoke Arabic, Persian, Hebrew, Greek, Latin and Sanskrit alongside his native Bengali. He read most of the religious scriptures from around the world and discovered that there was little difference between them. In 1828, he founded the Brahmo Samaj, based on the teachings of the Upanishads.

Whilst he based much of his work on the teachings of the Upanishads, his social outlook was progressive and he was keen to develop education and particularly the establishment of western sciences into Indian culture. Rammohan Roy died in Bristol of meningitis while on a visit to Europe. There is a statue of him at College Green in Bristol.

Ramakrishna Paramahamsa

Another school of Hinduism developed under the influence of Ramakrishna Paramahamsa (1836-86) who put much greater emphasis on devotion to God. He combined the trend of popular Hinduism with its many images with a belief in a loveable Almighty God, for he could see God in many forms. He preached without a complicated theology and without an over-reliance on the scriptures. It was a pluralist approach to Hinduism which helped it to find its feet in the modern world.

Swami Vivekananda

The work of Ramakrishna Paramahamsa was continued and extended by Swami Vivekananda (1863-1902) who, after 12 years of ascetic study and discipline, was responsible for promoting the Hindu tradition and thought in the west. He taught that the divine is in everything and promoted the Ramakrishna Mission which is well known for its social work as well as being a focus for Hindu religious thought.

International Society for Krishna Consciousness

More often known as the Hare Krishnas, the movement is often recognised as the western face of Hinduism. Its origins can be traced back to Chaitanya, a fifteenth century devotee of Krishna, who chanted devotional songs to Krishna. His teachings were promoted in the 20th century by Bhaktisiddhanta Sarasvati, who had a vision of taking the message of Chaitanya to the west shortly before his death in 1936. This work was taken up by Prabhupada who took that message to the United States and eventually established bases around the world to promote those teachings.

ARYAN INVASION THEORY PROVED WRONG

One of the most controversial ideas about Hindu history is the Aryan invasion theory. This theory, originally devised by F. Max Muller in 1848, traces the history of Hinduism to the invasion of India's indigenous people by lighter skinned Aryans around 1500 BCE. The theory was reinforced by other research over the next 120 years, and became the accepted history of Hinduism, not only in the West but in India. There is now ample evidence to show that Muller, and those who followed him, were wrong.

Why is the theory no longer accepted?

The Aryan invasion theory was based on archaeological, linguistic and ethnological evidence. Later research has either discredited this evidence, or provided new evidence that combined with the earlier evidence makes other explanations more likely. Modern historians of the area no longer believe that such invasions had such great influence on Indian history. It's now generally accepted that Indian history shows a continuity of progress from the earliest times to today. The changes brought to India by other cultures are not denied by modern historians, but they are no longer thought to be a major ingredient in the development of Hinduism.

Dangers of the Theory

The Aryan invasion theory denies the Indian origin of India's predominant culture, but gives the credit for Indian culture to invaders from elsewhere. It even teaches that some of the most revered books of Hindu scripture are not actually Indian, and it devalues India's culture by portraying it as less ancient than it actually is. The theory was not just wrong, it included unacceptably racist ideas:

- it suggested that Indian culture was not a culture in its own right, but a synthesis of elements from other cultures
- it implied that Hinduism was not an authentically Indian religion but the result of cultural imperialism
- it suggested that Indian culture was static, and only changed under outside influences
- it suggested that the dark-skinned Dravidian people of the South of India had got their faith from light-skinned Aryan invaders
- it implied that indigenous people were incapable of creatively developing their faith
- it suggested that indigenous peoples could only acquire new religious and cultural ideas from other races, by invasion or other processes
- it accepted that race was a biologically based concept (rather than, at least in part, a social construct) that

provided a sensible way of ranking people in a hierarchy, which provided a partial basis for the caste system

- it provided a basis for racism in the Imperial context by suggesting that the peoples of Northern India were descended from invaders from Europe and so racially closer to the British Raj
- it gave a historical precedent to justify the role and status of the British Raj, who could argue that they were transforming India for the better in the same way that the Aryans had done thousands of years earlier
- it downgraded the intellectual status of India and its people by giving a falsely late date to elements of Indian science and culture

JAINISM AND BUDDHISM IN SOUTH INDIA

In South India, Jainism is little more than a name. Even serious students of religion in India paid little attention to it. In a population of nearly 60 crores of people, Jainas may constitute nearly some 3 million people. But the influence it wields, its contribution to the development of Indian couture, commerce and industry is out of proportion to their population. Jainological material is so rich and varied and so much extended in time it is impossible to write about it in few pages. Because of this limitation the paper will be simply a fringe study and a general survey.

In this brief paper an attempt is made to trace the rise of Jainism as religio-philosophical system, its contribution to Indian Philosophy, Religion, Metaphysics and Logic, Art and Architecture, languages and literatures, and also a brief summary of its history in Andhra Pradesh.

The Jainas claim hoary antiquity for their religion. Vishnu and Bhagavata Puranas also mention this fact. The tradition says that during the time of the Mahabharata War Jaina order was led by Neminatha, the 22nd Thirthankara and he belonged to Yadava family. The order gained strength during 8th century B. C., under Parsvanatha, the 23rd Thirthankara.

In Parsvanatha we have the first historical beginnings of Jainism. Mahavira was born in the middle of the 6th century B. C. It appears he was influenced to a great extent by Gosala and the followers of Ajivaka sect also. According to one tradition there were 5 heretical sects. They are:

1. Akriyavadins of Purana Kassapa,
2. Anuvadins of Pakuda Kaccayana,
3. Ajivakas of Makkhali Gosala,
4. The materialists of Ajita Kesa Kambalin, and
5. The sceptics of Sanjaya Belattiputta.

All these systems including Buddhism and Jainism were considered as Non-Brahmanic or Sramanic systems. The common feature of these systems are:

1. They challenged the Vedas
2. Admitted all members to their community
3. Observed a set of ethical principles
4. Practiced detached life to get liberation
5. Accepted renunciation.

These sects indicate there were two trends of thought, Brahmanic and Non-Brahmanic even from earlier times and these two trends influenced Indian Philosophy and Religion equally.

The records of the Buddhists and Jainas about the philosophical ideas of those days are of great importance to the historian of religions. The similarity between some of those heretical doctrines of the one side, and Jaina or Buddhist ideas on the other, favours the assumption that the Buddha as well as Mahavira owed some of their conceptions to these very heretics.

CONTRIBUTION TO THE DEVELOPMENT OF LANGUAGES

The Jainas have played a very important role in the linguistic development of the country. Sanskrit has all along been the medium of sacred writings and preachings of the Brahmanas and Pali that of the Buddhists. But the Jainas utilized the prevailing language of the area for religious purposes. Thus they developed Prakrit and other regional languages.

Of late rich literature produced by the Jainas came to light. The literature in Apabhramsa is worth mentioning. This language is a link between the Sanskrit, Prakrit, the classical languages on the one hand and modern Indian languages on the other. It is surprising to note that the earliest literature in Kannada and Tamil is also of Jaina authorship.

Jaina Ethics: Contribution of Jaina ethics to Indian ethical theories is also note worthy. It is different from the Bhakti Marga of the Bhagvatas, Jnana Marga of the Vedantins and Karma Marga of the Mimamsakas. Jainism holds that all the three must coexist in a person, if he is to walk along the path of salvation. Taking the analogy of medicine, faith in its efficacy, knowledge of its use, and the actual taking of the medicine. All these three are essential to effect a cure. Similarly the suffering soul can be cured by Ratnatraya, the three principles of Right faith, Right knowledge and Right conduct. The doctrine of Ahimsa though found in the epics, was preached on extensive scale, by the Jainas and Buddhists. Ahimsa must be observed both by the saints and the laymen according to Jainas and Buddhists, where as in classical Hindu tradition it was meant only for the Sanyasis.

Metaphysics: The tenets of Jainism are not always easy to grasp mainly due to two reasons. Firstly on account of our relative unfamiliarity with the ancient background and secondly on account of highly complex and perplexing system of innumerable divisions and sub divisions in the Jaina order.

In metaphysics there in some general likeness between Sankhya and yoga on the one hand and Jainism on the other. Dualism of matter and Soul is accepted by all these systems. Souls are like substances like Monads and they are characterized by intelligence. The actual difference between the souls is caused by their connection with the matter. Jainas and Sankhyas believe matter to be of indefinite nature and it can become anything.

The summarize Jaina philosophy the living and the non-living, by coming into contact with each other forge certain energies which bring about birth, death and various experiences of life. This process could be stopped and energies already forged destroyed by a course of discipline leading to salvation. a close analysis leads to 7 propositions:

1. There is something called living,
2. Something called non-living,
3. The two come into contact with each other,
4. The contact leads to production,
5. This process of contact could be stopped,
6. The existing energies could be exhausted,
7. The salvation could be achieved.

These seven propositions are called seven tattvas or realities by the Jainas. "The first two great truths are that there is a jiva or soul and that there is an ajiva or non-soul. These two exhaust between them all that exists in the Universe.

CONTRIBUTION TO LITERATURE

The contribution of the Jainas to Sanskrit and other Indian languages is noteworthy. Dr. Winterniz says that there was a close connection between Jaina nd post Vedic literature. The story of Jajali and Tuladhara (M. bh. XXII, 261-64) the fable of the Hunter and the pigeons (M. bh XXII, 143-49) and the legend of Mudgala in Mahabharata (V, 23-40) indicate this close relation.

Prof. Hertel has shown that their contribution to narrative and story literature is much. He says that the Jainas have preserved much of Indian tales that otherwise would have been lost to us. They have also compiled great collection of tales. Kathakosa by Subhasilagani, Kathankakosa by Jinesvara, Kathamahodadhi by somachandra (1448 A. D.) Katharatnakara by Hema Vijaya (1600 A. D.) are some of them. They wrote many charitas and Prabhandas. The charitas are legendary biographies of the Thirthankaras, Chakravartins and Rishis. Prabhandas contain stories of famous monks and laymen of historical times. Sthaviravalicarita, Prabhandhacintamani of Merutunga and Prabandhakosa of Rajasekhara gives us a glimpse of the social and cultural history of those times.

Some of the novels are Somaraiccakaha of Dhanavala (romantic epic in Apabhramsa) and Somadeva Suri's (959 A.D.) Yasastilaka are of this type. It has also been shown by Prof, Hertel that the popular recessions of Pancatantra are the works of the Jainas. Dhananjaya Srutakirti wrote to prove his mastery in sleshas by writing Raghavapandaviya (1123-1140 A. D.)

The Jainas have some books written in drama styple also. Mohaparajaya of Yasopala narrates the story of Kumarapala's conversion to Jainism. Many of the poetical works are written in the apabhramsa dialect. The Jainas also have lexicographical writings. Their contribution to grammar is also noteworthy. According to some scholars the grammatical writing Siddha-Hemachandra by Hemachandra is in many respects better than that of Panini's Grammar. The oldest Prakrit lexicon is the work of a Jaina scholar, Paiyalacchi Namamala of Dhanapala (972 A. D.)

Jaina's philosophical literature is rich. Umasvati whom Prof. Suali would place as early as 300 A. D., in his Tattvarthanthigama Sutra expounds the doctrine of categories and theory of Pramanas.

Siddhasena Divakara in his Nyayavatara wrote for the first time a treatise on the means of proof (pramana) and the methods (Naya) of comprehending things from particular stand points. Devasuri (1086-1169 A. D.) wrote Syadvada Ratnakara. Even in 17th century we have great logician in Yaso Vijaya Gani who wrote great number of works on Logic.

Another commendable thing is some of these Jaina philosophical works is their liberal attitude towards other religious beliefs. A study of Shaddarshanasamucchaya reveals this. They dealt about many of the sciences and even on politics Jaina contribution is noteworthy. Somadeva Suri, the author of Niti Vakyamrta can be compared well with the classical Indian Niti writers like Kautilya and Sukra.

ARTS AND ARCHITECTURE

The Jaina have a due share in the development of Arts in the country. In honor of their saints they erected Stupas as the Buddhists with their accessories of stone railings, umbrellas, decorated gateways and pillars and statues. The Gomateswara statue at Sravana Belagola (10th Century), the collosal reliefs carved on the rock face near Gwalior (15th Century A. D.), the Hathi Gumpha caves in Orissa, Pava Puri, Rajagiri in Bihar, Girinar and Palitana in Kathiawar, possess temples and architectural monuments of different ages. The Jaina marble temples at Mount Abu in Rajasthan belonging to the eleventh century and later. carry to its highest perfection the Indian genius for the invention of graceful patterns and their application to the decoration of Masonry.

Andhra's Contribution to Jainism: For the spread of Jainism the south played a vital role. We find evidence for it in Jaina literature. During the reign of Chandragupta Maurya (4th Century B. C.) Magadha was ravaged by a 12 year long famine. Some Jainas under the leadership of Bhadrabahu came to the South and by that time Jainism was a flourishing religion in the South.

In "Hari Bhadriya Vritti" it is written that the King of Kalinga who ruled during the time of Vardhamana Mahavira was a friend of Vardhamana's father and Mahavira came to Kalinga and preached his religion.

Dharmamrita, a classic of 12th century A. D., mentions that even during the times of 12th Thirthankara, Vasupujya Jainism was prevalent in the Andhra country. Tradition also says an Anga king come with his three sons to Vengi who later became Jainas and built a city known as Pratipalapura which is some where near modern Bhattiprolu.

The Jaina tradition also mentions that Asoka's grandson Samprati became a Svetambra Jaina and spread the religion in Kalinga. The Andhra and the Kalinga countries might have been strongholds of non-vedic religions for long, for Bodhayana says that whoever goes to Kinga must perform Prayschitta.

During the regime of Kharavela (2nd century B. C.), Jainism spread into many regions of Northern Andhra and Orissa. The rock caves at Khandagiri and Udayagiri bear testimony to the same. The Satavahana rulers of Pre-Christian era who ruled a vast territory which now comprises of Andhra, Maharashtra and Karnataka states were also influenced by Jainism. 'Kalakasuri prabandha' writes that one of the Satavahana rulers of Pratistanapura used to attend a Jaina monk's discourse.

JAINISM IN KARNATAKA

Even before the reign of Chalukya king Pulakesi the (17th Century A. D.) Jainism was a dominant religion in the Karnataka. All the later kings like Vinayaditya, Vijayaditya helped Jaina saints in spreading their religion. During Vatapi Chalukyas and Rashtrakutas in whose kingdoms much of Andhra (mainly Rayalasemsa and Telangana regions) was a territory influenced by Jainism as these kings were great patrons of this religion.

During the Rashtrakuta king Nitya Varsha Indra Vallabha (915-927 A. D.) Bodhan was his capital and even now it is considered by the jainas as one of their Adima Thirthas. The famous Jaina Acharya Somadevasuri of that time wrote many bocks and spread the faith the Telangana region.

From 2nd century B. C. upto 800-900 A. D., there were no inscriptions bearing the dates of that period. It might be the period of Jaina decline in Kalinga and it was only during that period of Jaina decline in Kalinga and it was only during that period the Vedic and the Buddhistic religions began to flourish in Kalinga.

Tradition says that in a village known as Gangaperulu in Rayalasema, a Jaina monk known as Simhanandi Acharya lived. The princes who fled from a town known as Vijayapura in northern India, sought his protection and later founded the famous Ganga dynasty with is blessings. Excavations conducted at Danavulapadu in Cuddapah district revealed the extent of spread of Jainism in that area.

The founder of Eastern Chalukya dynasty Kubjavishnuvardhana (624-641 A. D.) was brother of Pulakesi II. During his period Vijayawada was a great Jaina centre. His Danasasana (762 A. D.) indicates that he was a great portion of Jaina religion.

Ramatirtham in Visakhapatnam district was both a Buddhist and Jaina Kshetra and now it is a famous Hindu Kshetra. Excavations at Penugonda in East Godavari districtrevealed that it was once a Jaina religious centre. At the time of Kullotunga Chola son of Raja Rajanarendra, Munugodu in Sattenapalli taluq was a Jaina kshetra. Another inscription of 1178 A.D., reveals that Bhogapuram in Visakhapatnam Dt. was having Jaina temples. In Nellore district upto 13th Century there were Jaina temples.

Spread of Saivism and Vaishnavism and decline of Jainism: During the 12th and 13th centuries Saivism began to spread in Andhra and there used to be religious debates over these religious faiths. There were many clashes between the followers of these faiths and of the Jaina Bastis (centres) were destroyed by the Saivites. Panditaradhyacarita and Palkuriki Somanatha and Sivaratrimahatmya of Srinatha gives evidence to this fact.

It is a wonder that though Jainism was prevalent for more than 1500 years in Andhra only one book written a by a saint of this area is available now. It is Jinendra Kalyanabhyudaya by Appayacharya (1241 Saka era).

While Saivism became popular during Kaltiya kings, Vaishnavism became popular during Vijayanagara kings. Spread of these religions led to the decline of the Jaina faith. Bur Jainas have their piligrim even now. Kollipaka in Nalgonda district is jaina kshetra and Penugonda in Anantapur district is one of the Jaina Chaturdasa mahavidya sthnams.

For an Archaeologist and epigraphist who wishes to study Jaina history Andhra provides a rich source.

'Padu' were all Jaina villages. In many places in Andhra we find wells known as Jainabavulu. They are of a particular type of construction. They are covered by lids so that animals in the streets may not fall in the nights. Similarly in many villages we find idols called as 'Sanyasi Demullu. All such villages were once Jaina villages. Many such villages are found in Coastal Andhra.

Its Relevance: To understand Indian Philosophy and culture in broader perspective study of Jainism in essential. As Prof. Hopkins puts it, Jainism "represents a theological mean between Brahmanism and Buddhism. Then assuredly a serious study of Jainism becomes incumbent on all who may seek to understand aright either the early. Brahamnic ritual or the trenchant and for long effective Buddhist protest which that elaborate ritual evoked".

The interest of Jainism to the student of religion lies in the fact that it goes back to a very early period and to primitive currents of religious and metaphysical speculations, which also gave rise to the oldest Indian philosophies like Sankhya, Yoga and Buddhism. It also shares their theoretical passimism and the pratical ideal of liberation.

Jaina approach to truth saying that it has many facts leads to relativism though not to pluralism. Their acceptance of the uniqueness of each soul and stress on individual effort to reach kaivalya makes it a humanistic religion. The ills of the 20th century are absolutism and ideological dogmatism. These attitudes will lead the world to catastrophy and more so in a nuclear age.

The Jainas say our affirmative predication is dependent on Svadravya, Svakshetra, Svakala and Svabhava. If it is paradravya, parakshetra, parakala and parabhava it can be negatively predicated. This approach to understand alien religions, cultures, political and social systems will lessen the tensions in the world and improve our quality of life and make this planet a better place to live. As Ratnasekhara in Sambodhasattari says "No matter whether he is a Svetambara or a digambara, A Buddhist or a follower of any other creed, one who has realized the self sameness of the soul, i. e., looks on all creatures as his own self, attains salavation".

Avadhu Atmajnan Men Rahana

Avadhu, live in the realization of soul never say anything to anyone

One who realizes the self, known all beliefs fighting

In the heats does not keep one-sidedness, sees tow-coloured wings

All sorrows and sickness end, becomes immortal and unchanging

Does not believe in muum and tuum breaks the worldly bondage

He keeps in his mind and soul the form which is invisible, incomparable, ultimate

He forsakes the pleasures of physical sight, with determination follows intuition

One thief is very active and militant he is found all over the world in sly

One has to keep vigilent and not permit him to enter the house secretly

One who leaves one and takes up the other only fans the fires of passion

Suri Rajendra's saying you ponder keep yourself on vigil, well-equipped.

The Tamils can be defined as people, having Tamil as their mother tongue. Tamil language is a member of the Dravidian/ South Indian family of languages. The four southernmost states of India-tamiz Nadu, kERaLa, karNAdaka, and Andra Pradesh-are predominantly linguistically Dravidian, each state carved out on the basis of predominance of the four major Dravidian languages. The Dravidian languages are mother tongues of about a quarter of the Indian population. Though about 80% of the speakers are found within the borders of these four South Indian states, a number of Dravidian languages have been identified in other parts of South Asia. Among the tribal languages of Central India, almost extending to the borders of Bengal, distinct from the Austro-Asiatic family of languages, many Dravidian languages have been identified. The northern reaches of this family have been located in isolated settlements in Nepal and Pakistan. The Brahui speakers are found in the hills of Baluchistan, almost on the borders of Pakistan, Afghanistan and Iran. So, the Dravidian family of languages is a South Asian family of languages in one sense. About 22 languages are classified as belonging to the Dravidian family and on linguisic criteria, sub-division as North, Central and South Dravidian are made. Tamils alone number about 60 million people.

South India and Sri Lanka have been homelands of the Tamils, from the beginning of recorded history. The region, roughly covered by the modern states of tamiz NAdu and Kerala are identified as ancient tamizakam up to about 10th century AD. Even though some evidence exists for Tamil influence, and Tamil presence in Sri Lanka is noticeable from very early times, strong Tamil presence and influence in Sri Lanka, from about the 10th century.

In the 19th and early 20th centuries, Tamils migrated to some British colonies in search of employment and thus there are substantial Tamil populations in Malaysia, Singapore, Mauritius, Fiji and South Africa. After the World War II, a movement of Tamil professionals to UK, USA, Australia and New Zealand is proceeding continuously. Due to the recent civil war type situation in Sri Lanka, many thousands of Tamils in about 20 countries, with large numbers in Canada, Germany, France, and Switzerland. Within the Nordic countries, Norway and Denmark have more Tamils than Sweden.

Present Situation Regarding Religious Affiliations of the Tamils

Hinduism, Christianity and Islam are the major religions among the Tamils in that order: Hindus are counted as forming more than 80% of the population and the other religions are reckoned to be less than 20% of the population. Some of the other religions like Jainism, Buddhism have relatively few adherents. The Tamil Christians include both Roman Catholics as well as the Protestants. The Muslims are mainly Sunni. The situation is fairly stable, only Christian missions, said to be marginally successful in making new converts. The general atmosphere is religious toleration and harmony.

The official policy of India is secularism. Overall, Hinduism is neither a missionary nor an exclusive religion. To put it in a negative way, the Hindus withdraw into themselves and don't react except when they feel threatened. Many scholars have commented on the tolerant attitude of the Hindus. Some recent developments in India challenges this view. But tamiz Nadu and the Tamils, generally keep up the Tamil tradition of tolerance, There is no Hindu extremism worth mentioning among the Tamils. No serious claim is put forward that Hinduism should have special privileges, compared to other religions.

DRAVIDIAN HYPOTHESIS ABOUT THE INDUS VALLEY PEOPLE

The Tamils have legends that their ancient history extends up to about ten thousand years, sea swallowing up their lands twice and kings establishing new capitals and fostering Tamil in three successive academies. The legend is first mentioned in the commentary of kaLavijal, which is assigned to about 8th century AD. This legend is one of the reasons-one of the excuses-for connecting up the Tamil civilization with some prehistoric ancient civilizations, whose identity and continuity poses special problems.

The records of the Indus Valley Civilization have not been satisfactorily deciphered. Material remains have been interpreted by archeologists. There cannot be finality, till a satisfactory reading of the records. Material remains are generally interpreted in the light of elements in the later Hinduism. Siva worship in the form of pacupati and NadaRajA, Sakti worship and some other deductions are made. In the 1950s, Father Heras argued for the Dravidian identity of the Indus Valley people. In the 1960s, the Scandinavian Institute of Asian Studies issued many announcements, trying to establish this identity. This hypothesis is still defended seriously by Japanese Professor Noboru Karashima, President of the International Association for Tamil Research in 1994.

The Dravidian Identity of the Sumerians

This is another hypothesis that is strongly advocated by certain scholars. The Sumerian records have been deciphered and material remains have been interpreted satisfactorily. Linguistic and cultural affinities between the Sumerians and the Tamils, separated by much more than a millennia, are pointed out. The late Professor A. catAcivam (A.Sathasivam) from Sri Lanka and Dr. ulakaNAtan muttarAjan (Loganathan Muttarayan) from Malaysia are examples. Eminent historians of the caliber of K.A. Nilakanda cAttiri (Nilakantta Sastri), have pointed out similarities in temple worship. A hypothesis, connecting the ancestors of the Dravidians, if not the Tamils. to the Mediterranean area, is still advocated by certain scholars.

6

A STUDY BASED ON THE HISTORICAL TIME AND EVENTS

Literary, epigraphical and archeological sources existt for the study of religious traditions of the Tamils for about 2000 years. As materials exist for such a long period of time, it is only fitting that we pay just passing attention to doubtful prehistoric connections and concentrate on the historical period. Tamil is one of the two classical languages of India, along with Sanskrit. There are Tamil literary texts and Tamil inscriptions, dated roughly, round about the beginning of the Christian era. As in most of ancient and medieval Indian texts, controversies exist on the exact dates of early Tamil records and documents. We have to be dependent on rough calculations and the most probable dates. Some distinct historical periods:

(1) 100 B.C to 300 A.D.;

(2) 300 A.D. to 600 A.D.;

(3) 600 A.D. to 1200 A.D.;

(4) 1200 A.D. to 1800 A.D.; and

(5) 1800 A.D. to today.

CANGKAM (ACADEMY) PERIOD

The general designation for the early period is cangkam period, because of the strong tradition that three academies existed in the remote past and that what we get as early literary texts were those approved by those academies. The main source for the early period is literary evidence. From a study of the literary evidence, some scholars argue that the Tamil society was secular then. It is only a relative term in the sense that when compared to early North Indian literature and later Tamil literature, a distinctiveness of relative secularism can be pointed out.

Some indigenous elements of religion, peculiar to the Tamils, have been noticed in the earliest available stratum of Tamil literature. A portion of this early Tamil poetry is identified as Heroic poetry. There were three Tamil Kingdoms-cEra, cOLa and pAnhdija-and many independent chieftaincies in the early period and there were intermittent and internecine wars and battles for violent state formation. maRam (valour) was the celebrated theme.

NADUKAL (PLANTED STONE)

The worship for the fallen brave warriors is one of the popular forms of worship in early Tamil poetry. tolkAppijam gives an elaborate description in six stages in the planting of stone, beginning with looking for a suitable stone and ending in the institution of formal worship. The portrait of the hero is often decorated with peacock feathers. Some poems refer to spears and shields erected around the planted stones. Offering of Naravam (toddy = alcohol) to the spirit of the fallen hero, represented in the planted stone, is mentioned in some verses.

Verijadal (Dance in Ecstasy)

The dance in ecstasy is found mainly in the worship of murukan/muruku (youth, beauty, god-head). He was the god of the hilly region. The name of god or archetype was different in each landscape among the five different landscapes of the Tamil land. mAjOn (dark male)/ mAl (great one) was the god of the forest or pastoral landscape. koRRavy (lady of victory) was the goddess of ferocious appearance for the arid or waste land. vEl (spear) was the main weapon of murukan. He is a warrior-hero par excellence, but is often mentioned in akam (love) poetry, the other main theme of the earliest stratum of Tamil literature. Love-sickness of young girls in separation from their lovers seem to be generally interpreted as caused by murukan who needs propitiation in worship. The organizer and chief priest of the worship was vElan (man with spear). A number of verses refer to the sacrifice of the blood of ram and offering of toddy in the ritual. The veRijAdal occurred in koRRavy worship also, Later, murukan was considered son of koRRavy. A group dance of girls, known as kuravyjAdal, is also associated with murukan worship. Some elements of ecstasy were also involved in this dance. This dance occurred in mAjOn worship also. murukan has continued to be very popular among the Tamils and he is frequently hailed as the T^mil god. Kamil Zvelebil had chosen to name his first volume on Tamil literature, as The smile of murukan.

CINYC CURAVIN KODU (PREGNANT SHARK BONE)

A solitary verse mentions this worship in the littoral region. On full moon day, fishermen and families get drunk and worship. This may be the peculiar worship of Nejtal, (littoral) landscape.

KANHDU (POST, STONE)

This worship is often mentioned in connection with manRu (public meeting place). Lighting of lamps by women is specifically referred to in some verses. Floor of the manRu was smeared with cow-dung.

INFLUENCE OF NORTH INDIAN RELIGIOUS TRADITIONS

Jaina monks lived in hills around maturai, the capittal of the pAnhdijAs and in a few other places. Early Tamil Brahmi inscriptions of round about the beginning of the

Christian era, testify to this. Some kings and chieftains were responsive to Brahmins and Vedic sacrifices. Many instances can be quoted to show that beliefs in the existence of the ujir (soul), maRu piRappu (rebirth) and vAnOr ulaku (world of celestial beings) existed among the Tamils even in that early period.

Post-cangkam Period 300 A.D. to 600 A.D.

Politically in this period, the Tamils were under foreign kalabhra domination. Their political history is characterized by many historians as a dark period. Buddhism and Jainism appear to have prospered during this period. Some notable literary works are assigned to this period. The early Tamil kAppijangkaL, (epics) are assigned to this age, as for examples, cilappatikAram, a Jaina epic and manhimEkaly, a Buddhist epic. aRam, the equivalent of Sanskrit dharma, becomes the main theme of literary works. Eleven didactic works were written in this period. Their main purpose seems to be reformation of the society-bringing back values which were reversed during the Heroic Age.

Tirukkural the most outstanding work in Tamil, belongs to this period. This sets the tone of didactic works. According to Albert Schweitzer's evaluation in his book, Indian Thoughts and its Development, tirukkuRaL represents a synthesis of much of the best in Indian thought up to that time with a positive approach to life. The positive approach to life, also called life-affirmation, seems to owe its influence to the literary traditions of the Academy period. varnAcirama dharma, the central concept of the Brahminical religion, prescribing different rules for the four-fold castes and for the four stages of human life, has not even been mentioned in this work. This work is of universal appeal.

The Tamil society never had the varnha system. There was no cattiryjAs, and the vycijAs. The ruling kings and their ancestors, were sometimes eulogized and flattered as the cattirijAs, but there was no consequent development from this position. The non-Brahmin high caste Tamils resented the term-cuttiras, the name of the fourth caste. So, what we get in the Tamil works, equivalent to the Sanskrit dharmasastras, is sAmAnija dharma applicable to every human being. Religious affiliation of the author is not known.

ThiruvaLLuvar, the author, has kept himself clear of external trappings of different religions. The Hindus, the Jains, and the Buddhists have claimed this work as their own. Many Christian missionaries and British administrators have praised this work, even tracing Christian influence in the work. This work, consisting of 1330 verses, has been translated into many languages. Other didactic works, follow the lead by tirukkural. The authors are identified as Jaina or Brahminical, mainly by their invocation verses. Otherwise, there are no deep differences in the contents of these works. NAladijAr the second most important work with 400 verses, ascribed to Jaina authorship and with a noticeable slant to life-negation, had been translated into English by G.U. Pope almost a century ago. tirukkuRaL and NAladijAr can be said to constitute the ethical core of the religious traditions of the Tamils. It is important to note here that varnAcirama dharma had not been brought into Tamil literature. Though the Tamils also developed an evil and pernicious caste system, in certain respects, quite distinct from the varnha system, in subsequent periods, that system had no sanction either in Tamil or in Sanskrit texts.

BHAKTI PERIOD 600 A.D. TO 1200 A.D.

The Tamils were under the Pallava and the pAnhdija kingdoms during the earlier half of this period and under the cola Empire during the latter half of the same. The Tamil power reached its zenith under the chola Empire, which also ruled many non-Tamil communities in South India and Sri Lanka. In the history of religion and literature, this period is referred to as the bhakti period. Bhakti is a Sanskrit word, meaning devotion. This Sanskrit word and the Tamilicised form patti became popular quite late. The bhaktti poetry seems to be a curious transformation of literary traditions of the Academy period. Both akam tradition, dealing with love between man and woman and puRam tradition, dealing with heroism and generosity of warriors are combined in a strange manner and the position of man as well as hero goes to god, while the position of woman and hero-worshipper go to the devotee.

A. K. Ramanujan has recently brought out a good translation into English of some of these early poems. Though the origins of the concept of bhakti are traceable in Sanskrit sources, bhakti movement as such originated in the Tamil land. Personal relationship between the devotee and the god was its main characteristic, and worship became a fervent personal experience in response to divine grace. Religion for the devotees is no longer a matter of contemplation of a transcendent, impersonal absolute, but of ecstatic response to an intensely personal experience. This leads to a profound sense of the devotee s own shortcomings and to a trustful recourse to the god s forgiveness, with the whole personality being surrendered to the deity. It is this position which inspired the scholar-missionary G. U. Pope's evaluation-which seems to be somewhat superficial-of this religion as the religion, closest to Christianity, among Indian religions. Norman Cutler has worked on the poetics of Tamil devotion.

The vedic religion-the Brahminical religion-becomes a popular religion of the Tamils, through the bhakti movement. The Sanskrit sources contributed another important element for this religion. This religion owes a massive debt to the Sanskrit purAnhAs and epics. The temple rituals, prescribed in the Sanskrit AkamAs, became very important. From the very beginning, sectarian differences are noticeable, may be because of the influence of purAnhAs. Saiva and Vaishnava movements were presented to the Tamil people as Tamil religions This was made possible by religious synchronism. murukan becomes identified with Skanda and karttikeja and related to Siva as a son, korravy becomes identified with umA, Siva's consort and as murukan s mother, and majon becomes identified with Vishnu. Saivism is the form of Hinduism, very popular among the Tamils.

The Saiva movement was relatively more involved in religious conflicts and controversies. Saint Appar, a convert from Jainism to Saivism, converted the Pallava ruler from Jainism to Saivism. His poetry seems to be a strange mixture of Jaina world-view and Siva bhakti. Even though he expresses his regret for having wasted much of his life as a Jaina monk, his poetry seems to be a form of synchronism between Jainism and Saivism.

The Jaina world-view and Jaina didactic works become acceptable to the Saivites. Saint Campanthar, a younger contemporary of saint Appar, converted the pAnhdija ruler from Jainism to Saivism.. He defeated the Buddhists in another controversy. As a Brahmin, he was a champion of Vedic religion against the Jains and the Buddhists. There are plenty of polemical references about the Jains and the Buddhists in his bhakti poetry. Saint Manikkavasagar was also said to have defeated the Lankan Buddhists in a controversy, but there is no trace of polemics in his compositions.

For about a millennium, Hinduism, Buddhism, and Jainism were the three important religions among the Tamils. The triangular contest for the loyalty of the Tamils led to the growth of polemical literature to which adherents of all religions contributed. The Buddhist contribution is seen in the manhimEkaly and the kunhdalakEci, the Jaina contribution in the NIlakEci and the Saiva contribution in the civagnAnacittijAr. But overall, conflicts are rare, especially after Hinduism consolidated its position. The Saiva or Vaishnava rulers, were generally generous to all the Hindus, irrespective of their personal inclinations and also patronized the Jaina and Buddhist religious establishments of their subjects.

A very important text for Tamil Saivism is the periya purAnham, the Saiva hagiology of 63 NajanmAr, (saint lords), all of whom lived in South India and attained heaven through their bhakti to Siva. This work influenced vIra Saivism of Karnataka. Saint Manikkavasagar's devotional poems are acknowledged as the most moving in Tamil literature. G. U. Pope brought a translation of the tiruvAcakam into English. almost a century ago. Glenn Yocum has published a study of tiruvAcakam recently. The devotional poems of Saint cuNtarar, numbering about a tthousand verses, had been translated by David Shulman recently. The Twelve Sacred Books of the Tamil Saivas were complete in the 12th century A.D. For the vast majority of the Tamil Saivites, the basic works of their religion are these Twelve Sacred Books. They don't look to any Sanskrit work for guidance.

The Vaishnava bhakti movement was dominated by twelve AzvArs-those who contemplate deeply on Vishnu. They were authors of tivvijapirapaNtam (sacred composition) of four thousand verses. Compared to the saiva devotional poems, the Vaishnava devotional poems make greater use of akam tradition and less of puRam tradition of the classical period. Friedhelm Hardy had brought out a fine publication recently on the history of this movement. Some important saints are AdAL, kulacEkarar, tirumangky and NammAzvAr. The works of the last one are very important and are sometimes referred to as Tamil Vedas. Though less influential in Tamil land, the Vaishnavite bhakti movement exerted great influence throughout India, during the later periods.

The temple worship seems to be a prominent feature from the beginning of the bhakti movement. Temples, built of durable material, first rock-cut and then made of stone, made their appearance from the 8th century. Huge stone temples were built by the cola Emperors and their successors throughout tamilnadu. The temples became the centres, around which many aspects of life of the people were organized. Architects and sculptors were needed in the construction activities. Music, dance, and drama were patronized by the Hindu temples. These temples were generally rich, having been owners of land other forms of wealthy. They employed people and helped them in times of distress. The big temples are still great pilgrim centres to which the Tamil Hindus from all over the world yearn to visit. Most of the big temples in tamiz Nadu have myths of their own. David Shulman has made an interpretation of these myths recently. The big temples are the main attraction for the modern tourists in tamiz NAdu.

AGE OF RELIGIOUS PHILOSOPHY. 1200-1800 AD.

The beginnings of philosophical speculations in India are traced to the Upanishads, which originated in North India and which are in Sanskrit. Buddhism dominated the philosophical field for many centuries and South India began to make significant contributions. The definitely identifiable contribution from tamizNAdu can be said to start from the 8th century A.D. Many religious philosophical doctrines of South Indian origin have been written in Sanskrit, may be because that language was the lingua-franca throughout the South Asian sub-continent in that age. In the eighth century, Sanskrit the propounder of Advita (monoism) hailed from Kerala, a part of ancient Tamil land. His Vedanta philosophy assimilated much of the world-view of the Buddhists and gave it a new twist. He is said to have toured throughout the sub-continent and engaged in debates with the Buddhists. What he had taken over from Buddhism is said to have helped him to win over large number of adherents of Buddhism which was already in decay in India at that time.

In the eleventh-twelfth centuries, Ramanuja, the propounder of (Visistadvita-qalified monoism) hailed from the present tamizNAdu. He was strongly influenced by the Vaishnava bhakti literature, based on the Puranic religion. He was better received in Karnataka than in tamiz Nadu. Ramanuja wrote in Sanskrit, so his impact among the Tamils is relatively limited. The history of Vaishnavism in tamizNAdu becomes a little complicated as the later Vijayanagar Emperors and the Nayak kings who were mainly Telugu origin gave it sustenance. They patronized Sanskrit and gave importance to Sanskrit sources. Soon, there was a schism in tamizNAdu Vaishnavism into vadakaly, (northern school) and tenkaly, (southern school) sects. The southern school, looks mainly to the Tamil Vaishnava texts for inspiration.

The thirteenth and the fourteenth centuries saw the appearance of the fourteen works of Saiva Siddhanta philosophy in Tamil.The basic Tamil work is civagnanapOtam. There is still a big controversy on whether this work is a translation of twelve aphorisms from an obscure or unattested portion of (Rauravagama). Saiva Siddhanta is a South Indian religion, found among the Tamils only. Besides the canonical fourteen works, there are subsidiary works and commentaries in Tamil only. Agamas are accorded a special status while the Vedas only a general status as basic works to the philosophy. The importance given to the Agamas makes South Indian Saivism, a distinctive form of Hinduism, in some respects. The Tamils try to derive the basic framework of the system from their own Twelve Sacred Books.

The development of many philosophical schools led to development of sectarian conflicts and later attempts to patch them up, especially by mystic poets like Saint tAjumAnavar in the 18th century and Saint IrAmalingkar in the 19th century. camaracam, (harmony) becomes the main theme. The former praises the CLEVER cittar, (poets of powers) who found harmony between Vedanta and Siddhanta. The latter founded cutta camaraca canmArkka cangkam, a Society for Religious Wisdom of Pure Harmony.

Modern Period

Islam and Christianity are important minority religions in this period. Islam came to Tamils in two ways. Arab traders intermarried with local people and built up a community, who now speak Tamil or Malayalam. Muslim invaders from the North had temporary success in the South and their descendants speak Urdu. As in Vaishnavism, there is some split in the attitude of the Muslims towards Tamil. Many of them are proud to claim Tamil as their language and they have made substantial contributions to the development of Tamil for more than six hundred years.

The Syrian Christian community, in the West coast, claims that they were the descendants of native converts of the Apostle Saint Thomas, from the first century A.D. They have preserved some copper plates, which according to them, were received by Saint Thomas from native rulers of his time. Modern epigraphists have dated the these plates in the ninth and the thirteenth centuries. It is now clear that this community is enjoying certain privileges in Kerala at least from the 9th century. Like the Christian trading community, a small Jewish trading community also in the West coast, gained privileges from the native Hindu rulers in the 10th century, as testified by a copper plate in the possession of their descendants. Roman Catholicism was introduced by the Portuguese in the 16th century. Protestantism was introduced by the Dutch in the 17th century. The British ruled over the entire Tamil homeland for 11/2 centuries-roughly from 1800 to 1950. Westernization and Modernization are going on, especially from the beginning of British rule and they are powerful forces even now. Christian missionaries have been very active and have considerable success in proselytisation. There was again Tamil polemical literature, reflecting a triangular contest among the Hindus, the Roman Catholics and the Protestants, especially between 1850 and 1925.

As for Jainism and Buddhism, the former continues to flicker, while the latter disappeared completely and has taken a new birth recently. Its rebirth is as a religion of protest, as a religion of the down-trodden. The people who became underprivileged and untouchable in the Hindu society felt that even Islam and Christianity could not bring them salvation and chose to accept Buddhism, on the advice of the late Dr. Ambedkar, their leader. Only a section of the underprivileged community called Dalits in India became converts. Their problem of integration into the rest of the population cries for solution.

The appeals to fundamentals of Brahminical Hinduism, as it is understood in North India, do not seem to have its echo among Tamils, because of the character of Hinduism in tamizNAdu. A few months ago, Prof. Saraswathy Vijayavenugopal, a folklorist from Madurai University in South India, in a lecture in Uppsala, made the observation that there seem to be many folk religions among the Hindu Tamils. Synchronization-continuing synchronism of different religions-seems to be a living process within what is called Hinduism among Tamils. The influence of political Hinduism, exemplified by Bharatiya Janata Party and Vishva Hindu Parishad, which champion Brahminical values, is negligible among Tamils.

The last half century in tamizNAdu is dominated by a powerful socio-political Dravidian movement, against North Indian influences, including Sanskrit and Hindi domination, but particularly Brahmin domination and oppression. among the Tamils in South India. Though the movement is split into many political groups. of which two are the two dominant political parties of tamiznadu, there are still no indications that parties which don't subscribe to the ideology of the Dravidian movement can make headway in tamiznadu. A small Brahmin community at the top is very vulnerable. Christians, Muslims, Buddhists and Jains find comfort in identifying themselves with the vast majority of the Hindus in the Dravidian movement. A kind of secularism is fostered as the ideology of the movement. tirukkuRaL is held up as the embodiment of Tamil Culture. The classical Cangkam period literature is idealised as the literature of the Golden Age of the Tamils.

ANCIENT PERIOD OF BENGAL

Our knowledge of Bengali life in this ancient period is fragmentary. Some descriptions of Bengali people, and some aspects of bengali food habits, culture, transportation, possessions, dress, society, religion, technology, literature, and arts are discussed in the respective pages. A brief outline of this period is supplied below.

History begins by definition in the historic period, the early phase is thus defined as the period from the beginning of the historic period (before the 5th century AD) till the Gupta period (ending in 550 AD). After the decline of the sarasvati-sindhu civilization, direct foreign trade with India restarted only in the centuries before the birth of christ, when trade with the Ptolemaic Egyptian ports (like Berenice, Nechesia, and Myos Hormos) allowed the Indians major benefits instead of the Arab intermediaries. The importance of the Indian trade increased in the first century BC when the Romans took over Egypt, and is underscored by Pliny's mention that the trade balance with India was draining the Roman empire, and in the laments of emperor Tiberius. In addition, in the maurya period, the trade route from eastern china through the desert and pamir, Afganisthan and Persia, all the way to the mediterranean was accessible to the major Indian empire.

This contact increased during the saka and kusana period. In fact this foreign trade was the major reason for the continuing power struggles in western India. The eastern ports of Gange and Tamralipti find mention from the very first century AD; sounagoura (possibly wari/vaTeshvar near DhAkA with occupation dating back to at least 450 BC) is mentioned in the early second century AD, and trade with Tibet, Myamar, and the southeast asian states like suvarNadvIpa is attested from a later period. Because of all this trade, the period from the 2nd centuy BC to the 7th century AD found the rise of international cross-influence and a pan-Indian culture: in literature, in language, in the scripts, and in arts. Overall, even though Bengal was never as rich as the western and southern parts of the country, trade seems to have been an important component of the economy in addition to farming, which, of course, had been the mainstay since the prehistoric period. The society was basically feudal, and like elsewhere in India, the Gupta period is a golden age in Bengal, with trade and well-minted gold coins.

No doubt the Hindus, Jainas and Buddhists preachers brought the aryan influence to Bengal early in this period, in addition to the influence that came through the mauryyas and the shuGgas; and local religious traditions started becoming discernible in Bengal. However, the complete aryanization probably had to wait till the age of the Guptas who were Hindu but supported the Buddhists and Jainas as well. It is to be noted however that aryanization here refers to the introduction of the aryan caste system and hindu religious ceremony into Bengal; and was equally accepted by the hindus and majoity of the jains and buddhists leading family lives.

The term is somewhat misleading as much of the hindu tradition all over India including Bengal and including some of the ceremonial structure and most of the pantheon of modern hindu gods largely traces its origins to non-'aryan', (dravidian and tribal) cultures as much as to the culture shared with other Indo-European people.

The golden period in Indian history was, however, not to last. The fall of Rome in 475 AD, the wrenching away of the chinese trade route by the Huns in the fifth century, and the rise of the Islamic power around the eighth century and them capturing the major western trading posts, and the slow decay of the eastern ports led to a major change in the economic and social landscape. The resulting fall in the centralized power, and the return to a more agricultural pattern led to the rise of insular and local identities.

Coming on top of the advent of the foreign influences not only through trade but also directly with the Yueh-chi zaka kusana, Ahira (2-3 cent AD), huNa (5-6 cent AD), and gujar-gurjar turaSkas (7-9 cent AD), and this rise of the regional kingdoms in the second half of the 7th century, the regional characteristics started dominating, in religion, arts and language, and it is counted as the beginning of medieval times in Indian history.

So also in Bengal, After the fall of the Guptas, different small kingdoms arose, and, some bengalis spread out into the rest of India in search of fortunes. For example, the gadAdhara of vArendrI, who in the 10th century founded a small kingdom in belari in South India under the suzerainty of rasrrakuta krsna III was probably a descendant of these expatriates. However, in Bengal, except for shashAGka, no powerful kings arose here, but bengal was very much in the fray of North Indian politics. As opposed to the situation under harSavarddhana in the UP region, the increasing influence of brahminism in Bengal in this period precluded state support for buddhism and jainism, even though they were popular religions, and the buddhist vihAras started. The only exception were the possibly foreign origin khad, gas.

During shashagka, the buddhists were probably actually persecuted, and some religious artifacts destroyed. But, three things need to be stated in this context. First, brahminical hinduism in the early period was very strongly against religions like buddhism which did not follow its rituals, and often explicitly criticized all ritual as meaningless or worse. Buddhists were considered inauspicious and their houses unclean. Many kings and kingdoms tried to expel them. Second, destruction of religious property in the ancient world was not uncommon; through the ages it was indulged in by such great rulers as puSyamitra Sunga, sri harsa of kashmir, pulakeshI II, subhata varmana of the parmars, mahendra varmana, and rajendra cola. The aims were varied: it was sometimes political as when at the end of the 12th century the malva parmars destroyed the jain temples and mosques for arab traders in the trade dominated chalukya gujarat, it was sometimes symbolic as when the rashtrakutas sent elephants to mow down pratihara temples in the 10th century, it was sometimes economic as when harshadeva of kashmir decided to appoint deva utpatana nayakas to loot hindu and buddhist temples at the end of the 11th century, and it was sometimes religious like karnataka jaina temples being taken over by the shaivaites who destroyed the original and put idols of shiva in it. As shashagka was fighting the buddhist harSavarddhana, the motives mght not have been entirely religious vengeance.

Third, it seems that traditional stories of extreme religious intolerance such as the one about the southern shaivaite king srimaravarman killing 8000 jains on a single day in late 7th century are not told about this reign, even though only accounts by religious and political opponents of shashagka have survived to date.

In general, vaishnava hinduism was on the rise among the populace. Trade seems to have reduced and currency devalued (even during shashAGka, land is being valued in cowries, not gold dInAra or silver drahma). In fact, during the last hundred years, metal currency disappeared. The trading post of tAmralipta is hardly ever mentioned after this period. But the state still seems rich.

Following this period, much of Bengal was ruled by the palas for about four hundred years (8th-11th century AD). Stories of gopAla's election, dharmapAla's conquests, the kaivarta revolt, and mahIpAla's popular policies fill Bengali folklore. However, during this period, trade seems to have further reduced and the region became mainly agricultural, though traders still seem important personages in the society. The feudal structure became more ornate along with increased bureaucracy. Poverty becomes apparent in Bengal at least in some selections from caryagIti (10th-12th cent AD) and saduktikarnamrta (11th-12th cent. poems collected in 1206 AD). Even though the pAla and candra states were mahayani buddhist (as was the first kamboja ruler) in name and in deed at least till the early 11th century, the society in all of Bengal (excepting, naturally, those of the buddhists who had renounced the worldly life and lived in the sagghas) followed the brahminical class division; but was quite tolerant. Land grants to buddhist organizations are found alongside those to brahmins. The buddhist vihAras at nalanda, vikramashIlA, odantapurI and sAranAtha flourished. Bengali language and literature rose to prominence in this period.

When however the sena and barman kings (12th-13th cent A.D.) came from the south (karnata and probably kaligga respectively), replaced the pala and candra dynasties respectively, and established a strict hindu (but otherwise similar) regime much more characteristic of their home regions (since the time of andhra-satavahana period though the times of pallava-cola-calukya) and north India than Bengal of that period, the tolerance reduced and the caste system became very rigid and the influence of buddhism reduced, and to some extent was forcibly reduced. This intolerance extended to the extant kamboja kingdom as well. The documents of this period reflect that the lower castes are not even mentioned in the royal edicts. The trading class no longer seems socally respectable, beaureaucracy seems to have reached new heights and feudal lords becomes very powerful. This is the period when Bengal developed its own brahminical tradition, rules and laws.

Islam also started spreading slowly, especially in the magadha region. When the turkish invaders started coming in to bengal, the society was ill-prepared to deal with the threat. The slow corruption of the sena era and its religious rigidity had made it inflexible, slow, poor, and too dependant on fatalism and astrology; to the extent that the horse-riding swift-moving turks were almost seen as the inevitable future brought about by kalki, the last incarnation of visnu.

But, Bengal, by this time had a self-sufficient village agrarian economy, almost no long distance trade, a feudal system and a distinct regional identity, its own language and script, artistic and cultural styles, and distinct religious tradition. The vedic rituals were weak and knowledge based philosophies were less important, emphasis was rather on the very physical feelings and aesthetics. This, in turn, led to a very humanistic religious streak, a bigger recognition of property rights of women, and a coupled rise of the romantic and physical aspects of the lore of rAdhA and kRSNa, and the slow but steady rise of the cult of feminine shakti which played such an important role during the medieval period ushered in by the Turkish conquest.

EXTENSION OF JAINISM-EARLY PERIOD

The Epigraphic Evidence

Eastern India-Bengal: We consider Bengal first, not because it was an important center of Jainism, but because it is easy to trace the growth and extinction of this religion in this part of the country. We have seen that Mahavira himself had gone to Ladha (West Bengal) in his pre-Kevalin days and had met with uncivil behavior from the inhabitants. It is likely that during Mahavira's time the cultural level of the people in that part of the country was not high enough.

The conditions seemed to have changed dramatically only two centuries later. At the time of Chandragupta Maurya, Bhadrabahu was the head of the Jain church in Magadh. One of Ghadrabahu's disciples Godasa had formed the Godasa Gana. This Godasa Gana according to the Kalpa Sutra had been divided into four Shakhas. It is interesting to note that three of these four Shakhas were named after three important cities of ancient Bengal. These Shakhas were Tamraliptika (after Tamralipta in south Bengal), Kotivarisiya (after Kotivarsha in north Bengal). It seems that the center of Jainism must have shifted towards Bengal at that time. Otherwise the Shakhas would not have been named after these Bengal cities. Some of the Shakhas, Ganas, kulas, etc., mentioned in the Kalpa Sutra have been found to occur in the inscriptions discovered in Mathura. These inscriptions belong to the first a few centuries of the Christian era. This proves that the Shakhas, etc., mentioned in the Kalpa Sutra actually existed. It is likely therefore, that the Shakhas named after the Bengal cities were also actual ones, and not later fictitious additions.

The first epigraphic evidence of the existence of Jainism in Bengal is a copper plate inscription at Paharpur in the Rajshahi district of Bengal. The date of the inscription is Gupta year 159 (AD 479.) It mentions the existence of a Vihara established by the disciples of the Nirgrantha Guhanandi. Hiuen Tsang who stayed in India between AD 629 to 645 also visited Bengal. He wrote that among the non-Buddhists in Pundravardhana the majority were Digambara Nirgranthas. This strong influence of Jainism appears to have abruptly declined immediately after this time for none of the copperplate inscriptions of the Pala and Sena kings of Bengal mentions Jainism. It is to be noted that practically no stone images of Gods of a date prior to the ninth century have been found in Bengal. By that time Jainism had almost disappeared from Bengal and, therefore, very Jain stone images have been found in this area. Among the Jain stone images found in Bengal the following are note worthy:

(1) An image of Rishabhanatha has been found in the Dinajpur District. The image built perhaps in the early Pala period, is one of the most beautiful images found in Bengal. Rishabhanatha is shown here in the sitting position of dhyanamudra.

(2) Another image of Rishabhanatha was found in the Barabhum village in the Midnapur district. Here the image is in standing, e.g., kayotsarga-posture.

(3) A dhyana-Mudra image of Parahvanatha has been found in the Deulbhir village of the Bankura district.

(4) A kayotsarga image of Parshvanatha has been found in Datta-Benia village of the Twenty-four Parganas district.

(5) A kayotasarga image of Shantinatha has been found in Ujani village of the Bardhamana district.

All these images have been identified definitely as those of Jain Tirthankaras. Kshitit Mohan Sen3 however thought that, there were many other Jain images in West Bengal. These have lost their identification marks. Their Jain connection has been forgotten and, the villagers worship these images to day as Bhairavas.

Sen also traces some Bengali words to their Jain origin. For instance the upper garment of the Jain monks is called 'pachheri'. This in Bengali has become 'pachhari'. Similarly the broom used by the Jain monks is called 'pichhi'. In East Bengal a broom is a 'pichha'.

It must, however, be admitted, that Jainism which was quite strong in Bengal fifteen hundred years ago, has now disappeared from this area leaving few traces among the indigenous population.

Bihar

From a reading of the Parishishtaparvan of Hemachandra it would appear that Jainism nearly disappeared from Bihar when Smaprati the grandson of Ashoka started ruling from Ujjayini in the 3rd century BC. This is not so. The Jains continued to exist in Bihar, and carried on building their temples and images all over South Bihar for many centuries. Many Jain images have been found in Bihar especially in the Manbhum district. "Among the other old Jain remains in Manbhum district, particular mention need be made about the Jain temples and sculptures at the small village Pakbira, 32 km. North-east of Bara Bazar or 50 km. by Purulia-Ranchi road in Manbhum district. They had attracted the attention of the archaeological department in the last century.

Report of the Archaeological Survey of India, Vol. VIII, mentions about the remains at Pakbira as follows: 'Here are numerous temples and sculptures, principally Jain; the principal object of attention here is a colossal naked figure, with the lotus as symbol on the pedestal, the figure is 2.25 meters high;...'"

It is surmised that Jainism was quite active in Bihar up to the 12th century. Since most of the images found are nude it is possible to conjecture that the majority of the Jains then in Bihar were Digambaras. Also since they have left behind no literature we may assume that they were ordinary people with no intellectual pretensions. The community must have been financially well off. Otherwise they would have been able to build so many images.

Orissa: It is difficult to say whether Jainism had ever been a strong force in Orissa. Our evidence from the early period is the two inscriptions found in the Udayagiri caves near Bhubaneswar. One of these is by King Kharavela in the Hathigumpha cave. The other is by his chief Queen (Aghamahisi) in the Manchapuri cave. On palecgraphic evidence D. C. Sircar had suggested that the inscriptions belong to the first century BC.

The Queen's inscription is a short one dedicating the cave for the use of the Jain shramnas. Thus it may be concluded that she was respectful towards the Jain religion. The Hathigumpha inscription of King Kharavela has been the subject of many learned comments by eminent historians. Among other reasons for the interest in this inscription is the fact that the inscription is quite a long one, and gives details of a number of occurrences of historical interest. Here, however, only those aspects of this inscription that relate to Jainism need be discussed.

The inscription starts with the benediction Namo arhantam namo sava-sidhanam. This is the Jain formula of veneration and therefore, Kharavela was either a Jain by religion or he had great respect for this religion. In the 12th year of his reign Kharavela brought back the (image of) Kalinga Jina to Orissa, this had been taken away by Nandaraja of Magadh.

This was either a religious act or a matter of prestige for Kharavela. In the thirteenth year of his reign he mentions the erection of a shrine in the vicinity of the relic depository of the Arihanta cn the Kumari Parvata.

These exhaust the list of references to Jainism in the Hathigumpha inscriptions.

Except for these inscriptions' one by Kharavela and the other by his queen, we know nothing about Jainism in Orissa in that period. Schubring is not inclined to give much importance to the Kharavela inscription from the Jain point of view. He said: "This much mutilated inscription it is true, begins with a Jinist formula of veneration, but what tangible deeds in favor of the Jains the scholars were inclined to interpret from it have turned out to be untenable or remained inexplicable. We may presuppose that Jain communities flourished within Kharavels's reign." One is inclined to agree with this view of Stubbing, for if Kharavela, an important king of Kalinga according to his own reckoning, was a Jain, he would surely find mention in the old Jain literature. But Jain literature does not contain even a hint that Kharavela existed.

Another significant thing about the Hathigumpha remains is that "except for Kharavela's inscriptions we could not attribute these to the Jains, for nothing of the decoration reveals their Jain character: the deities depicted are early Hindu, e.g. the sun-God Surya and the lotus Goddess Gaja-Laksmi (Padma-Shri); the figural relief in the Rani-Gumpha have been interpreted by some as scenes from the life of Parshvanatha and by others as episodes from the popular stories of Vasavadatta and Shakuntala; and the whole building is even thought to have been a theater......"

In short, we know that Kharavela's chief queen was a patron of the Jains and Kharavela himself also had a friendly attitude towards them.

There is positive evidence that in the 11th century some caves of the Khandagiri group, specially Cave no. 11, were used as Jain sacred places. "......a few of the old cells were converted into sanctuaries by the carving of relief of Tirthankaras and the Shasanadevis on the walls". A large number of nude chlorite images of the different Tirthankaras all belonging to this period have also been found here. "The prolonged Digambara association of the Khandagiri caves during the reign of the Gangas and their successors, the Gajapatis, is proved by the crude relief of the Tirthankaras on the walls of the cave, which are not earlier in date than the 15th century and may be even later. Evidence regarding the cells being tenanted in this period and monastic fraternities is, however, lacking."

Influence of Jainism seems to have disappeared from Orissa after the sixteenth century.

We thus know that Jainism existed in Orissa for a Period of about seventeen hundred years from the first century BC to the 16th century. For a large part of this period the Khandagiri caves were used as a religious center by them, as resting places of the monks and perhaps also as temples, but we do not know whether the occupation of these caves by the Jains was continuous or intermittent. The Existence of the nude images of the Tirthankaras in the eleventh century proves that at least in the later days the Jains who occupied the caves belonged to the Digambara sect.

Spread of Jainism in South India-early Period

We do not know when and how Jainism entered South India. Traditionally Shravana Belgola in South West Karnataka is said to be the earliest Jain center in South India. Unfortunately, however, there is no epigraphic evidence to support this theory. The Earliest Jain inscription found at this place is believed to be about AD 600, though some Jain inscriptions older than this have been found in areas near about this place. One of them, a copper plate inscription found in Mercara (Coorg) and dated AD 466-67 mentions the gift of the village Badaneguppe to the Shrivijaya Jain-temple at Talvananagara. This proves that Jains were established in this area in the 5th century, but Shravana Belgola itself might not have been their first center in South India.

The inscription of AD 600 found at Shravana Belgola, is one of the most important records in the history of Jainism. A summary of this inscription is as below:

> *"After Mahavira the succession of pupils was Gautama, Lohacharya, Jambu, Vishnudeva, Aparajita, Govardhana, Bhadrabahu, Vishakha, Prothila, Kritikarya (?), Jaya, Siddhartha, Dhrtisena, etc. Bhadrabahu who belonged to this list, with his knowledge of the past, present and future, came to know that a twelve-year famine (vaisamya) was about to occur in Ujjayini. The whole Sangha then moved towards the South (Daksinapatha). They reached a prosperous area. Acharya Prabhachandra knowing his end was near stayed on the Katavapra hill with one disciple, and asked the rest of the Sangha to proceed further. Prabhachandra then started his samadhi aradhana....*

Thus it would appear that it was Prabhachandra who had led the first (?) Jain Sangha to South India and the Sangha, which went there, started from Ujjayini. In later Digambara works the story was modified. "The Bhadrabahu-Katha (about AD 800) and the Brihatkatkosha (AD 931) report that towards the end of his life Bhadrabahu ordered his followers to move away to Punnata (South-Karnataka), whereas Bhadrabahu-Charitra (2nd half of the century) says that he himself took the lead and died on the way". Since the Digambaras believe that there were two Bhadrabahus, the first of whom died 162 years after Mahavira's Nirvana (i.e. in 365 BC), and the second 515 years after the Nirvana (i.e. in 12 BC), it is not clear which Bhadrabahu these later authors were talking about.

The Shvetambara tradition as recorded in Hemachandra's Parishishtaparvan was, as we have seen, quite different. There the Sangha was said to have moved to the seacoast when a dreadful dearth prevailed in the Magadh area, and came back to Magadh when the famine ended. Bhadrabahu himself did not go to the seacoast with the Sangha but had actually gone to Nepal where he undertook the Mahaprana vow. He came back and joined the Sangha in Magadh after performing the austerities.

Also it was Samprati, the successor of Ashoka, who according to Hemchandra prepared the ground for the spread of Jainism in South India (Andras and Dramilas). Ujjayini was at that time the capital of Samprati. Hemchandra's version appears to be more plausible than the later Digambara traditions.

Epigraphic evidence available so far would tend to show that Jainism entered the Deccan through the West. Halsi, known in ancient times as Palasika in the Belgaum district was the most important Jain center in the Deccan in the fifth century. The Kadamba kings of Palasika were patrons of Jainism at that time. They themselves were Brahmans, but some of them made grants of land to Jains, and erected Jain temples. This also supports the view that Jainism entered South India through the west and perhaps from Ujjayini itself.

Another important Jain center in the Deccan was Altem in the Kolhapur district. We have there an epigraph of Shaka 411 (AD 489) which records the erection of a Jain temple by a feudatory of the Calukyas. He is styled as Samiyar.

Tamil Nadu: No definite evidence of the existence of Jainism in the early period has been found in Tamil Nadu. "A large number of caverns have been discovered in the hills and mountainous regions in the Pudukkottai area and Madura and Tinnevelly districts. The two last named areas are particularly rich in these antiquities and the Madura district is known to possess numerous monuments of this kind. These caverns are found generally containing inscriptions. These epigraphs are in the Brahmi characters of the 3rd century BC. These antiquities and records are attributed to the Jains."

This point that the caves perhaps belonged to the Jains, was made by K. V. Subramnia Iyer, a few decades ago. At that time the inscriptions had not been deciphered. In 1966 I. Mahadevan 23 was able to read most of these inscriptions (which number about 75). The inscriptions mention the dedication of the caves by the rulers or their servants to religious people. What exactly was the religion of these people to whom the caves were dedicated is not clear. Some of the terms used in the inscriptions are 'Asiriyan' (archarya), 'Upasakam', 'Palli' (non-Hindu temples), etc. In one place viz., Pukalur, the word 'Ammanam' (naked one) is also found.

It will not perhaps be correct to attribute the dedication of the caves to the Jain monks on the basis of these few words only. Clearly the Donees were religious people, but they could have belonged to any of the non-orthodox sects such as the Buddhists, Ajivakas or the Jains. The 'naked one' could in fact be an Ajivika monk, for we know that according to their rules the monks had to remain naked. Thus this cave could have been dedicated to the Ajivikas. Jainism, however, in later centuries became an important religion of the Tamil Land, and left its mark on the Tamil literature.

Andhra: Andhra is virtually devoid of all traces of Jainism in the first few centuries AD.

NORTHERN AND WESTERN INDIA

The earliest epigraphic evidence of the existence of the Nigantha sect in northern India comes from a solitary inscription of Ashoka (3rd century BC). This is the Seventh Pillar Edict Ashoka and it is recorded on the pillar Firoze Shah Kotla in Delhi. This pillar was originally in Topra in the Ambala district of Haryana, and was brought to Delhi by Firoze Shah Tughlak. Ashoka mentioned in this edict that he had appointed senior officers to look after the affairs of the religious people of the various sects.

These officers had been directed to occupy themselves with matters concerning the (Buddhist) Sangha the Brahmans, the Ajivikas, and the Niganthas. (There are other edicts of Ashoka that mention the Sangha, the Brahmans and the Ajivikas, but Niganthas have not been mentioned in any other Ashokan inscription.) Since the officers were directed to look after the Niganthas, clearly this sect existed in this area in sufficient number. Otherwise the specific mention of this community was not necessary. However, we have no Jain literary records to show the existence of this community in Haryana at that time, and Mahavira himself, perhaps never traveled west of Shravasti that is in eastern Utter Pradesh. But the epigraphic evidence is clear. The Jain religion had by the time of Ashoka spread in northern India at least as far as Haryana.

It appears from the genealogy of the pontiffs given in the Kalpa Sutra that within a hundred years of Ashoka, Jainism had spread as Far West as Pathankot. The Jain pontiff at the time of Samprati, the grandson of Ashoka, was Suhastin. Suhastin's disciple Rohana who became the next pontiff had founded the Uddeha gana that was divided into four Shakhas. One of these shakhas was Udumbarika. Now the country of Audumbara is the present district of Gurudaspur, and its capital was Pratisthana (Pathankot). Thus we know that a substantially large group of Jains was settled in the Pathankot area by the 2nd century BC.

Ujjayini: The next two centuries appear to be quite dark so far as any information about the Jains is concerned. There are no contemporary epigraphs or literary records. The later

Jain historians say that Jainism had spread to Ujjayini at the time of Ashoka's grandson Samprati. Hemachandra (12th century) wrote that Suhastin the head of the Jain Church at that time was living in Ujjayini 25 when ruled from his capital there, and Samprati was a patron of the Jains. This might have been actually so but there is no epigraphic or other independent proof of Samprati's affinity to Jainism.

Ujjayini, however, was the scene of an important event which is said to have occurred in the first century BC This legend is connected with the Shaka conquest of Ujjayini and the origin of the Vikram era.

The legend mentions Gardabhilla, a king of Ujjayini. He had abducted the sister of Kalakacharya, a celebrated Jain teacher (Kalaka was a king's son and had later become Jain. His sister whose name was Saravati was herself a Jain nun). Kalakacharya approached one of the Scythian kings, the Shahis, in Shakasthana for help. But that king was afraid of attacking Gardabhilla, a powerful ruler enjoying the protection of the goddess Rasabhi, who by the spell of her voice made it impossible for an enemy to approach within 24 kilometers of the king. On his part Kalaka had magic powers and could produce wealth at will. He persuaded the Shaka king to raise an army and march against Ujjayini. When he encamped at a distance of 24 kilometers from Ujjayini, the goddess began to raise her voice for the protection of Gardbhilla, but the shaka army stopped her mouth with their arrows, and she became unable to utter a sound. The Gardabhilla was easily made captive and Kalaka's sister was recovered. When he was later forgiven and released, Gardabhilla retired to a forest where he was devoured by a tiger.

Some years afterwards, the son of Gardabhilla, according to some accounts the glorious Vikramditya, came up from Pratisthana with an army, expelled the invaders from Ujjayini, and ruled there for many years in great splendor and established the era that goes by his name (58-57 BC).

Though the exact historical foundation for this legend cannot easily be ascertained, its setting fits the first century BC very well, as it was clearly a period of Shaka inroads into India and of the attempts of Indian rulers, particularly the Satavahanas to resists them. The Hindu Puranas which describe the Satavahanas as Andhras, count Gardabhilla among the feudatories (bhrityas) of the Andhras. Thus the Jain story is partly corroborated. There might thus be some historical truth in this legend of Kalakacharya.

It is possible that the legend existed in some form since the first century but its first recorded form is found in Kalakacharya Kathanaka, a work by Mahesara Suri who probably existed at the time of Hemachandra Suri (12th century). Thus the legend or history of Kalakacharya was put down in writing about 1200 years after the alleged event.

Mathura: The inroads of the Shakas into northern India was followed by those of other foreigners such as the Greeks, and the Kusanas, and these inroads continued for a few centuries from the beginning of the Christian era. The political center of northern India moved to Mathura. It was in Mathura that we find the existence of a large prosperous Jain community at this time.

A large number if Jain relics have been dug up from a mound called Kankali-tila in this town. The relics include one Jain stupa, two temples, and many inscriptions recording the dedication of images of Tirthankaras, and other religious things by pious Jains. Some of these inscriptions bear dates, which mention the years in Kusana era. These dates lie between year 5 and year 98 of this era. Since we do not know the year in which this era started, it is possible only to assign an approximate period of these Mathura relics.

Scholars hold different opinions about the beginning of the Kusana era. Some hold the opinion that it is the same as the Shaka era and started in AD 78. Other dates given for the beginning of the Kusana era are AD 102, AD 128,

AD 144, etc., R. C. Majumdar has, however, suggested the date AD 244 and this suggestion appears to be getting more and more support. If this is correct then the years in which a flourishing Jain community lived in Mathura lie between AD 250 and AD 350.

Mathura during the rule of the Kusanas was the most important city of northern India. There were in Mathura rich people of many communities, Buddhist, Jain and Brahman. The inscriptions dug out in many localities in Mathura show that religious monuments were built and grants were given by all these communities. So far as Kankali-tila was concerned, it seems to have been at this period the exclusive preserve of the Jains. Some centuries before that period, the Buddhists, who had built a stupa here, perhaps occupied the tila. One Jain inscription (59) clearly mentions that the Jain image was established on a Vodve (Buddhist?) stupa, which had been built by the gods. It has been conjectured that the stupa at that time was already so old, that people had forgotten who its builders were. They, therefore, thought that the Gods built it. In the Kusana period, the Buddhists seem to have moved on to the Jamalpura mound in Mathura.

We may now consider the Jain inscriptions of Mathura belonging to the Kusana period. (Altogether 78 inscriptions have been given in the Jain Shila-Lekha Sangraha, Vol. II. It appears that the compiler of this volume might have missed a few more inscriptions. For instance, the Lucknow Museum Jain Image Inscriptions of Havisha---year 48 appears to have been missed. In any case, the total number of Jain inscriptions discovered here should not be many more than 90).

Rulers Named in the Inscriptions: Mathura before it came under the Kusanas was a part of the Shaka-Pahlava empire. The provincial governors under these emperors were called Mahakshatrapas. We have only one Jain inscription (5) of a Mahakshatrapa, the one belonging to Mahakshatrapa

Sodasa in Mathura. It is dated year 72 but we do not know the era. It appears that Mathura came under the Kusanas after Sodasa. These are three inscriptions (19, 24 and 25) of Kaniska, six of Huviska (37, 39, 43, 45, 50 and 56) who succeeded Kaniska's immediate successor Vasika who had a very short reign, and three of Huviska's successor Vasudeva (62, 65 and 69) in the Kankali-tila group. The names of the rulers in the other inscriptions at this place were either not recorded or are unreadable.

Tirthankaras: The following Tirthankaras are mentioned by name:

1. *Vardhamana*---eleven inscriptions (5, 8, 9, 19, 30, 34, 36, 37, 75, 79 and 84);

   Mahavira--one (16); Mahavira and Vardhamana---One (67).
2. *Sambhava*---One (in the Lucknow Museum Jain image inscription of Huviska--year 48).
3. *Rishava*---One (56); Usabha--One (82).
4. *Arishtanemi*---One (28).
5. *Shantinatha*--One (29).

Apart from these there are donative inscriptions, one to Nemesa (13), who may be Negamesa, and one to Nand (ya) varta (59) which is said to be meant for the 18th Tirthankara Arantha, Nandyavarta being his symbol. There are four donations (22, 26, 27, and 41) to the sarvatobhadra images. These are four-sided sculptures with images of one Tirthankara on each side.

It is quite clear from the above that Mahavira was the most popular Tirthankara among the Jains in Mathura at that time. Absence of Parshva's name is noticeable.

Many of the donors have mentioned their professions. In the case of the women donors, the professions of their husbands are sometimes mentioned. We know from these that most of the donors belonged to the trader class, though some of them were artisans such as goldsmiths or (iron) smiths. The list of professions or occupations and the inscription numbers where they occur are these:

Profession or Occupation	Number in the Jain *Shila-lekha Sangraha*
1. Shresthi (Merchant)	19, 26
2. Vanika (Trader)	71
3. Manikara (Jeweller)	31
4. Lohavaniya (Iron trader)	31
5. Hairanyaka (Gold smith)	67
6. Sarthavaha (Caravan guide)	33
7. Gandhika (Perfume seller)	41, 42, 62, 69
8. Lohikakaraka (Smith)	54, 55
9. Ganika (Courtesan)	08
10. Na(r)taka (Dancer)	15
11. Vacaka (Reciter, Priest?)	22
12. Gramika (Village headman)	44
13. Cotton dealer (35)	56

We thus get an idea as to how people of all such occupations as were common in a large provincial capital were living in Mathura in those days. At least one courtesan was not ashamed to disclose her profession as a stone tablet. Not much can be gleaned about social customs from these inscriptions. Inscriptions' number 14 is interesting. Here a woman named (Ba) Lahastini declares that she along with her parents and parents-in-law, had put up a religious arch. According to the present Indian custom, a woman for all religious purposes belongs to her husband's family and she has nothing to do in religious matters with her parents. Performance of a religious act of a married woman with her own parents in Mathura at that time perhaps shows that these people were foreigners (Shakas or Kusanas) newly converted to Jainism and were still maintaining some of their old customs.

The names of a few of the donors also show foreign influence. Some of these names are Mosini (22), Bubu (52), Vadhara (31), Huggu (31), Jabhaka (35), Nada (08), etc.

Another Shaka influence is shown in the mutilated Sarasvati image found at Kankali-tila. Two small figures of attendants are shown on each side of the Goddess. One of these attendants is in Shaka.

The present Jain custom of women keeping long fasts was known in Mathura of Huviska's days also. We have in inscription number 52, the statement that one Vijayasiri who was the wife of Rajyavasu had kept a fast for a month.

One Jain iconography practice had already been standardized in Mathura. The images of Tirthankaras all bear the shrivatsa 37 symbol on the chest as an auspicious mark (and perhaps also to distinguish them from the Buddha images that do not bear such marks on the chest).

It is perhaps not possible to state definitely whether the people who donated the images and the other religious objects at Mathura were Svetambaras or Digambaras. The donors have mentioned their ganas, kulas, etc., in the accompanying inscriptions. Some of these ganas, kulas, are similar to those found in the Kalpa Sutra. Now the Kalpa Sutra is a Shvetambara work and is not recognized by Digambaras. Similarly, it is the Svetambaras only who believe that the God Harinegamesi transferred the embryo of Mahavira to the womb of Trishala. The Digambaras completely reject this story. If, therefore, the name Nemesa read in one of the Mathura inscriptions, is the short form of "Harinegamesi", the Jains of Mathura would definitely have to be called Svetambaras. On the other hand, all the images of the Tirthankaras found at Kankali-tila are nude. All the Jain images of these centuries, for instance, those found at Kahaum (AD 460) in the Gorakhpur district, depict the Tirthankaras as nude. Added to this is the fact, that most of the Jains of Uttar Pradesh and Bihar today are Digambaras. Thus it is difficult to be sure about the sect of the Jains of Mathura in the Kusana period. It is likely, however, that the Shvetambara-Digambara split had not become clear-cut by that time. In any case the Svetambaras even if they existed, as a separate sect had not started worshipping non-nude images of the Tirthankaras, for no non-nude image of a Tirthankara prior to the fifth century has been found so far.

Mathura continued to be a center of the Jains for a long time. Many Jain sculptures belonging to the Gupta and the early medieval period have been discovered there.

7

BUDDHISM: GROWTH AND EXPANSION

INRTODUCTION

Soon after the Buddha's death, the monks gave up the practice of begging for alms and wandering from place and place. They settled down for a sedentary life in monasteries, built by kings and wealthy merchants who were inspired by the teachings and the events of the Buddha's life and became his ardent followers. With generous donations and material contributions from these patrons, the monasteries thrived as Buddhism took deep roots in the subcontinent, despite stiff competition from sectarian movements within the Vedic religion and other religious movements such as Jainism.

During his life time on earth, the Buddha attracted the attention of many people. His exemplary life, the fact that he descended from a princely family, the simplicity of his teachings and his opposition to ritualism and casteism, drew the attention of many from all ranks and contributed to the immense popularity of Buddhism. The Buddha was aware of the problems of monastic life that could surface within the monastic order over a period of time. He therefore established well defined code of conduct for the monks to ensure that they followed the right way of life during their practice of the Dhamma in general and the eightfold path in particular.

His parinirvana must have left a big vacuum in the Order. None of his followers had his great stature and his personal appeal, though they had an infinite capacity to remain loyal to his teachings and the discipline he established. They were incapable of filling the void he left behind and needed a leading and guiding source of inspiration that would keep them firmly abide by the Buddha, the Dhamma and the Sangha, the three cardinal principles of Buddhism.

The best that they could do in such circumstances was to preserve the teachings of the Buddha in a systematic manner and use them as points of reference in times of doubt and confusion. This would help them preserve his teachings for the future generations, strengthen the roots of Buddhism and create a universal code of conduct that could be implemented uniformly in all the monasteries that were know during that period.

And this was probably one of the objectives of the First Buddhist Council which was convened by the early followers of the Buddha after the Buddha's parinirvana. We understand that soon after the Buddha's parinirvana, his chief disciples, Ananda and Upali recited his teachings to the gathered assembly and thus laid the foundation stone for the Buddhist Canon, that was to emerge later in the form of three Pitikas-Vinaya, Sutta and Abhidhamma.

The Buddha admitted all types of people into the Order, irrespective of their social and religious backgrounds. This practice contributed greatly to the popularity of the religion. But in many respects it also proved to be its weakness, for it admitted into the Order many who were ill qualified for a strict monastic discipline. It helped the Order to grow into an organized body of huge proportions. But at the same time it sowed the seeds of internal dissension and divisions, that finally led to the break up of the Order into various sects and sub-sects.

It is difficult to say how far the immediate disciples and followers of the Buddha succeeded in their efforts to preserve his teachings. The early history of Buddhism does not offer many clues. It is possible that during the life time of the

Buddha, his followers might have done some ground work to organize his teachings and preserve them for posterity. True to the ancient Indian tradition, some of the teachings might have been preserved through the oral tradition and in the form of descriptive fables and parables.

We do not know much about the relationship the followers of Buddhism and the Buddha himself maintained during the early days of Buddhism with other religions and faiths. We know that there were occasions in the life of the Buddha when he personally engaged himself in religious debates and discussions with other sects such as the Jainas and the Ajivakas to disprove their theories and beliefs. It is hard to attribute any reason for such debates and discussions on the part of the Buddha, other than unbound compassion the Buddha had towards others and his attempts to bring them to the Dhamma and Sangha in order to help them in their salvation.

The fledgling new faith needed immunity from the corruption of teachings, a strong leadership and a distinct identity of its own to distinguish itself from other religions, gain a strong foothold in the subcontinent, keep the Dhamma and Sangha intact and attract new followers and converts to the faith.

As a scion of a ruling family, and having been tutored in the early part of his life, the Buddha was familiar with the art of leadership, organization and administration. He was also aware of the implications of creating a large body of Buddhist monks who would have to stay together and practice Dhamma under the most challenging circumstances. We know that at times he was disappointed with the behavior and insincerity of some of his followers. He knew the evils of decay and disintegration inherent in all component things, which he reminded his followers to remember even from his death bed. He therefore organized the Buddhist Monastic Order on the basis of an established code of conduct, a hierarchy with in the Order and a daily and seasonal routine for the community of the monks within the Order. He also maintained a rigid stance when it came to admitting women who he believed would disturb the Order with their very presence and created a procedure to admit them. He exhorted his followers to be wary of the temptations of samsara by remaining focused on the Four Noble Truths and the Eightfold path. He did not designate a successor as he truly believed his followers to be lamps unto themselves and follow the Dhamma as it was taught to them.

One of the new practices that began after his passing away was the veneration of the chaityas or the sacred spots. This practice was already prevalent in ancient India in some rudimentary form and the Buddhists adopted it as their own. Another new practice adopted by The Buddhists was the building of the stupas.

Originally stupas were built to designate the places where the ashes of the Buddha were buried as a mark of honor and symbols of veneration. In course of time stupas were being built for other reasons as well such as to express devotion or to honor the relics of a Buddhist monk. The third development was the development of sacred places and objects like the Bodhi tree, the Deer Park etc., which were associated with the Buddha's life and activities. These places became sacred places of pilgrimage and veneration for the followers of Buddhism.

These new developments contributed to the popularity of Buddhism outside the monastic order. But rituals were still looked with disfavor and the worship of the Buddha or his images, perhaps, did not yet begin.

These changes gradually led to the emergence of a new schools of Buddhism that were radically different in several respects from the original teachings of the Buddha. The changes helped the new religion adapt itself to the growing demands of a wider population and helped it emerge as a major world religion.

HISTORICAL AND ARTISTIC DESCRIPTION OF SANCHI

The history of Sanchi starts during the reign of Asoka in the third century B.C., and covers a period of some fourteen centuries, thus synchronising almost with the rise and fall of Buddhism in India. The political story of Eastern Malwa during these fourteen centuries is known to us only in the barest outline, and is beset with many uncertainties. Such as it is, however, it enables us to follow the chief dynastic changes and the chief religious movements which affected this part of India, and which are necessarily reflected in the changing character of the monuments.

To make this history and its bearing upon the architecture and sculptures of Sanchi more easily intelligible, I shall divide it into three periods, the first extending from the reign of Asoka to the overthrow of the Kshatrapa power, about 400 A.D., by Chandragupta II; the second from the advent of the Imperial Guptas to the death of the Emperor Harsha in 647 A.D.; and the third embracing the later mediaeval period down to the close of the twelfth century.

Early Period

The ancient name of Sanchi was Kakanada but the name is known only from inscriptions and does not occur in any ancient author. It seems probable, however, that Sanchi is referred to under the name of Chetiyagiri in the 'Mahavamsa'-the Buddhist chronicle of Ceylon-where it is recorded that Asoka, when he was heir-apparent and was journeying as Viceroy to Ujjayini (Ujjain), halted at Vidisa, and married the daughter of a local banker, one Devi Mahendra, and a daughter Sanghamitra. It is further narrated that, after Asoka's accession, Mahendra headed the Buddhist mission, sent probably under the auspices of the Emperor, to Ceylon, and that before setting out to the island he visited his mother at 'Chetiyagiri ' near Vidisa, and was lodged there in sumptuous vihara or monastery, which she herself had erected. Now, assuming that the story of Mahendra as told in the Sinhalese chronicleis correct, it would be reasonable to identify this 'Chetiyagiri' with the hill of Sanchi; for it was at Sanchi that Asoka set up one of his edict pillars as well as other monuments; and it is at Sanchi alone in this neighbourhood that any remains of the Maurya age have been found. Unfortunately, however, there is another version of the legend, which makes Mahendra the brother, not the son, of Asoka, and which fails to connect him in any way with Vidisa. It would manifestly be unsafe, therefore, to deduce from the Mahavamsa version any conclusions as to the age or origin of the monuments of Sanchi. Be the story true or not, there is good evidence, as we shall presently see, to show that the Buddhists established themselves at Sanchi for the first time during the lifetime of Asoka, and it is clear also from the memorials which the Emperor erected there, that the sangha at Sanchi was an object of special interest and care to him.

Asoka had probably become a convert to Buddhism early in life, and during the last thirty years of his reign (B.C. 273-232) he seems to have employed his almost unlimited powers in propagating his religious ideas throughout the length and breadth of his dominions (which comprised practically the whole of India except the Madras Presidency), and in sending missionaries of the faith to foreign lands as far remote as Egypt and Albania. In fact, it is upon his zealous patronage of Buddhism that the fame of this Great Emperor mainly rests; and it is not surprising, therefore, that most of the monuments of his reign which have come down to us relate to that religion. Among these monuments are some of the most perfect and highly developed specimens of sculpture in India, but the particular specimens referred to, including the edict-bearing pillar at Sanchi, are Perso-Greek in style, not Indian, and there is every reason to believe that they were the handiwork of foreign, probably Bactrian, artists. In the time of Asoka indigenous art was still in the rudimentary state, when the sculptor could not grasp more than one aspect of his subject at a time, when the law of 'frontality ' was still binding upon him, and when the 'memory picture' had not yet given place to direct observation of nature.

On the death of Asoka in 232 B.C. the Empire of the Mauryas rapidly fell to pieces: the central power declined, the outlying provinces asserted their in dependence, and about the year 185 B.C. the throne of Magadha passed to the Sungas. Of this dynasty our knowledge is meagre in the extreme. Its founder was Pushyamitra, who had murdered Brihadratha, the last of the Mauryas, and it appears from Kalidasa's drama the 'Malavikagnimitra' that during Pushyamitra's reign his son, Agnimitra, was ruling as Viceroy over the Western dominions, with Vidisa as his Capital. Pushyamitra himself is reputed by later writers to have persecuted the Buddhist church, but his successors must have been more tolerant; for an epigraph on the gate way of the Buddhist stupa at Bharhut records its erection 'during the supremacy of the Sungas,' and it is to the period of their supremacy, also, that several of the most important monuments at Sanchi probably belong, namely: the Second and Third Stupas with their balustrades (but not the gateway of the latter), the ground balustrade and stone casing of the Great Stupas, which had originally been of brick and of much smaller dimensions, and pillar No. 25.

The sculpture of these and other monuments of the Sunga period is full of promise, but still in much the same primitive and undeveloped stage in which the sculpture of Greece was at the beginning of the 6th century B.C. The influence of 'frontality' and of the 'memory image' continues to obtrude itself; the relief-work is lacking in depth; the attitudes of the individual figures are as a rule stiff and awkward, and are portrayed as sharply defined silhouettes against a neutral background; and there is rarely any effort made at bringing them into close mutual relationship one with another. On the other hand, a great advance is effected during this period in the modelling of the contours and interior details, and in many other respects, also, art begins to profit from the direct observation of nature. Here and there the reliefs of the Sunga period at Sanchi, as well as at Bharhut and Bodh-Gaya, reveal the influence which foreign, and especially Hellenistic ideas, were exerting on India through the medium of the contemporary Greek colonies in the Panjab; but the art of these reliefs is essentially indigenous in character and, though stimulated and inspired by extraneous teaching, is in no sense mimetic. Its national and independent character is attested not merely by its methodical evolution on Indian soil, but by the wonderful sense of decorative beauty which pervaded it and which from first to last has been the heritage of Indian art.

The power of the Sungas endured for a little over a century, i.e., until about the year 70 B.C., but whether they were supplanted by the Kanvas or the Andhras, is open to question. The Andhras had long been dominant in the west and south of India, and it is known that they had extended their sway over Eastern Malwa at least two or three decades before the beginning of the Christian era. It was under their dynasty that the early school of Indian art achieved its zenith, and that the most splendid of the Sanchi structures were erected, viz., the four gateways of the Great Stupa, and the single gateway of the Third Stupa, all five of which must have been set up within a few decades of one another.

On the Southern Gateway of the Great Stupa (the earliest of the five) is a donative inscription recording the gift of one of its architraves by a certain Anamda, foreman of the artisans of the Andhra king Sri Satakarni. Unfortunately for the identification of this king, the title of Satakarni was borne by many members of the dynasty, and it is not practicable to determine which particular one is here designated. Hitherto he has generally been identified with the Sri Satakarni who was reigning in the middle of the second century B.C. and who is mentioned in the Nanaghat and Hathigumpha inscriptions; but this view conflicts not only with what is now known of the history of Eastern Malwa (which in the second century B.C. was ruled by the Sungas and not by the Andhras), but with the history also of early Indian plastic art, which has recently been established on a much firmer basis.

It may now be regarded as practically certain that the king referred to is one of the Satakarnis who appear later in the Pauranic lists, and we shall not be far wrong if we assign his reign to the middle or latter half of the first century B.C. Of the monumental art of this period the gateways of Sanchi are by far the most important survivals. Between the times when the ground balustrade of Stupa 2 and the earliest of these gateways were erected, it is probable that not more than a few decades intervened, yet the advance made in relief work during this short period is most striking. In the decoration of the gateways there is little of the clumsy immature workmanship that characterises the balustrade in question. Though they exhibit considerable variety in their composition and technical treatment, their style generally is maintained at a relatively high level. They are manifestly the work of experienced artists, who had freed themselves almost entirely from the ' memory pictures ' of primitive art, and had learnt how to portray the figures in free and easy postures, how to compose them in natural and convincing group, how to give depth and a sense of perspective to the picture, and how to express their meaning both dramatically and sincerely.

That Hellenistic and Western Asiatic art affected the early Indian school during the Andhra even more intimately than it had done during the Sunga period, is clear from the many extraneous motifs in these reliefs, e.g., from the familiar; bell capital of Persia, from the floral designs of Assyria, or from the winged monsters of Western Asia; and it is clear also from the individuality of many of the figures, e.g., of the hill-men riders on the Easter Gate, from the symmetrical character of some of the compositions, and from the 'colouristic' treatment with its alternation of light and dark, which was peculiarly characteristic of Graeco-Syrian art at this period.

But though Western Art evidently played prominent part in the evolution of the early India school, we must be careful not to exaggerate its importance. The artists of early India were quick with the versatility of all true artists to profit by the lessons which others had to teach them; but there is no more reason in calling their creations Persian or Greek, than there would be in designating the modern fabric of St. Paul's Italian. The art which they practised was essentially a national art, having its root in the heart and in the faith of tie people, and giving eloquent expression to their spiritual beliefs and to their deep and intuitive sympathy with nature. Free alike from artificiality and idealism, its purpose was to glorify religion, not by seeking to embody spiritual ideas in terms of form, as the mediaeval art of India did, but by telling the story of Buddhism or Jainism in the simplest and most expressive language which of the chisel of the sculptor could command; and it was just because of its simplicity and transparent sincerity that it voiced so truthfully the soul of the people, and still continues to make an instant appeal to our feelings.

The rule of the Andhras in Eastern Malwa was interrupted for a few decades by that of the Kshaharatas, probably towards the end of the first century, but it was re-established about 125 A.D. by Gautamiputra Sri Satakarni, and survived until about 150 A.D., when it was finally overthrown by the Great Satrap Rudradaman, after which Sanchii and Vidisa remained in possession of the Western Kshatrapas until the close of the fourth century, when both Malwa and Surashtra were annexed to the Gupta Empire.

The Kshatrapas of Western India, including the family of the Kshaharatas as well as the later Satraps, were of foreign origin and, as their name implies, were in the position of feudatories to a supreme power, that power being, first the Scytho-Parthian, and later the Kushan empire of the North. In Eastern Malwa itself these Satraps do not appear on the scene until after the establishment of the Kushan Empire, and the only remains at Sanchi in which any connexion with the suzerain power of the north can be traced are a few sculptures, in the Kushan style from Mathura, one of which bears an inscription of the year 28 and of the reign of the King Shahi Vasishka. There are various other monuments, however, of local workmanship, which belong to the epoch of the Satraps and which indicate that Buddhism was as flourishing at Sanchi under the Satraps as it was elsewhere under their overlords the Kushans, though the art in which it found expression was then at a relatively low ebb.

THE GUPTAS OR EARLY MEDIAEVAL PERIOD

Although the rapid expansion of Gupta power under Samudragupta had brought the Western Kshatrapas into contact with it as early as the middle of the fourth century, it was not until the close of that century that the actual annexation of Eastern and Western Malwa was achieved by Chandragupta II. An echo of this Emperor's conquest occurs in an inscription carved on the balustrade of the Great Stupa, dated in the year 93 of the Gupta era, that is, in A.D. 412-13. It records the gift by one of Chandragupta's officers named Amrakardava, apparently a man of very high rank, of a village called Isvaravasaka and of a sum of money to the Arya-Sangha or community of the faithful at the great vihara or convent of Kakanadabota, for the purpose of feeding mendicants (bhikshus) and maintaining lamps.

In A.D. 413 Kumaragupta succeeded Chandragupta II, and was himself succeeded by Skandagupta in 455. It was towards the close of the reign of the latter Emperor (480 A.D.) that the Gupta Empire was overrun by invading hosts of White Huns, and shorn of the greater part of its western dominions. Eastern Malwa, however, was still unconquered in the reign of Skandagupta's successor, Buddhagupta, and it was not until about 500 A.D. that it passed into the hands of a local chief named Bhanugupta, and not until a decade later that it became feudatory to the Hun King, Toramana.

The rule of the Guptas lasted for little more than a hundred and fifty years, but it marks in many respects the most brilliant and striking of all epochs in Indian history. It was the age when the thought and genius of the Indian people awakened, and when there was an outburst of mental activity such as has never since been equalled. What precisely were the causes which underlay this sudden development of the nation intellect, we cannot say, any more than we can say what brought about similar developments in the golden age of Greece or in Italy during the Renaissance. Possibly, contact with other civilisations made have had something to do with it; for during this epoch there was close intercourse with the Sasanian Empire of Persia, and there was intercourse also with China and the Roman Empire.

Possibly, too, the invasions of barbarian races and the sufferings they inflicted may have been contributing factors; for Northern India had suffered long beneath the yoke of the Kushans, as well as of the Parthians and Scythians. Whatever the causes may have been, the effects of the new intellectual vitality were conspicuous and far-reaching. In the political sphere they resulted in resuscitating the Imperial idea, which had been dormant since the time of the Mauryas, and the outcome of this idea was the consolidation of an empire which embraced the whole Northern India as far south as the Narmada river In the sphere of religion, the new activity found expression in the revival of Brahmanism, and along with Brahmanism, in the revival of Sanskrit, which was the sacred language of the Brahmans. It was during this period that Kalidasa-the Shakespeare of India-wrote his immortal plays, and that other famous dramas were produced; and during this period, also, that the Puranas were finally redacted, that the laws of Manu took their present form and that mathematics and astronomy reached their highest perfection.

Thus, the Gupta age marked a re-awakening-a true 'Renaissance'-of the Indian intellect; and the new intellectualism was reflected in architecture and the formative arts as much as in other spheres of knowledge and thought. Indeed, it is precisely in their intellectual qualities-in their logical thought and logical beauty-that the architecture and sculpture of the Gupta age stand pre-eminent in the history of Indian art, and that they remind us in many respects of the creations of Greece eight hundred years earlier or of Italy a thousand years later.

Of early Indian art the keynotes, as I have already noticed, were spontaneous naturalism and simplicity. In the more advanced and cultured age of the Guptas these qualities were brought under the constraint of reason, and art became more formal, more self-conscious arid more complex. Necessarily it lost much of the naiveté and charm of the earlier work, but it gained in qualities which appealed to the conscious intellect as well as to the subconscious aesthetic sense: in symmetry and proportion, for example; in the structural propriety of its forms; in the reasoned restraint of ornament and in the definition of detail. In another important feature, also, the art of the Gupta period differed radically from all that had gone before.

For, whereas the Early School had regarded the formative arts merely as a valuable medium in which to narrate the legends and history of its faith, in the Gupta age a closer contact was established between thought and art, and sculptor and painter alike essayed to give articulate expression to their spiritual and emotional ideas by translating them into terms of form and colour. The types of the Buddha which this age produced and in which it succeeded in combining beauty of definition with a spirit of calm and peaceful contemplation are among the greatest contributions which India has made to the World's Art.

The 'Renaissance' of India did not come to an end with the break-up of the Gupta power, nor was it limited by the geographical boundaries of that Empire. Its influence was felt not only throughout the length and breadth of India, but in countries far beyond, and the strength which it had gathered in the fourth and fifth centuries did not exhaust itself until the close of the seventh. These three centuries of India's Renaissance (circa 350-650 A.D.) are commonly known as the 'Gupta period,' though during the latter half of this period the Guptas themselves were reduced to a petty principality in Eastern India.

For two generations Northern India lay under the yoke of the Huns, and it was not until 528 A.D. that their power was shattered by the victories of Baladitya and Yasodharman over Mihiragula-the bloodthirsty and ruthless successor of Toramana, who well earned for himself the title of ' the Attila of India. ' Then followed a period of quiescence, while the country was recovering from the savagery of the barbarians. During this period, which lasted until the beginning of the 7th century, there was no paramount authority in Northern India capable of welding together the petty states, and the latter were probably too weak and exhausted by their sufferings to make a bid for imperial dominion.

The ideals, however, of Gupta culture, though necessarily weakened, were still vital forces in the life of the people, continuing to manifest themselves alike in their science, their literature and their art; and it needed but the agency of a strong, benevolent government to bring them once more to their full fruition.

In Northern India, this agency was found in the government of Harsha of Thanesar (606-647 A.D.), who within five and a half years of his accession established an empire almost coterminous with that of the Guptas, and for thirty-five years more governed it with all the energy and brilliancy that had distinguished their rule. The art of the 6th and 7th centuries is represented at Sanchi mainly by detached images, which will be described in a separate catalogue, when the Museum now in course of erection is complete.

They are infused with the same spirit of calm contemplation, of almost divine peace, as the images of the fourth and fifth centuries, but they have lost the beauty of definition which the earlier artists strove to preserve, and, though still graceful and elegant, tend to become stereotyped and artificial.

The sculpture of this age, as we know from the caves at Ajanta, was not on so high a level as painting, and as a means of decoration was probably less popular than the sister art. At Sanchi, unfortunately, no trace is left of the chapels, and only those who know the grandeur of the Ajanta decorations, can appreciate how vastly different these buildings must have looked in ancient days.

Later Mediaeval Period

From 528 A.D., when the Huns were defeated, until 1023 A.D., when the Panjab was occupied by Mahmud of Ghazni, Northern India was left practically immune from foreign aggressions and free therefore to work out her own destinies. During these five centuries no need was felt of a central power to oppose the common foe; there was no voluntary cohesion among the many petty states; and, with one single exception, no sovereign arose vigorous enough to impose his will upon his neighbours.

It was a period, in fact, of stagnation, when the energy of the country was largely dissipated in internecine strife, and when its political weakness was reflected in the religion and arts of the country. The only ruler, so far as we know, who rose superior to his age and surroundings was Mihira Bhoja of Kanauj, who between the years 840-90 A.D. made himself master of an empire of which extended from the Sutlej to Bihar and which was maintained intact by his successors Mahendrapala and Bhoja II.

In this empire Eastern Malwa, which was then ruled by the Paramara dynasty, is known to have been included at the close of the 9th century, but the power of the Pratiharas of Kanauj rapidly declined during the early decades of the following century, and by the time that Raja Munja (974-95 A.D.) came to the throne, Eastern Malwa appears to have asserted its independence and to have become the predominant state in Central India.

Both Munja and his nephew, the celebrated Bhoja, who reigned over Malwa for more than 40 years (A.D. 1018-60), were liberal patrons of literature and art, and themselves writers of no small ability. A reputed monument of the latter king, that may have preserved his name, was the great Bhojpur lake to the S.E. of Bhopal, which was drained in the fifteenth century by order of one of the Muhammadan kings. With the death of Bhoja, about 1060 A.D., the power of the Paramaras declined, and, though the dynasty survived at Dhar, Malwa passed during the twelfth century into the possession of the Chalukya kings of Anhilwara. With the subsequent history of this district we need not here concern ourselves; for at Sanchi there are no Buddhist edifices of importance later than the twelfth century A.D., and it is probable that the Buddhist religion, which had already been, largely merged into Hinduism, died out in Central India about that time.

Of the architecture and sculpture of this later medieval period there are various examples at Sanchi, including the whole group of structures on the Eastern terrace, numbered from 43 to 50, besides a vast array of detached carvings, small votive stupas, statues and the like. One and all bear witness to the rapidly declining purity both of the Buddhist religion and of Buddhist art, but it is in Temple 45, which is by far the most pretentious monument of this epoch, that the visitor will most quickly recognise the overwhelming influence which Hinduism, and particularly the Tantric cult, had exercised on Buddhism before the 11th century A.D., and it is in the same temple that he will best appreciate the wide gulf which separates this architecture from that of the Gupta age.

During the later medieval times architecture aspired to greater magnificence and display, but what it gained in grandeur (and the gain in this respect was undeniably great), it lost in its aesthetic quality. There is no longer the same sense of proportion and of balance between form and ornament which was so conspicuous in Gupta work. The purely decorative impulse which the Gupta artist had kept under the control of reason, reasserts itself, and ornament is allowed to run riot, destroying thereby the unity and coherence of the design. Carving loses its plasticity and vitality, and cult images become stereotyped and lifeless-mere symbols, as it were, of religion, devoid alike of spirituality and of anatomical definition.

Sanchi in Modern Times

From the 13th century onwards Sanchi appears to have been left desolate and deserted. The city of Vidisa had fallen to ruins during the Gupta period and had been superseded by Bhilsa (Bhailasvamin); but, though the latter town played an important part in local history during Muhammadan times, and though it was thrice sacked by Moslem conquerors, and its temples destroyed for a fourth time in the reign of Aurangzeb, yet amid all this devastation the monuments of Sanchii, in spite of their prominent position on a hill only five miles away, were left unscathed, and when visited by Gen.

Taylor in 1818, proved to be in a remarkably food state of preservation. At that time three of the gateways of the Great Stupa were still standing erect, and the southern one was lying where it had fallen; the great dome was intact; and a portion of the balustrade on the summit was still in situ. The second and third stupas were also well preserved, and there were remains of eight minor stupas, besides other buildings, in the vicinity of the Second Stupa, but no record of their condition is preserved. The beauty and unique character of these monuments was immediately recognized; and from 1819 onwards there appeared various notes, illustrations and monographs descriptive of their architecture and sculpture, though too often marred by the fanciful ideas or inaccuracies of the authors.

Most notable among these works were Cunningham's Bhilsa Topes, (1854), Fergusson's Tree and Serpent worship (1868) and Gen. Maisey's Sanchi and its Remains (1892). But the widespread interest which the discovery and successive accounts of the stupas excited, proved lamentably disastrous to the monuments themselves; for the site quickly became a hunting-ground for treasure seekers and amateur archeologists, who, in their efforts to probe its hidden secrets or to enrich themselves from the spoils supposed to be hidden there, succeeded in half demolishing and doing irreparable harm to, most of the structures. Thus, in 1822, Capt. Johnson, the Assistant Political Agent in Bhopal, opened the Great Stupa from top to bottom on one side, and left a vast breach in it, which was the cause of much subsequent damage to the body of the structure and of the collapse of the Western Gateway and portions of the enclosing balustrade.

The same blundering excavator was probably responsible, also, for the partial destruction of the Second and Third Stupas, which until then had been in perfect repair. Then, in 1851, Major (afterwards Gen. Sir) Alexander Cunningham and Capt. F. C. Maisey together contributed to the general spoliation of the site by hasty excavations in several of the monuments, and, though they succeeded in recovering a most valuable series of relic caskets from the Second and Third Stupas, their discoveries scarcely compensated for the damage entailed in their operations, since the caskets themselves were subsequently lost.

During all these years the idea of repairing and preserving these incomparable structures for the sake of future generations seems never to have entered anyone's head, and, though in 1869 (as an indirect result of a request by Napoleon III for one of the richly carved gates) casts of the East Gate were prepared and presented to the principal national museums of Europe, it was not until 1881, when still more havoc had been wrought by the neighbouring villagers or by the ravages of the ever encroaching jungle that the Government bethought itself of safeguarding the original structures. In that year Major Cole, then Curator of Ancient Monuments, cleared the hill top of vegetation and filled the great breach in the Main Stupa made by Capt. Johnson nearly sixty years before, and during the two following years he re-erected at the expense of the Imperial Government the fallen gates on the south and west, as well as the smaller gate in front of the third stupa.

No attempt, however, was made by him to preserve the other monuments which were crumbling to ruin, to exhume from their debris the monasteries, temples and other edifices which cover the plateau around the Great Stupa, or to protect the hundreds of loose sculptures and inscriptions lying on the site. These tasks which involved operations far more extensive than any previously carried out were left for the writer to undertake in 1912, and during the five years that have intervened since then they have been steadily and systematically pushed forward: The building which were at that time visible on the hill top were the Great Stupa and the few other remains which the reader will find indicated in the plan on Pl. XV by hatched lines.

For the rest, the whole site was buried beneath such deep accumulations of debris and so overgrown with jungle, that the very existence of the majority of the monuments had not even been suspected. The first step therefore, was to clear the whole enclave of the thick jungle growth in which it was enveloped. Then follower the excavation of the areas to the south and east of the Great Stupa, where it was evident that a considerable depth of debris lay over the natural rock, and where, accordingly, there was reason to hope (hope which has since been abundantly justified) that substantial remains might be found.

The building which have been exposed to view in the southern part of the site are for the most part founded on the living rock; but those in the eastern area constitute only the uppermost stratum, beneath which there still lip buried the remains of various earlier structures. Then I have been well content to leave to the spade of some future explorer, having satisfied myself by trial digging at different points that they are mainly monastic dwellings similar in character to those already brought to light in other parts of the enclave and likely, there fore, to add but little to our present knowledge of the monuments.

The third task that awaited me was to put one and all of the monuments into as thorough and lasting a state of repair as was practicable. Most important and most difficult of achievement among the many measures which this task entailed have been: first, the dismantling and reconstruction of the south-west quadrant of the Great Stupa, which was threatening to collapse and to bring down with it the South and West Gateways, as well as the balustrade between them; secondly, the preservation, of Temple 18, the ponderous columns of which were leaning at perilous angles, and had to be reset in the perpendicular and established on secure foundations; and, thirdly, the repair of Temple 45, which had reached the last stage of decay and was a menace to anyone entering its shrine.

Other measures that are also deserving of particular mention, are the rebuilding of the long retaining wall between the central and eastern terraces; the reconstruction of the dome, balustrades and crowning umbrella of the Third Stupa; the re-roofing and general repair of Temples 17, 31 and 32; the effective drainage (involving the relaying of the old fragmentary pavement) of the area around the Great Stupa; and the improvement and beautifying of the site generally by roughly levelling and turfing it by the (planting of trees and flowering creepers.

Finally, there remained the question of protecting the numerous moveable antiquities which lay scattered about the site. For this purpose a small but adequate museum is now in course of construction, where sculptures, inscriptions and architectural fragments can all be duly arranged and catalogued, and where the visitor will find plans, photographs and other materials to assist him in the study of these unique monuments.

THE SOCIO-ECONOMIC ROOTS OF AHIMSA

Most Supporters of Buddhism and Jainism were from the Merchant Classes

As we know that Buddhism received royal patronage right from its inception. Apart from the romanticised tale of King Ajatashatru and the courtesan Amrapali, the reason why kings like Ajatashatru, traders like Anathapindaka, Kosiyagotta and Mendaka, patronised Buddhism was that the new faith advocated principles that suited their way of life. Even Jainism, (which was contemporary of Buddhism) found ardent supporters among the landed nobility and the mercantile community. Many principles are common to Buddhism and Jainism. Both religions deny the authority of Vedas and disown Vedic rituals of animal sacrifice. This earned them the support of the mercantile and agrarian classes. Their concept of ahimsa and non-violence, directly benefited agricultural and pastoral activities both of which require conservation of animal (bovine) life.

But with its excessive emphasis on non-violence, Jainism stood in the way of agriculturists whose activities require the killing of insects and pests. Nor did Mahavira's ideas become entirely acceptable to the agrarian community due to its ban on the ownership of property in the form of land. Hence those who accepted Jainism were mostly those who were engaged in mercantile pursuits, traded in commodities and who hence confined themselves to financial transactions without owing any landed property.

This is the possible explanation behind the predominance of Jains in ancient times (and even today) in trade and maritime pursuits.

India's western coast had widespread trade contact with foreign countries since ancient times, therefore it is not surprlsing why a significant portion of the population there opted for Jainism. Even today the Jain community is concentrated in Gujarat, Rajasthan and Karnataka and many Jains are till today engaged mainly in trading and mercantile activities.

Buddhism and Jainism Adopted Favourable Attitudes Towards Trade

Both Buddhism and Jainism adopted an attitude favourable to trade and commerce. As contrasted with this, the early Vedic law books prescribe the mercantilc and agrarian professions to the Vaishyas who were ranked after the Brahmins and Kshatriyas.

Brahmins were allowed to undertake trading activities only during times of distress. A Hindu lawgiver, Baudhayana condemns voyaging by sea as a sinful practice. The Hindu dogmas that a voyage across the seas caused the person to lose his religion (dharma) and his caste were born out of this attitude. As against this, Buddhism encouraged sea voyages. As Buddha's attitude towards trade was favourable he received generous gifts from the trading community for his Sangha (monastic order).

It was natural for the trading community to turn to the new faiths as compared to the Vedic religion which looked down upon mercantile activities. It is not surprising that the first two followers of Buddha-Sariputta and Mogallana were two merchants passing through Bodh Gaya.

A Person had to Pay Off his Debts before Joining the Buddhist Sangha

Signifiantly the Buddhist scriptures nowhere condemns the practise of usury (money-lending with interest). On the contrary they advocate the right to livelihood through mercantile activities. There seems to be an intimate relationship between the Buddhist order and the urban based Setthis who perhaps lent money on interest and were looked down upon in the Brahminical scriptures. Buddha himself enjoins that a person pay off his debt before joining the Buddhist Sangha and no debtor is allowed to join. Thus indirectly though by enjoining payment of debts, Buddhism supported usury which is a corollary of mercantile activities.

There seems to be an intimate relationship between the Buddhist order and the urban based Setthis who perhaps lent money on interest and were looked down upon in the Brahminical scriptures. Buddha himself enjoins that a person pay off his debt before joining the Buddhist Sangha and no debtor is allowed to join.

Other corollaries of mercantile activities also received support from Buddhism. For instance while the Brahminical law giver Apastamba prohibits the higher castes from taking food cooked at eating houses located on trade routes, the Buddhist texts apparently support this practice. Buddhism also placed emphasis on unlawful practices harmful to trade like robbery, deception and intimidation. At one place Buddha himself equates the food earned by unlawful means with the leavings of a Chandala. Thus Buddhism and Jainism which provided a creed that preached non-violence, forbadc burglary and brigandage of property, timely payment of debts served the interests of the trading community.

Thus the emergence of Buddhism and Jainism at a particular Juncture of social development cannot be explained only as a pious humanistic revulsion against violent practices of animal sacrifice. They were a result of the friction between established social Practices and an emerging way of life whose requirements these practices violated. As Indian society passed from the hunting to the pastoral and to the agrarian stage, livestock which formerly was a usual item of diet became an essential means of production, whose preservation became an economic necessity.

The propertied trading and agrarian community had much to gain from a creed that preached prohibition of the waste of productive resources through animal sacrifice as most of these animals and other items like graio milk, honey, etc., must have been taken by the priests from these trading and agrarian communities as a social obligation having religious sanction.

This was the reason why Buddhism, Jainism and other similar doctrines could take root at one particular juncture of social development with ardent support from the agrarian and trading communities. Although the natural human instinctive revulsion against violence exists wherever violence which ls not essential for human survival is practiced. Nevertheless, with their prescriptions of non-violence, along with universal brotherhood, love, compassion and a general charitable attitude, these religions apart from serving the interests of merchants and traders also had a salutary effect on society in general. The following story of a bandit named Angulimala brings out this aspect.

Bandit Angulimala's Conversion

Angulimala was a dreaded dacoit who also lived during Buddha lifetime. He was a terror of traders and merchants travelling from one city to another. Angulimala's activities had given him the notoriety of being a ruthless bandit who would suck his victims clean of all their money, jewellery, valuables and merchandise. Even their horses and bullocks would be taken away and those unfortunate victims who were unwise enough to resist Angulimala and his accomplices would be maimed and even done to death.

Traders Formed Big Groups of Caravans defended by Armed Troops to Protect Themselves from Angulimala

He had become such a terror that the very mention of his name brought a chill in the spine of many traders whose profession required them to travel from one city to another. Even a waft of rumour that Angulimala was lying in wait on any trade route brought about Ehe cancellation of caravan journeys of merchants. Many kings of the Gangetic valley had made attempts to capture the dacoit, but Angulimala had eluded all of them. As his notoriety spread merchants started getting more cautious and travelled only in big groups accompanied with a strong battalion of armed guards. This brought about a fall in Angulimala's earnings and day by day he grew more desperate.

Angulimala Robs Buddha

One day during such despondency Angulimala and his gang of dacoits spied on a group of monks going though the forest. The monks were unarmed and seemed easy prey for Angulimala. But the only disappointing aspect was that they did not appear to have anything worthwhile to rob. Most of them were barefooted and apart from a single loincloth draped across their bodies, a walking stick and a begging bowl they had nothing else with them.

Angulimala suspected that they were either rich merchants who had come in the guise of monks to deceive him or were troops in disguise sent to apprehend his gang of dacoits. Out of caution Angulimala decided not to set upon them immediately but to watch their activities and then attack them if advisable. He tracked the group of monks throughout the day. Towards nightfall the monks settled down in one clearing in the forest and one of them, who was no other than Gautama Buddha himself started speaking before the group of monks.

The Deer Park where Buddha gave his first sermon. The Buddha used to say that the wealth we accumulate during our lives is not really our wealth, thus we have to leave it behind when we commence our eternal journey. A person's real wealth are his acts of charity and service to others which are cherished by the beneficiaries even after the person is no more. Thus even after a bodily death, such a person remains alive in the memories of others.

Angulimala who was hiding within earshot, heard Buddha saying that the wealth we accumulate during our lives is not really our wealth, thus we have to leave it behind when we commence our eternal journey. A person's real wealth are his acts of charity and service to others which are cherished by the beneficiaries even after the person is no more. Thus even after a bodily death, such a person remains alive in the memories of others. Thus a person who gives his material wealth to others becomes a really rich person and not one who aims at depriving others of wealth by cheating or robbery.

These words struck Angulimala as a block of ice to a roaring fire. For the first time Angulimala pondered introspectively on his acts. He not only decided to leave the monks alone but in the days to come he became increasingly remorseful while indulging in acts of brigandage. One day he decided that he had enough of the wretched robber's life, he left his accomplices and started living the life of a secluded monk. He wanted to join Buddha's Sangha (Monastic order) but wondered if he would be admitted into it due to his past activities One day he decided that he would leave his secluded abode and go to meet Buddha personally.

With this objective he entered the town of Shrtvasti in which Buddha was camping at that time. Angulimala was dressed like a monk and also looked like one, but he still was the same person who till a few days back was a feared bandit. Unfortunately for him, he was recognised by some residents of Shravasti who had been his victims once upon a time. His sudden appearance in the city filled the residents with fear, and looking at him dressed like a monk, made some feel that he had come with some new nefarious intention.

Ultimately a group of merchants got together and with the help of some city ruffians caught hold of Angulimala and began mortally beating him up. They left a profusely bleeding Angulimala to die the same gory death which he himself had brought upon many others. Severely wounded, Angulimala managed to make his way to his master, Gautama Buddha, who we are told instantly recognised Angulimala and personally attended to Angulimala's wounds.

But the wounds proved fatal. And although the touch of Buddha cleared Angulimala's conscience; shortly after reaching Buddha's camp Angulimala passed away and attained Nirvana.

This episode illustrated the widespread effect that the teachings of Buddha were having on people from literally all walks of life.

8

BUDDHIST INFLUENCES ON HINDUISM

Through its effect on the thinking of the general population, the rise of Buddhism also dealt a severe jolt to the Vedic religion. Many practices which became characteristic of later Hinduism were a result of this jolt. The Hindu insistence on vegetarianism was the most important one.

In the post-vedic period, with agriculture becoming the main occupation, the continuing practice of slaughtering the much needed livestock in the Yagnas put a heavy strain on the agrarian economy. Thus a new ethic was needed to curb this practice. The emergence of Buddhism and Jainism fulfilled this need. (Seen here is the monolithic statue of Bahubali worshipped by the Jains)

As discussed in the chapter on the fire sacrifice of Yagna could have been a ritualisation of the cooking function of the tribal period of early Aryan society in which the yagna fireplace was the central fire (hearth) of the common tribal kitchen. (Refer Chapter on The Rise and fall of the Caste System, section on Brahmins-Those Baptised by Fire). That mostly meat must have been cooked (roasted) on the central fireplace of the Aryan tribe is evident as meat was the main item of food available and essential to conserve energy in those days of collective hunting. The logical corollary of this is that meat eating must have been associated with the original activity which later got ritualized in to the Yagna fire sacrifice in the post Vedic days when hunting was no longer the main occupation and its place was taken by pastoral and agricultural activities. But even after the Yagna had become a ritual in the Post Vedic times, the sacrificing of animals must have been an essential part of the Yagna ritual. even the eating of meat during a Yagna was an established practice in those days. This is borne out by the statement in the Manusmriti according to which "He who performs the Yagna but does not eat the sacrificial meat is condemned to be born as an animal whose meat he refuses to eat for 21 future rebirths." But in the changed circumstances, with agriculture becoming the main occupation, the continuing practice of slaughtering the much needed livestock in the Yagnas put a heavy strain on the agrarian economy. Thus a new ethic was needed to curb this practice. The emergence of Buddhism and Jainism fulfilled this need.

The determined support which these new faiths received from society at large, but especially from the mercantile community which was the rising class of that age, gave these religions a strong social base. The Vedic religion had to change to adapt itself to the new material conditions, if it was to survive. The Mitakashara treatise by the law giver Vidnyaneshwara written after the practice of meat eating had fallen into disgrace, forbids the regular eating of flesh in Kaliyuga (dark age), but simultaneously concedes permission for meat eating during performance of the Yagna. This represents the ambivalent attitude of the later Vedic religion towards meat eating. Gradually came the taboo on meat eating, initially on those animals which were important for the agrarian economy-the cow and the bull, this was later made into a general ban on eating meat as well as fish and eggs. But an exception was made for milk and milk products. This process reached its climax with the deification of the cow (Gomata) and bull (Nandi). But such deification or at least glorification is not peculiar to Indian society alone, it had existed in many agrarian societies. It seems to have existed even in the pre-Aryan Indus culture as is brought out by the appearance of the bull on many Indus seals. But the acceptance in the Dharmashastras of an attitude prohibiting animal sacrifice and meat eating was inevitable for thc Vedic religion if it was to stem the tide of the propertied merchant and agricultural classes towards Buddhism and Jainism. If the Vedic religion was to survive in a changing society, the support of the dominant classes had to be retained. And for which those practices which violated the interests of this class had to be dropped.

In place of the actual sacrifice of living creatures during the Yagna, what was now done was the symbolic breaking of a coconut and the offering of small figures of bulls and horses (Pista-Pashu) representing the animals that had formerly been sacrificed during a Yagna. Consumption of beef was replaced by the consumption of the five elements issuing from the cow, viz. the cowdung, cow's urine, milk, curds and clarified butter mixed together in a liquid (slurry) called Pancha-Gavya. The constituents honey and sugar later replaced cowdung and cow's urine! when vegetarianism was further refined, to give us the Panchamrita of today.

The acceptance of the Buddhist and Jaina doctrine of ahimsa by the Vedic religion with the continued the Yagna ritual characterised the later Hindu religion. The Yagna ritual in an altered version was a combination of convenience. This peculiar but convenient combination became characterized of later Hindu theology. So much so that today we have forgotten that the ideals of non-violence and vegetarianism came into being as a reaction against animal sacrifices of the early Hindu religion of the Vedic period.

ANTIQUITY OF JAINISM

The origin of Jainism is shrounded in considerable obscurity. The available evidence ot decide the questions is scanty, dubious and capable of different interpretations. Scholars have therefore come to widely divergent conclusions. Mrs. Stevenson is of opinion that Jainism originated as a protest against the sacrifice and casteism of the Brahmanism in the eighth century B. C. According to Jacobi, there are even traces of Jainism even in the Vedic period. Dr. Zimmer and Farlong observe that there was the existence of the Sramana culture before the Aryans in India. Dr. Zimmer calls it by the name of the Dravidan religion while Farlong considers it to be different from the religion of the Dravidans.

The divergence of views among the Scholars about the antiquity of Jainism is thus almost bewildering. The question has therefore to be examined and considered carefully, critically and exhaustively in order to arrive at some conclusion.

JAINISM OLDER THAN BUDDHISM

From the Buddhist and Jain records, it is clear that Jainism is older than Buddhism and was firmly established at the time of the origin of Buddhism. Mahavira was not the founder and author of Jain religion but simply a reformer. Many abuses had crept into Jainism at that time and he simply tried to remove them. His parents had, according to a tradition which seems to be trustworthy, been followers of Parsva. He himself, when he became a monk, returned to the chaitya of his own lawn called Duipalasa. The chaitya seems to be of the Jains. Even Buddha after giving up the worldly life lived in the company of the saints who practiced austerities and were possibly Jains.

In the Samannaphala Sutta of the Dighanikaya, there is a reference to the four vows (Chaturyama Dharma) in contradiction to the five vows of Mahavira. The four vows of Parsva were:-not to take life, not to tell a lie, not to steal and not to own property. To these Mahavira was forced to add the vow of chastity when the abuses had crept into the Jain church. The Buddhists could not have used the term Chaturyama Dharma for the Nigranthas unless they had heard it from the followers of Parsva. This is the proof for the correctness of the Jain tradition that the followers of

Parsva actually existed at the time of Mahavira. This sect of the Nigranthas was an important sect at the rise of Buddhism.

This may be inferred from the fact that they are frequently mentioned in the pitakas as opponents of Buddha and his disciples. This conclusion is further supported by another fact. Mankkhali Gosala, a contemporary of Buddha and Mahavira divided mankind into six classes, of these the third class contained the Nigranthas. Gosala probably would not have ranked them as a separate class of mankind if they had recently come into existence. He must have regarded them as a very important and at the same time an old sect.

The Majjhima Nikaya 35th records a dispute between Buddha and Sakdal, the son of a Nigrantha. Sakdal is not himself a Nigrantha Now, when a famous controversialist whose father was a Nigrantha, was a contemporary of the Buddha, the Nigranthas can scarcely have been a sect founded during Buddha's life.

The Uttaradhyayana Sutra 23rd relates a meeting between Gautama Indrabhuti, the disciple of Mahavira and Kesi Kumara, the disciple of Parsva at Sravasti which brought about the union of the old branch of the Jain church and the new one. This again points out to the existence of the older Jain faith than that of Mahavira.

HISTORICITY OF PARSVANATHA

These discussions clearly show that Parsvanatha is a real historical figure. He must have been of a genial nature as he is always given the epithet Purisa-daniya 'beloved of men.' He is supposed to have attained liberation about 246 years before Mahavira at Sammetasikhara which is known by his name Parsvanatha hill. If 526 B. C. is taken as the year of Lord Mahavira's Nirvana, in 772 B. C. must have occurred the death of Parsvanatha. According to the tradition, he dwelt in the world exactly one hundred years and left home at the age of thirty of become an ascetic. From it, we may conclude that he was born about 872 B. C. and left this world in about 772 B. C. The Kalpasutra states that Parsva like other Tirthankaras was a Kshatriya and the son of the King Asvasena of Banaras and his wife Vama. His chief disciple was Gubhadatta who was succeeded by Haridatta. Then, came Arya Samudra and his disciple Prabhasuri. Next Kesi Kumara succeeded to the headship of the church who was the contemporary of Mahavira. Thus the history of Jainism goes back to 872 B. C.

There seems to be no doubt about the existence of Jainism in the nineth century B. C. but the history of Jainism goes back even earlier than of Parsvanatha. The Jain record mentions the names of twenty two Tirthankaras before him. Neminatha, the 22nd Tirthankara of the Jains, was the son of Samudra Vijaya and grandson of Andhakavrishni. He is said to be a cousin of Krishna, the lord of the Bhagvadgita. Krishna negotiated his marriage with Rajamati, the daughter of Ugrasena but Neminatha taking compassion on the animals which were to be slaughtered in connection with the marriage feast, left the marriage procession suddenly and renounced the world. If the historicity of Lord Krishna is admitted, we may as well admit that Lord Neminatha, the 22nd Tirthankara is not a mere myth.

The Andhakavrishnis of Dwaraka in Kathiawar as a republic is referred to in the Mahabharata, Arthasastra and Ashtadhyayi of Panini. The name of the Vrishni corporation is also found on a coin which on paleographical grounds belongs to the first and second1 century B. C. It seems that the republic was named after Andhakavrishni, the grand father of Neminatha. As this republic is mentioned in the Ashtadhyayi of Panini who according to Gold Stucker must have lived in the seventh century B. C. at the latest. It must have been well known at this time and must have come into existence long before eighth century B. C. If Andhakavrishni is the real person, there seems to be little doubt that his grand son Neminatha was a reality.

There is a mention in the Chhandogya Upanishada III, 17, 6, that the sage Ghora Angirasa imparted a certain instructions of the spiritual sacrifice to Krishna, the son of Devaki. The liberal payment of this scarify was austerity, liberality, simplicity, non-violence and truthfulness. These teachings of Ghora Angirasa seem to be the tenets of Jainism. Hence, Ghora Angirasa seems to be the Jain saint. The writers of the Jain scriptures say that Tirthankara Neminatha was the master of Krishna. Now the question arises whether Neminatha and Ghora Angirasa a are the names of the same individual.

The word Ghora Angirasa seems to be an epithet given to him because of the extreme austerities undertaken by him. It may be possible to suggest that Neminatha was his early name and when he had obtained salvation after hard austerities, he might have been given the name of Ghora Angirasa.

Infact the Jaina traditions about Neminatha or Arishtanemi as incorporated in the Harivamsa, Arittha Nemi Chariu and other works may be corroborated to some extent by the Brahaminical traditions. He is mentioned in some of the hymns of the Vedas but their meaning is doubtful. In the Yajurveda, he seems to be clearly mentioned as one of the important Rishis. He is described as one who is capable of crossing over the ocean of life and death, as the remover of violence, one who is instrumental is sparing life from injury and so on. The Yajurveda probably beolongs to the twelfth century B. C. This indicates that Neminatha seems to be known at this time and flourished even before.

The literary evidence seems to be supported by an epigraphic evidence.1 In Kathiawar, a copper plate has been discovered on which there is an inscription. The king Nebuchadnazzar (940 B. C.) who was also the lord of Revanagara (in Kathiawara) and who belonged to Sumer tribe, has come to the lace (Dwarka) of the Yaduraja. He has built a temple and paid homage and made the grant perpetual in favour of Lord Neminatha, the paramount deity of Mt. Raivata. This inscription is of great historical importance. The king named Nebuchadnazzar was living in the 10th century B. C. It indicates that even in the tenth century B.C. there was the worship of the temple of Neminatha the 22nd. Tirthankara of the Jains. It goes to prove the historicity of Neminatha.

Thus, there seems to be little doubt about Neminatha as a historical figure but there is some difficulty in fixing his date. He is said to be the contemporary of Krishna the hero of Mahabharata. The scholars differ in their opinions as to the exact date of the Mahabharata which vary from 950 B.C. to 3000 B.C.

Jainism in the Ramayana Period

The period of Ramayana is earlier than Mahabharata. The majority of the scholars believe most of the events and persons connected with the story of Ramayana to be real and historical. The oldest available Jain version of Rama epic is Paumachariya in Prakrit which was composed in 530 years after the Mahavira-nirvana according to the statements of the author named3 Vimala Suri. It belongs to about the same period as the oldest Brahaminic version, the Ramayana of Valmiki i.e. to the first century B. C. No doubt Vimal seems to be acquainted with the other works on the life of Rama but he criticizes them as giving false and fantastic statements. On the other hand, he himself claims to give a real and true account of the life of Rama, based on the words of Tirthankara Mahavira. The story of Ramayana as stated in the Jain Puranas is substantially similar to the account of Valmiki. But the way in which the Jain version differs from the Brahaminic Ramayana throws a very significant light on the position of Jainism. According to the Jain version, Ravana and Raksas were highly cultured people belonging to the race of the Vidyadharas and were great devotees of Jina.2 But the Hindu tradition depicted them as evil natured and irreligious demons because they were antagonistic to the sacrificial cult of the Vedic sages. At the same time, they were defeated, therefore, they become the demons in the hands of the poets. Considering these two accounts together, it seems that the Vedic people denounced the Rakshas because they were the followers of Jainism. F. E. Pargiter also asserts the Jains were treated as Asuras and Daityas by the Hindus. Rama, his brother Laksamana and their enemy Ravana were 63 prominent personages (the trisastisalaka purushas) of the Jain traditions where in the Raksas and Vanaras of the Ramayana have been described not as semihuman or demons but as highly civilized and cultured human beings of the Vidyadhara race who were mostly devotees of the Jina.

Even in the Yoga Vasistha Ramayana in the Chapter of Vairagya, Rama expresses to be of a peaceful nature like Jinendra. There is also mention in the Ramayana of Valmiki that the king Dasaratha, the father of Rama entertained the sramanas as the guests. The word sramana indicates the Jain saints and not saints of Buddhism which is of late origin.

Thus, it seems that Jainism was in existence in the period of Ramayana according to the Jain traditions. Lord Munisuvarta, the 20th Tirthankara is said to be the contemporary of Rama. Munisuvratanatha seems to be as real person as Rama himself.

JAINISM IN THE RIG VEDIC AGE

In the Vedic period, there were two kinds of saints-Yati, the enemy of Indra, the Vedic God and Muni-the friend of Indra. It seems that the saints of the Aryans who honored them were called the Munis while persons corresponding to the saints among non-Vedic people were probably called the Yatis. In the Tai. S. VI. 2. 75, we read 'Indra threw Yatis to the Salavrikas (wolves), they devoured them to the south of the Uttaravedi. The same words and story occur in the

Kathaka Samhita VIII 5, the Ait. Br. 35. 3 and the Kausitaki Up. III, 1; in the last, Indra said to Pratardana, " do know me only. I regard this as the most beneficial thing to man that he should know me. I killed the three headed Tvashtra, I gave to the Salavrikas, the arunmukh yatis" In the Kathaka Samhita 10 and the Tai. S. II 4, 9, 2, it is stated that the heads of the Yatis when they were being devoured, fell aside and they (the heads) became the Kharjuras (date palms). Atharvaveda II, 53 says 'Indra who is quick in his attack, who is Mitra and who killed Vritra as he did the yatis.

In the Tandya Mahabrahmana VIII 1, 4, Brihadgiri is said to be one of the three Yatis who escaped from slaughter and who were then taken under his protection by Indra. All these passages taken together suggest that the Yatis were the people who had incurred the hostility of Indra, the patron of the Aryas and their bodies were therefore thrown to the wolves. A few of them who escaped slaughter were subsequently won over and became the worshippers of Indra. They therefore, in Rg. VIII, 6, 18; are described as praising Indra.

These Yatis may probably represent the Jain Saints. Some of the saints are described as naked which indicates that they were Jain saints. It seems that at the coming of the Aryans in India, the austerity was practiced by the natives. This idea of renunciation did not appeal to the society of the Aryans who had the optimistic outlook on life which is clearly reflected in hymns. The Rig-Veda is full of prayers for long life, freedom from disease, heroic progeny, wealth, power, abundance of food, drink, the defeat of the rivals etc. The people who liked renunciation were few in society. It seems that the invasion of the Aryans brought the destruction of the native culture and religion. The natives were forced to give up their own religion and to accept the culture of the invaders.

The Aryan invasion which overwhelmed the North Western and North Central provinces of the Sub-continent in the second millennium B. C. did not extend beyond the middle of the Ganges valley. The possession of the Aryans at the Rig-Vedic time was probably confined to Sapta Sindhu. The pre-Aryan nobility of the north eastern states were therefore not all annihilated.

Many of the old families survived. Probably, the people of Kasi, Magadha and other neighboring countries were the followers of a different culture on whom curses used to be showered and troubles used to be invoked. Jainism was probable popular in the east where the Tirthankaras were born. Even when the eastern part of India was aryanised, it preserved considerable differences from the midlands in the points of language, ethnic elements and culture. Probably, the Vratyas mentioned in Atharva Veda and Panchavimsa Brahmana of Samaveda lived there. The Panchavimsa Brahmana describes peculiarities of the Vratyas. They did not study the Vedas. They did not observe the rules regulating the Brahamanical order of life. They called an expression difficult to pronounce when it was no difficult to pronounce and spoke the tongue of the consecrated through un-consecrated. This proves that they had some Prakritic form of speech. The Prakrit language is specially the language of the canonical works of the Jains. Jayaswal states that they had traditions of the Jinas and Buddhas amongst them even before the sixth century B.C. It seems that they were the followers of the Jainism which is known to have come into existence even before the sixth century B. C.

JAINISM AS A DRAVIDAN RELIGION

Dr. Zimmer considers Jainism to be an older religion even than Vedic religion and called it the dravidan religion. Both are simple, unsophisticated, clear cut and direct manifestation of the pessimistic dualism. Jainism believes in pessimism, a conviction that human life is full of misery, no trace of which is to be found in the optimistic attitude of the Vedic Aryans. The doctrine of transmigration of the

Dravidans unknown to the early Brahmanas suddenly emerges in the Upanishads and forms an essential element in the Jain religion. What is more important, is the fact that the doctrine assumes it (x) peculiarly Indian form by its association with the doctrine of Karman and we know that the most primitive ideas of Karman are found in Jain Metaphysics. An atheistic attitude and a kind of dualism between soul and matter characterize both Dravidan religion and Jainism. From this religion also arose the heterodox sects namely Sankhya, Yoga and Buddhism.

Dr. Zimmer further observes that Jainism and Zoorastrian religions seem to be the forms of the Dravidan religion Both arose as a protest and as parallels against the Vedic religion and the religion of Avasta respectively in about 8th Century B. C. for the revival of the older religion which we may call the Dravidan religion. There are elements of similarity in both the religions. Parsvanatha and Zooraster were contemporary in time and they were against the sacrificial ceremony and polytheism of the gods. The enemy of Parsva was Kamatha, while of Zoorastra is Dahaka. Both gave troubles to Parsva and Zoorastra respectively for a long time but at the end, they were overcome by love. The serpents springing from the shoulders of both the images are well known. It seems that the snake played an important part in the lives of both.

Dr. Zimmer's arguments are held plausible but our main difficulty in accepting them is that our knowledge of the Dravidan faith is very meagre and perfunctory.

JAINISM IN THE TIME OF INDUS VALLEY CIVILIZATION

The discovery of the Indus Civilization seem to have thrown a new light on the antiquity of Jainism. The time assigned by the Scholars to this culture is 3000 B. C. on the archaeological evidence and on the evidence of the relations with the cultures of the other countries. The religion of the

Indus culture seems to be quite different from the religion of the Indus culture seems to be quite different from the religion of the Aryans in the Vedic period.

At Mohenjodaro and Harappa, iconism is every where apparent. But it is extremely doubtful whether images were generally worshipped in the ancient Vedic times. In the Rig-Veda and the other Vedas, there is worship of Agni, Sun, Varuna and various other deities. But they were worshipped in the abstract form as manifestations of a divine power. There are no doubt passages where the deities of the Rig-Veda are spoken of as possessed of bodily attributes.

R. G. VIII 175 speaks of the limbs and sides of Indra and prays Indra to taste honey with is tongue. In Rig. I. 155-6 Vishnu is said to approach a battle with his huge body and as a youth. It is possible to argue that all these descriptions are poetic and metaphoric. But there are two passages of time Rig-Veda that cause mush more difficulty than the above. Rg. VIII 1. 5. says, 'o Indra, I shall not give thee for even a great price, not even for a hundred, a thousand or ten thousand. It may be argued that here, there is a reference to an image of Indra.

But it is not convincing. It is equally possible to hold that these are hyperbolic or boastful statements of the great devotion of the worshipper to Indra and that there is no reference to an image of Indra. In most of the earlier and more authoritative Brahmanas which lay down in detail the rules of the rituals, associated with the Vedic sacrifices, there is no reference to images which would certainly have been explicitly mentioned, had they been regarded as necessary. In the subsequent period, when the image worship-had come to play a definite part in Brahamanic religion, detailed descriptions of these are not lacking. But the cult of symbols and images seems to have been current among the people who continued the traditional religious practices of the settlers of the Indus Valley region. These people seem to be the Jains because the image worship was prevalent among them in the times of Nandas and Mauryas. It seems that the image worship might have been copied by the Brahmanas from the Jains.

It is possible to suggest from the evidence of articles discovered that Jainism was not unknown among the people of the Indus Valley. Some nude images and the nude figures on the seals have been discovered at Mohenjodaro and Harrappa. Nudity has been the special characteristic of Jainism. Even Rishabha, the first Tirthankara observed the vow of nudity. The pictures 1. JBORS. Vol. III. Pt. IV, P. 458, & JBORS 1937 P. 130-32. Nos. 15 & 16 of plate XIII represent a seated image with a hood over its head attended by a half kneeling figure in respectful attitude. This may be the representation of the seventh Tirthankara Suparsvanatha. The bull is the cognizance of Rishabha Deva. The standing deity figured on seals three to five with a bull in the fore ground may be the proto-type of Rishabha. Some statues have been discovered also in the meditative mood, the half shut eyes, being fixed on the tips of the nose both in the sitting and standing poses. These statues and images on the seals may be taken to indicate that the people of the Indus Valley at this time not only practiced Yoga but worshipped the images of Yogis. In the Adipurana (Book XXI) there are the instruction given about the meditation. With regard to the eyes, it is stated that they should neither be kept wide open, nor totally shut up. The Kayotsarga posture of standing is peculiarly Jain. In the Adipurana Book XVIII, it is described in connection with the penances of Rishabha. This is also the characteristic of the Jain images at present.

These images have been described by Marshal as the proto-type of Siva. But with due difference to the illustrious scholar, an argument can be hazarded that the word Siva meaning the auspicious occurs as an epithet of Rudra in the Rigveda, Yajur Veda and Atharva Veda. It is only Rudra and not Siva who is praised in all hymns. He is represented in these hymns as a malevolent deity causing death and disease among men and cattle. The physical description of Rudra is found in a number of hymns in great detail. For instance in some places, he is said to be tawny in color and other of a very fair complexion, with a beautiful hair on his head. He carries in his hands a bow and arrows and is described in some hymns as wielding the thunderbolt. This type of Rudra can not be identified with the prototype Siva whose portraits are found on the seal because his attributes are quite different from the attributes stated in the Vedas about Rudra. Rudra occupies the minor position in the Vedic period but Siva seems to be dominant among the people of the Indus Civilizations. Siva with the puranic attributes can not be identified with the images on the seals because these puranas were composed about three thousand years after the Indus Civilization.

HISTORICITY OF SUPARSVANATHA

There are some legends about the Tirthankaras which may contain some historical matter. In the Mahavagga (1. 22. 13), there is a mention of a Jain temple of Lord Suparsva, the seventh Tirthankara situated at Rajagrih in the time of Lord Buddha. At Mathura, there is an old stupa of the Jains with the inscription of 157 A. D. This inscription records that an image of the Tirthankara Aranatha was set up at the stupa built by the gods. Thus, in 157 A. D., this stupa was so old that it was regarded as the work of the gods. It was probably, therefore, erected several centuries before the Christian era. The later authors give us some information about this stupa. Jinprabha in the Tirtha Kalpa, a work of the 14th century based on ancient materials mentions that the stupa originally of gold was erected in honor of the seventh Jina Suparsvanatha by the Kubera for two Jain Saints named Dharmaruchi and Dharmaghosh. In the time of twenty third Jina, Parsvanatha, the golden stupa was enclosed in bricks and a stone temple was built outside. Even Somadeva, the author of the Yasastilaka who is nearly four hundred years earlier than Jinaprabha refers to it as built by gods. From this type of legendary account, it seems that there was the worship of Suparsvanatha several centuries before the Christian era. The Yajurveda is also said to have mentioned the name of Suparsvanatha but the meaning is not definite. A seated image with a hood over its head attended by a half kneeling figure in respectful attitude in the pictures No. 15 & 16 of plate VIII may be the representation of the seventh Tirthankara Suparsvanatha.

Ajitanatha as a Historical Figure: The second Tirthankara is Ajitanatha, born in Ayodhya. The Yajurveda mentions the name of Ajitanatha but the meaning is not clear. His younger brother according to Jain traditions was Sagara who became the second Chakravarti. He is known from the traditions of both Hinduism and Jainism as found in their respective Purans. From the Hindu source, he is known to have many sons. One of them was Bhagiratha who brought the Ganges. From the Jain account, it is clear that Sagara in his last days adopted the life of asceticism from Ajitanatha and retired from the worldly life. Ajitanatha seems to be as real a person as Sagara.

HISTORICITY OF RISHABHADEVA

Even Rishabhadeva, founder of Jainism may be a historical figure. An image of Rishabha of V. S. 162 of the time of the Kushan Emperor Vasudeva has been discovered at Mathura. The inscription of Kharvela tells us that the image of Rishabha carried by Nanda three hundred years before was brought back by him to Kaling. There was thus the worship of Rishabha even in the fifth century B. C. in the time of Nandas. This points out that If mahavira or Parsva had been the founders of Jainism, it would not have been possible to find the images of Rishabha in the very early period. This indicates that he is not a mythical figure but a real personality. The name Vrishabha is mentioned in the Vedas, but the meaning is not certain. The different interpretations have been made by the scholars. The standing deity figured on the seals with a bull in the foreground may be the proto-type of Rishabha as we have already discussed. His parents were Nabhiraja and Marudevi. The name of his son was kept Bharata after which India said to be named.

LEGENDARY ANTIQUITY OF JAINISM

The Jain religion, according to the Jain scriptures is eternal, revealed in every cyclic period of the world. The time is divided into two equal cycles namely Utsarpini Kala and Avasarpini Kala. Each cycle is again divided into six divisions into six divisions known as aras. (Spoke of a wheel).

Avasarpini	Utsarpini
1. Sushama-Sushama	1. Duhshama-Duhshama
2. Sushama	2. Duhshama
3. Sushama-Duhshama	3. Duhshama-Sushama
4. Duhshama-Sushama	4. Sushama-Duhshama
5. Duhshama	5. Sushama
6. Duhshama-Duhshama	6. Suhshama-Sushama

Each Utsarpini and Avasarpini Kala extends over ten Kota-Koti sagaropama years. The first ara Sushama-Sushama of four Kota-Koti sagaropama years, the second ara Susama of three Kota-Koti Sagaropama years, the third ara Sushama-Duhshama of two Kota-Koti sagaropama years, the fourth Duhshama-Sushama of the duration of forty two thousand years less in one Kota-Koti sagaropama years, the fifth are Duhshama of twenty one thousand years and the last ara Duhshama-Duhshama will be twenty one thousand years duration.

At present, Duhshama is going on of which nearly twenty four hundred and eighty one years have passed. In the Utsarpini Kala, the order of the aras is the reverse.

During the first ara of Sushama-Sushama of the Avasarpini Kala, the age of the yugalika people was three palyopama years. They took their food on the fourth day, their bodies were very tall and were marked by auspicious symbols. They were devoid of anger, pride, deceit, greed and other sinful acts. Various kinds of the kalpa trees fulfilled their wishes.

During the second ara named Sushama, the yugalika lived for two palyopamas. They took their food at an interval of three days. They were also tall. The kalpa trees less supplied their wants than before. The objects of land and water became less sweet and fruitful than they were during the first ara.

During the third ara of Sushama-Duhshama, the age limit of the yugalikas became one palyopama. They took their food on the second day. The earth and water as well as height and strength of the body went on decreasing and they became less than they were during the second ara.

During the fourth ara Duhshama-Sushama, the height of the human being became five hundred dhanushyas and with ever progressing decrease it was reduced only to seven hands at the end of the fourth ara. Even the period of age limit was reduced approximately to one hundred years and less at the close of this ara. At this time, there was much happiness but the slight misery. People were happy and prosperous. The land was fertile and produced the abundant fruits.

At this time, the Tirthankaras were born and propagated Jainism. Lord Rishabha Deva, the first Tirthankara lived in the later part of the third ara and the remaining twenty three Tirthankaras lived during the forth ara. In the time of Rishabha, the Kalpa trees seized to fulfill the wishes, placing the people under difficulties. Under these circum stances, Rishabha instructed them to get on with the different occupations such as trade, agriculture etc. The people engaged In different occupations, formed different social groups. Lord Rishabha is very often described as a creator of the world in the sense of laying the socio-economic foundation.

In the fourth ara, Nami died 5,00,000 years before Nemi, Munisuvrata 11,00,000 or a krore; the following intervals can not be expressed in definite numbers of years but are given in palyopamas and sagaropamas. The length of the life and the height of the Tirthankaras are in proportion to the length of the interval. In connection with these proportion to the length of the interval. In connection with these items of the mythical history of the Jains, it may be added that they relate the life-length of twelve universal monarchs (Chakravartins); of nine Vasudevas, nine Baladevas, and nine Prati-Vasudevas who lived within the period from the first to the second Tirthankara together with the 24 Tirthankaras. They are the 63 great personages of Jain history.

During the fifth are named Duhshama, the present age during which we are living, the height, age limit and the strength of the human beings will be reduced. The majority of the people will be miserable and there will be reduced. The majority of the people will be miserable and there will be little piety and honesty. After that, there will be the sixth ara Duhshama-Duhshama in which there will be no sense of reason and morality among the people. The age, height and strength of the human beings will decrease to a great extent. People will suffer from the various diseases and thus, their lived will be miserable. Similarly, to the sixth and fifth aras of the Avasarpini Kala are first and the second of the Utasarapini Kala. At the end of the second ara named Dushama of the Utsarapini Kala, there will be seven Kulkaras. After the lapse of the Duhshama ara of the Utsarapini Kala, there will be sixty three excellent personages. This is only an imaginary theory similar to several such theories in the Purans and it can not be scientifically proved and historically demonstrated. It is only based on the firm faith of the authors and the strong traditions of Jainism. According to them, Jainism is eternal and came into existence with the very dawn of the civilization.

9

A Comparative Analysis of the Asian Religions

INTRODUCTION

The study of a religion other than one's own is a modern, and Western, phenomenon. The earliest reference to "the religions of the world" that Wilfred Cantwell Smith could find after a diligent search (discussed in his recent The Meaning and End of Religion) was in 1508 in Dyalogus Johannis Stamler Augustñ. de diversarum gencium sectis et mundi religionibus. That was followed a century later, in 1614, by Brerewood's Enquiries touching the diversity of languages, and religions through the chiefe parts of the world, which ran through some thirteen editions in the seventeenth century, in English, French, and Latin. The Enlightenment showed an interest in Asian religions, but it was not until the second half of the nineteenth century, beginning with Max Muller in 1867, that serious scholarly study of the religions of the world, of religions other than the scholar's own, was undertaken. The first article on Buddhism in the Encyclopaedia Britannica appeared in the ninth edition, in 1875.

By the beginning of the twentieth century there were chairs devoted to the study of the history of religions, or comparative religions, in about a dozen European universities, and today research in at least some of the Asian religions is being done in most of the universities of Europe and

America. A recent survey showed that there are over four hundred college professors in the United States giving undergraduate courses in the religions of the world. Opportunities for graduate study and research in the religions of Asia have expanded rapidly in the United States and Europe since the war, using the techniques of linguistics, history, literary criticism, sociology, anthropology, psychology, the arts, theology, and philosophy.

There has been no such development in Asia. Japanese scholars have greatly expanded their studies within the Buddhist context, covering Tibet, China, and the Buddhism of India and Southeast Asia, but have done little with Hinduism, Judaism, Islam, and Christianity. Some work has been done in India, courses have been offered in religions other than Buddhism in Ceylon, there was a chair of comparative religions for a time in Turkey, but in general the scholars of Asia have not turned to a study of religions other than their own.

Various reasons have been given for the interest in the religions of the world. Some suggest that the very idea of religions, in the plural, came from a pluralistic society with a democratic form of government. Some attribute the interest to improved methods of communication and transportation, together with more widespread education, saying that the desire to know more about other religions is inevitable when educated people have frequent opportunities to observe their differences and similarities throughout the world. Some of the studies seem to have been motivated by a desire to establish an underlying unity in all religions, or to prove the superiority of one religion over the others, or to develop more effective methods for conversion.

The time is past for easy comparisons, oversimplifications, stress on the exotic, or smug superiority in discussing religions other than one's own. The information at our disposal now makes so evident the complexity, the diversity, of the religious aspect of human experience in all Asian cultures that we can no longer use easy generalizations or traditionally accepted patterns in talking about other religions. As Professor Smith pointed out in the work referred to above, "Normally persons talk about other people's religions as they are, and about their own as it ought to be.... Those without a faith of their own think of all 'religions' as observably practiced. Hence insiders and outsiders use the same words while talking of different things" (p. 49). The aim in studying another religion should be to know it as it is and as its followers think it ought to be. It is a good rule always to speak of a religion other than one's own as if the speaker were in the presence of a good friend who is a follower of that religion. And, obviously, comparative evaluations should not be made, until one is sure that he understands accurately and perceptively the religion other than his own which he is judging--a level of understanding rarely attained by any of us.

We are concerned here with the place of Asian religions in the study of world history. When we study the history of Europe and America we can assume at least a minimal knowledge about the influence of Greek, Jewish, and Christian religious thought and practices, but for the study of the history of Asia we must prepare ourselves by gaining a sympathetic understanding of the quite different religious ideas and practices of that part of the world. We find ourselves guilty of errors of judgment and distortions of our sources when we apply to the history of Asia our own religious patterns and evaluations. This is to assume, as I do, that religious faith--the ways men find meaning for their lives and evaluate their relations to the natural world, to each other, and to the transcendent--is a factor of basic importance in shaping a culture and influencing the process of history; that religion is not just one of many aspects of the history of a people, to be taken up when, and if, convenient, but is fundamental to historical understanding; that it is a necessary, but not sufficient, basis for the interpretation of history. A knowledge of the religious background of the historical process under study will give meaning to much that would otherwise be obscure, will guard against possible misinterpretations, and might, even, lead to new perspectives on our own history and culture.

There is no easy way to get the background needed in Islam, Hinduism, Buddhism, Confucianism, and Taoism. It helps if one has a reasonably sophisticated and objective view of one's own religious faith, for that makes it easier to guard against attempting to force the religion studied into familiar molds. The first task in studying an Asian religion is to try to see the religion as it is seen by a believer; obviously, our judgments will be invalid if we see the religion through the eyes of German, or French, or American scholars, colored by the biases of Christian, Jewish, democratic, colonial or anti-colonial scholarship. We will not be altogether successful in gaining the Asian perspective, but we must try. For that, our basic resources are history and anthropology, with recent anthropological research proving to be of increasing value. Such descriptive studies must be the prelude to the study of the scriptures, the sacred writings, which are received as revelations or accepted as spiritual guides. Then we must turn to the other religious writings accepted as authoritative within the religion, and to the art and music when they play an important role. It may be objected that art and music cannot be conceptualized and are not therefore usable as facts in presenting religious history; from the point of view of religion, however, it must be insisted that the art and music are data which must be understood if the history is to be accurate.

As in other aspects of historical study, there is no getting away from the necessity to learn the relevant geography, to study the maps until the events have been placed spacially as well as temporally. Another chore is the learning of a new vocabulary. It is discouraging to think that one must understand the meaning of words which cannot be translated, such as karma, avatara, bodhisattva, anicca, Tao, shari'a, ijma, and dozens more; must recognize such names as Jalalu 'l-Din Rumi, Avalokiteswara, Vivekananda, 'Ali, Ananda, Ramanuja; must know the significance of such places as Sarnath, Karbala, Borobodur, Anuradhapura, Ajanta, Bamiyan, Hardwar, Mohenjodaro--but there is no short cut. One cannot understand the religions of Asia without having learned the basic religious concepts, the accepted religious writings, the important religious leaders, and the places which have sacred connotations for the people of Asia.

GENERAL

Unfortunately, there is no adequate, generally accepted introduction to the religions of Asia. The complexity of the field forces oversimplification when an attempt is made to cover all religions in one volume, and the attempt to be brief seems to create an irresistible tendency to force the religions into patterns. The classic in the field is History of Religions, by George Foote Moore, a scholarly introduction done some fifty years ago and still useful for factual material. The most widely used college textbook is Man's Religions, by John B. Noss; the author's preferences are frequently evident, and many passages would be questioned by followers of the religion under discussion, but it is widely used because of its extensive coverage and wealth of informative material. Readily available in paperback is The Religions of Man, by Huston Smith. It was not written as a textbook but as a response to a popular demand for an introduction to world religions after his brilliant television programs a few years ago. The Hinduism section gives the impression that Vedanta and Hinduism are synonymous, and the Buddhist section overemphasizes Zen, but the book is notable for the spirit of understanding of other religions expressed throughout. It is a good book to put in the hands of a beginner, for it gives much useful information with sympathetic insight and wise counsel on how to approach the study of a religion other than one's own. E. G. Parrinder, Reader in Comparative Religions at London University, has recently published What World Religions Teach, designed for high school students introducing them to Hinduism, Jainism, Buddhism, Confucius, Taoism, Shinto, the Sikhs, Bahais, Theosophy, African religions, Zoroastrianism, Judaism, Christianity, and Islam. It has a strong Christian bias. Modern Trends in World Religions, edited by Joseph M. Kitagawa, is not a systematic introduction to world religions but is useful as a general introduction for it is a collection of essays on current trends and problems in the study of world religions as seen by competent scholars who have been reflecting on the results of their research.

Teachers of Asian religions tend to look upon general introductions to the religions of the world as useful only for quick reference, and to prefer books dealing with a specific religion, supplemented with readings from original sources.

Many, but not all, of the sacred writings of the religions of Asia are now available in English translations, but the most complete collection is still The Sacred Books of the East, edited by Friedrich Max Muller, and published from 1879 to 1910 in fifty-one volumes. They are now out of print but some of them are being reprinted by Dover Publications.

Some books deal with an area, discussing more than one religion without aiming to be a general introduction to world religions. Anyone concerned with the religions of Southeast Asia would find it helpful to refer to A History of South-East Asia, by Daniel G. E. Hall, for it gives much information about the religions not readily available elsewhere. Brian Harrison's A Short History of South-East Asia is designed for high school students, giving less detail. Southeast Asia, Crossroad of Religions, by Kenneth Perry Landon, is a lucid, readable, somewhat simplified account of the Hindu and Islamic contributions to the culture of Southeast Asia. It is a fascinating story. The Wonder That Was India, by A. L. Basham, is a cultural history of India before the coming of the Muslims, with a great deal of information in small compass on the earliest culture, political history, social organization, the arts, language and literature, and over a hundred pages devoted to Hinduism and Buddhism. As a general introduction to the culture of India, it is widely used in American colleges. For Indian religions it is a convenient introduction to Harappa culture and the Aryans and gives a brief summary of Vedic and later Hinduism, Buddhism, and some other sects.

William Theodore de Bary and others have edited three volumes which are indispensable for students of Asian religions: Sources of Indian Tradition, Sources of Japanese Tradition, and Sources of Chinese Tradition. They have included explanatory sections by the editors, sections written by contemporary Asian scholars, and both classical and contemporary writings covering political, social, and literary aspects of the traditions of Hinduism, Buddhism, Sikhism, Jainism, Confucianism, Taoism, Neo-Confucianism, and Shinto. The editors and writers, basing their selections of topics and readings on their years of research and teaching, have brought together in these volumes valuable materials for the study of Asian religions which would not otherwise be readily available to teachers and students.

HINDUISM

The people of India would never refer to their religious faith and practices as Hinduism except as a concession to Western thought, for the Western label implies a pattern of beliefs and practices which is alien to their way of life. It is used here in the sense of the religion of the people of India, as distinguished from the Buddhists, Christians, Muslims and others who diverge from the predominant religious trends of the subcontinent. The attitude of the Hindus toward what seems to them an attempt to oversimplify and to impose Western religious categories and concepts on their religion should be borne in mind when evaluating books about the religion of India.

Hinduism, with four hundred million followers, is the oldest of the contemporary world religions, dating from at least two thousand B. C. It is primarily a religion of India; although it was known in the countries to the west, its major influence outside India was in Southeast Asia where it at one time was the dominant culture as far east as Indonesia.

While there are many sects within Hinduism, and numerous interpretations of the basic Hindu ideas, there would be general agreement that the world as we know it is an emanation from an original Source, Brahman, that ultimately the world as we know it will return to its Source; in the meantime, living beings go through numerous rebirths, their progress upward toward Brahman or downward toward material existence determined by the law of karma. Karma may be interpreted as a kind of cosmic justice, a moral law of cause and effect; or it may be seen as simply an orderly world in which every act has its inevitable consequence. For most Hindus, the final authority is found in the Vedas and the writings of great religious leaders capable of seeing the true nature of reality. There are many gods, all of them manifestations of the Supreme Being. Man's place in society is determined by his actions in his previous life, and in this life he is preparing the consequences for future existences. Yogic practices are designed to free men from the attachments of material existence and to develop their spiritual faculties so they can move toward the divine source from which they came.

Charles Eliot published in 1921 a three-volume work on Hinduism and Buddhism which is still a standard reference and dependable scholarly guide to Hinduism. Hindus detect in his asides frequent evidence that the book was written by a pukkha sahib in colonial times, but join in admiration for his scholarship and insight. The index to the three volumes is an amazingly complete reference source for looking up new words, strange titles, and definitions of terms. Even those who find the books too detailed for an introduction to Hinduism will discover that they will be coming back to Eliot as questions arise in their reading. It is a westernized interpretation of Hinduism, but an unusually able, scholarly work.

Hinduism, by K. M. Sen, is a small paperback of about a hundred pages written by a Hindu to introduce Hinduism to Europeans and Americans. Although occasionally defensive and apologetic in tone, it is generally a simple, straightforward description of Hinduism. It has the advantage that it presents the point of view of a follower of the faith. Another presentation of Hinduism by Hindus is The Religion of the Hindus, edited by Kenneth W. Morgan. After numerous interviews in India, seeking agreement as to what such a book should contain and who would be the most representative scholars to write it, the editor asked seven religious leaders to write on different aspects of the beliefs and practices of the Hindus. As they wrote, they made a conscious effort to present an accurate picture of contemporary Hinduism. The book contains a glossary of Hindu terms and a map showing the sacred places of the Hindus.

Sources of Indian Tradition, edited by William Theodore de Bary and others, has excellent sections on Hinduism written by two distinguished Hindu scholars, R. N. Dandekar and V. Raghavan, and readings from Hindu writings, carefully chosen to present Hindu beliefs and practices. It is one of the best available sources for becoming acquainted with the religion of the Hindus.

One of the best ways to gain an understanding of Hinduism is to study the Bhagavad Gita, especially if the reading of the Gita follows some introductory study of Hinduism so the ideas about Hinduism will be clarified and enriched as the Gita is mastered. Mahatma Gandhi found the basis for his faith in the Bhagavad Gita and found the inspiration and justification for non-violent direct action in its second chapter. One of the best editions of the Bhagavad Gita for the beginner is the translation by Swami Nikhilananda, for it is not only in good English but is provided with extensive notes, clarifying new concepts and giving a background for interpretation. The notes are Vedantic, and not all Hindus follow Vedanta, but with that warning in mind the commentary is one of the most useful available to Western students. For an understanding of Hinduism, it is better to have read a little introductory material and to have studied the Bhagavad Gita intensively than to have read more widely in secondary sources.

V. Raghavan's The Indian Heritage makes available a carefully selected volume of the most important passages from Sanskrit literature, covering the Vedas, the Upanishads, the Dharma Sastra, the Yoga Sutras of Patanjali, the Bhagavad Gita, and a collection of prayers not readily available elsewhere. It brings together in one volume the passages of the Hindu sacred writings which are treasured by an intelligent, devout Hindu.

There are multi-volumed studies of Indian philosophy by Radhakrishnan and Dasgupta, but one of the clearest and simplest introductions to the philosophy of India is The Essentials of Indian Philosophy, by M. Hiriyanna. He first wrote Outlines of Indian Philosophy, a somewhat fuller treatment, and then rewrote it as the Essentials, clarifying some passages. Another book of considerable merit is An Introduction to Indian Philosophy, by Satischandra Chatterjee and Dhirendramohan Datta. Either of these books will give Western students a good introduction to the philosophy of India. Having read about Indian philosophy, the next step is to read some of the sources, and for that Charles A. Moore of the University of Hawaii and Sarvepalli Radhakrishnan, India's philosopher President, have provided A Source Book in Indian Philosophy, a carefully selected collection of representative philosophical writings from Vedic to modern times.

To enrich the understanding of Hinduism, and to provide a dimension not found in the other writings, it is useful to read The Gospel of Sri Ramakrishna and Vivekananda, The Yogas and Other Works, both edited by Swami Nikhilananda. Ramakrishna played an important role in the revival of Hinduism in this century, and his work was carried on by his disciple Vivekananda, both in India and America. The stories of their lives and their teachings provide unique and illuminating source material for understanding contemporary Hinduism. Vivekananda's writings on yoga are useful for understanding one of the interpretations of the role of yoga in Hindu religious life.

For the study of yoga, one of the best books available is Yoga: Immortality and Freedom, by Mircea Eliade. It includes a discussion of yoga in Buddhism and in its Tantric forms and shows the relation of yoga to Hindu beliefs. It is a balanced, critical study by one of the great religious scholars of our time. For a somewhat simpler introduction, Yoga, A Scientific Evaluation, by Kovoor T. Behanan, is available in paperback. Behanan, as a graduate student at Yale, became interested in yoga and returned to India to study yogic techniques as a basis for his thesis at Yale. It is a clear statement of the basic principles of yoga, written with a Western reader in mind. Those who are interested in yogic exercises, Hatha Yoga, will find ample information in the little book Yoga for Perfect Health, by Alain, with illustrations of the postures by Sachin Majumdar.

The student who seeks to gain a sympathetic understanding of Hinduism will find that an appreciation of Indian art, literature, and music will be most helpful. For Hinduism, The Art and Architecture of India, by Professor Benjamin Rowland of Harvard University, is more than a merely adequate introduction, yet not too expensive for personal use. There are many recent novels in English, written by Indians, which reveal new dimensions of Indian religious life and illuminate the historical, philosophical, and religious studies of Hinduism: R. K. Narayan is one contemporary novelist whose works have excited students to further study of Hinduism and Indian culture. (Narayan's Financial Expert is the only one of his novels in paperback, but his other novels are now published in the United States.) For the theater, Theatre in India, by Balwant Gargi, gives an introduction to the traditional and the modern theater, with a wealth of information and perceptive interpretations. Indian music reveals much about Hinduism that is not conveyed by the written word or by reproductions of painting and sculpture; for an introduction to the music of India, Swami Prajnanananda has written Historical Development of Indian Music which, although it bristles with untranslated Sanskrit words, can be read with profit by anyone who has made enough of a study of Hinduism to be able to recognize its central concepts.

Recordings with helpful explanatory notes can be purchased from Folkways (P431, with notes by Alain Danielou) and from Angel (35468 and 35283, with notes by Yehudi Menuhin). The student of Hinduism who becomes familiar with those records by hearing them several times, who reads several Indian novels, and who becomes acquainted with some of the best examples of Indian art, will find that he understands Hinduism better and brings new insight to his study of the history of India.

BUDDHISM

The Buddha was a Hindu prince who rejected the Hindu scriptures, rituals, austerities, caste, and the Hindu teachings concerning creation and the Self, but remained close to Hinduism in his acceptance of the belief that existence continues through many lives and is controlled by the law of karma. The Buddha means The Enlightened One; he is the man who found the path by which all men may free themselves from suffering and despair. He rejected useless speculations which go beyond human experience, such as speculations about creation, God, and the nature of the future life, and urged a pattern of conduct and meditation leading to enlightenment, to freedom from sorrow. That enlightenment brings the recognition that all is change, that change ends in sorrow, that there is no soul, that man is only a combination of elements controlled by karma, and that when man is free from the illusory attachment to this world he becomes free from rebirth--what happens then is beyond our powers to know.

That basic pattern of Buddhism (now known as Theravada and based on scriptures written in Pali) was taught in India in the sixth century B. C. and spread throughout much of India and Southeast Asia. By the first century A. D., another form of Buddhism, known as Mahayana, had arisen in northern India with new writings mostly in Sanskrit, with much more elaborate speculative teachings. Theravada is found today in Ceylon, Burma, Thailand, Laos, and Cambodia; Mahayana spread to China, Korea, Japan, and Tibet; there is little Buddhism left in India. Not counting China, where it is impossible to know the status of Buddhism, there are about 150,000,000 Buddhists in the world today. It should be remembered when evaluating sources of information about Buddhism that the division between Theravada and Mahayana Buddhism has meant that there has been little communication between them for centuries, giving most writings either a Mahayana or Theravada bias.

Western scholars have been writing about Buddhism for about a century, not altogether to their own satisfaction or that of the Buddhists. Theravada Buddhists now point to What the Buddha Taught, by Walpola Rahula, a Ceylonese Bhikkhu (monk), as the best introduction to the central ideas of Buddhism, whether Theravada or Mahayana. Mahayanists might not agree, but it is a good book to read for it presents Buddhism with the emphases one would hear if receiving instruction in Ceylon. Another book which seeks to present Buddhism from the point of view of the Buddhists is The Path of the Buddha, edited by Kenneth W. Morgan and written by eleven Buddhist scholars, three Theravada and eight Mahayana, who were recommended by Buddhists as the religious leaders best able to speak for them. Its map of Buddhist pilgrimage places and its glossary of Buddhist terms are aids to the beginner in Buddhist studies.

For general introductions, all that was said under Hinduism about Sir Charles Eliot's Hinduism and Buddhism applies to the study of Buddhism, and de Bary's Sources of Indian Tradition, Sources of Japanese Tradition, and the Buddhist section of Sources of Chinese Tradition are equally useful. Edward J. Thomas has written two widely used books, The Life of Buddha as Legend and History and The History of Buddhist Thought, which, although inevitably reflecting the perspective of Western scholarship and primarily concerned with Theravada, are notable for their clarity and accuracy. And a classic in the field, James Bissett Pratt's The Pilgrimage of Buddhism, written thirty-five years ago, is still a dependable and thoroughly enjoyable introduction to Buddhism. He tells the story of the expansion of Buddhism, and with it the story of his own reactions as he traveled along some of the routes of that expansion. Thirty years after he made his own pilgrimage, as he calls it, many Buddhists in Asia remembered him and spoke of his friendly openness and understanding.

The complexity of the sacred writings of the Buddhists, both Theravada and Mahayana, discourages and puzzles the Western student who expects to find a clearly defined scriptural canon. One of the best introductory guides to the Buddhist sacred writings is Buddhism: A Religion of Infinite Compassion, edited by Clarence H. Hamilton, a collection which includes the stories of the life of the Buddha, the early teachings, the Dhammapada, and representative extracts from the Mahayana scriptures.

For the beginner, it is helpful to concentrate on the stories of the life of the Buddha and the Dhammapada, a summary of the teachings of early Buddhism. Another readily available and useful selection from the Buddhist writings, also a paperback, is The Teachings of the Compassionate Buddha, edited by Edwin A. Burtt. A larger collection of only Theravada sources is found in Warren's Buddhism in Translations. Edward Conze has recently published a Penguin paperback edition, Buddhist Scriptures, concentrating on the central tradition of Buddhism in an effort to bring together in one volume materials acceptable to all Buddhists. Somewhat earlier Conze published Buddhist Texts Through the Ages covering sacred writings from Theravada, Mahayana, and Tantric sources, arranged according to schools.

Much of the material basic to Buddhist philosophy can be found in the collections above, but Radhakrishnan and Moore in their A Source Book in Indian Philosophy included readings especially selected to illustrate Buddhist thought as it developed in India. In The Central Philosophy of Buddhism, A Study of the Madbyamika System, T. R. V. Murti of Banaras Hindu University makes a careful study of one of the most important schools of Mahayana philosophy. In reading that book it should be borne in mind that it is written by a Hindu and reflects the opinion that Buddhism is only a variant of Hindu ideas, an assumption not usually granted by Buddhist philosophers. Professor Murti has, however, undertaken a systematic exposition such as has not yet been made available in the West by Mahayana scholars. Although the exposition by the Japanese scholar Junjiro Takakusu is not by philosophic systems such as Abhidharma, Madhyamika, and Vijnanavada (or Yogacara), his The Essentials of Buddhist Philosophy is a standard guide to Mahayana thought. After a discussion of the fundamental principles of Buddhist philosophy, he discusses the chief sects of Japan: Kusha, Jojitsu, Hosso, Sanron, Kegon, Tendai, Shingon, Zen, Jodo, Nichiren, and New Ritsu. It is a concise and able introduction to Japanese Buddhist thought.

Since Buddhism has taken many forms and has adapted to different cultures in Asia, books dealing with limited areas are especially helpful as protection against too-easy generalizations. Thai Buddhism, Its Rites and Activities, by Kenneth E. Wells, for instance, by giving a general introduction to Buddhism in Thailand and then a description of the State ceremonies and the ceremonies in the temples and the homes, brings Buddhism in Thailand to life for the Western reader.

Theravada Buddhism in Burma, by Niharranjan Ray, is a history of Buddhism with emphasis on Burmese-Indian relations, and written by an Indian, but it, too, conveys the special character of Buddhism in one Theravada country. For a description of Buddhism in Ceylon, which carries all the flavor of conversations in a Buddhist monastery and presents Ceylonese Buddhism as it is seen by the Bhikkhus of Ceylon, see Walpola Rabula's History of Buddhism in Ceylon. There is also a recent journal article on Buddhism in Ceylon well worth the effort of looking up, not only for its insight into Buddhism in Ceylon but also for its value as an example of the contribution anthropology can make to the understanding of Asian religions. It is written by a Ceylonese anthropologist, Gananath Obeyesekere, and is one of the best explanations available of the relation between Buddhism and the customs of the country; it presents the Buddhism of the common people, not the Buddhism of the books: "The Great Tradition and the Little in the Perspective of Sinhalese Buddhism," The Journal of Asian Studies, February 1963.

Although Tibet does not now exist as an independent country, Tibetan Buddhism continues to be of special interest because it combines, more than anywhere else in the Buddhist world, the traditions of Theravada, Mahayana, and Tantra. Three popularly written books give an excellent introduction to Tibet: the Dalai Lama's My Land and My People; the autobiography by his brother, Thubten Norbu, Tibet Is My Country; and Heinrich Harrer's Seven Years in Tibet. The latter might be the first book to read since it gives a Western view of Tibet by an Austrian who lived there after escaping from a prisoner-of-war camp in India. Although the other two books deal primarily with recent events in Tibet, they manage to convey a great deal of information about the beliefs and practices of the Tibetans. The chapter in The Path of the Buddha on Tibet, by Lobsang Phuntsok Lhalungpa, an aide of the Dalai Lama, is a brief, systematic presentation of Tibetan Buddhism. A more arduous, but richly rewarding, path to an appreciation of Tibetan Buddhism would be a study of The Hundred Thousand Songs of Milarepa, recently translated by C. C. Chang. It is a classic Tibetan writing, full of stories and teachings which are part of the traditions of Tibet. For a more systematic description of the religious practices of Tibet, see Tibet and the Tibetans, by Tsung-Lien Shen and Shen-Chi Liu, two Chinese scholars who fled Tibet when the Communists arrived. It discusses the geography, history, organization of Lamas, government, customs and ceremonies of the Tibetans.

For a detailed history of Buddhism in China we will have to wait for Kenneth Chen's book which should be published by the Princeton Press in 1964. In the meantime, Arthur Wright's Buddhism in Chinese History gives a clear and discerning picture of the sweep of Buddhist history through the centuries and has a useful bibliography for further reading, especially in the journals. There are also two chapters in Wing-tsit Chan's Religious Trends in Modern China dealing with the development of Buddhist thought and modern movements in Chinese Buddhism which give a great deal of information and insight in a few pages.

For additional background which brings Buddhism in China to life, there are two fascinating, though rather specialized books: Reischauer's Ennin's Travels in T'ang China, and Waley's The Real Tripitaka. Ennin was a Japanese Buddhist monk who traveled in China between 838 and 847 and wrote an account of his journey which our present ambassador to Japan has made available in English, an account that transports the reader to the Buddhist world of China in the ninth century. Tripitaka (or, Hsuan Tsang) was a Chinese Buddhist of the seventh century who traveled with great difficulty to India to learn more of Buddhism in its native land and returned to translate many of the scriptures into Chinese. The story of his adventures and observations reads like a novel, and in the sixteenth century was made into a novel, Monkey, by Wu Ch'eng-en. It has been translated by Arthur Waley, is available in paperback, and has awakened in many a student in our times an interest in Buddhism and Chinese history.

After World War II, the military headquarters recognized the need for some guide to the religious groups in Japan and asked the Religious and Cultural Division of the Civil Information and Education Section to prepare a concise description of Japanese religious organizations for the guidance of occupation personnel. The report was circulated in mimeographed form for some years, and then published as Religions in Japan, by William K. Bunce. It is a quick introduction, but was carefully prepared by competent researchers with the aid of many Japanese scholars and is still useful for reference. The classical introduction to Buddhism in Japan was written by Sir Charles Eliot, that fabulous British civil servant, titled simply Japanese Buddhism. The information is there, flavored with his sympathetic, but Western, point of view. For a study in more detail of one period, we have Japanese Religion in the Meiji Era, written in part and edited by Hideo Kishimoto; it gives the Japanese viewpoint by competent scholars who understand Western historical methods.

Those who find Zen the most interesting form of Mahayana Buddhism should bear in mind that it is only one small sect, considered by some Buddhists to be almost heretical, and frequently distorted in the West. One of the best introductions to Zen is The Practice of Zen, by C. C. Chang, a Chinese Buddhist who received his Zen training in China before going to study Buddhism in Tibet. It makes clear the rigorous nature of Zen training, and gives many apt illustrations from Zen literature. D. T. Suzuki, who has lived much of his life in the United States and is well-known for his writings on Zen, has published many books explaining Zen to Americans, of which his Zen Buddhism is representative. Readers of his works should be aware of the feeling of some Japanese Buddhists that he tends to Americanize his explanations. Sohaku Ogata, a Zen monk in Kyoto who has visited the United States and has had many American disciples in Japan, has written Zen for the West, an explanation of Zen with an anthology of Zen writings selected with Western readers in mind. Nancy Wilson Ross, after many years of study of Zen, has published an anthology of Zen writings and writings about Zen, bringing together all the material she has found most useful, under the title The World of Zen. William Briggs, who calls his book Anthology of Zen, has edited a book of writings about Zen by leading Japanese Zen scholars, with a few articles by Westerners; it is one of the most useful explanations of Zen thought.

For Zen writings, the best book available is Zen Flesh, Zen Bones, a collection of Zen and Pre-Zen writings compiled by Paul Reps, and beautifully printed by Tuttle. There one finds the best of the Zen stories.

It is said that the Chinese were at first scornful of Buddhism--can anything good come from India? until they saw examples of Buddhist art. Certainly Buddhism is not understood until there is some appreciation for Buddhist art. As a supplement to the reading of the stories of the life of the Buddha, and an aid to understanding the role of the Buddha in Buddhism, Anil De Silva-Vigier's The Life of the Buddha Retold from Ancient Sources serves a unique function for it tells the life of the Buddha with illustrations of Buddhist art. For comprehensive treatment of Buddhist art, the three Penguin books on Asian art are most helpful: The Art and Architecture of India, by Benjamin Rowland; The Art and Architecture of China, by Laurence Sickman and Alexander Soper; The Art and Architecture of Japan, by Robert T. Paine and Alexander Soper. Langdon Warner's The Enduring

Art of Japan is a classic introduction by a great teacher and scholar. For superb reproductions of Japanese painting and sculpture, Yukio Yoshiro's 2000 Years of Japanese Art should do all that any book can do to explain the influence that art has had in Buddhist history.

Music is not a part of worship in Theravada Buddhism, but is used in sophisticated forms in many Mahayana sects. In Japanese Music and Musical Instruments, by William P. Malm, there is a brief chapter on Buddhist religious music, and a little information can be gleaned from the notes accompanying recordings of Japanese music by Folkways (FR8980), but the study of music in the Buddhism of China, Japan, Korea, and Tibet has not yet been written.

ISLAM

When studying or teaching Hinduism or Buddhism, the Westerner soon becomes aware of the rather wide differences of perspective and meaning between the Judeo-Christian and the Hindu-Buddhist ways of viewing the nature of man and man's relation to his world. The avatara of Hinduism is not the prophet of Judaism nor the Christ of Christianity; karma is not easily equated with destiny or divine will; tantric yoga differs noticeably from Sunday School exercises. The nature of the teachings and practices of Hinduism and Buddhism reminds the Westerner of the danger of trying to force new and strange ideas into familiar patterns. Rarely, and then only in contemporary writings, do Hindus or Buddhists refer to Christianity or Judaism, arousing defensive feelings which lead us to suggest that they would not have said what they did if they understood our religion better. But the situation is quite different when we come to Islam, for there the differences are not great, and may be missed, and there the references to Judaism and Christianity are frequent, and not always complimentary. Thus, although it should be easier to teach Western students about Islam than about Hinduism or Buddhism, for there is much in common, the burden of our neighborhood quarrels--not always impartially recorded--and the subtle differences of interpretation make Islam the most difficult religion to present fairly.

Muslims--who do not like to be called Muhammadans because they think it implies a misunderstanding of the place of the Prophet in their faith--have themselves tended to encourage oversimplification by claiming that Islam may be quickly grasped by accepting the Fundamentals and following the simple list of Consequences they imply. There is unity in Islam from Morocco to Indonesia and China, but there is also diversity which must not be slighted if the appeal of Islam to more than four hundred million followers is to be understood.

The Prophet Muhammad died in 632 A. D. after having received the revelations recorded in the Qur'an and having organized the Muslim community in Arabia. Following his death, Islam spread from Spain to the Indus river in India within a century, and by the fifteenth century had completed its expansion and major theological developments. One becomes a Muslim by repeating the Word of Witness, "I witness that there is no God but Allah and that Muhammad is His Prophet," and accepting the Fundamentals: belief in the existence and oneness of God, in Angels, in the Qur'an as the revelation of God, in the Prophets, in the Day of Judgment, and in the Divine Order.

Those Fundamentals require the acceptance of the Consequences, also known as the required Worship: repeating the Word of Witness, observing the five daily prayers, giving a fixed percentage of income to the poor, fasting during the month of Ramadan, and making the pilgrimage to Mecca if possible. There is no ordained clergy in Islam; they have as leaders men who have established their ability to guide by their learning and piety. The daily life of Muslims is guided by an elaborate code of laws worked out over the centuries, based first on the Qur'an, then on the traditions concerning the Prophet, then the consensus of the Islamic community, and finally in a limited area on individual interpretation. Most Muslims are Sunnis, but in Iran and Iraq and a few other areas there are about 30,000,000 Shi'as who believe that the leadership of the Muslim community should rest in the descendants of the Prophet, particularly through his nephew Ali.

Mohammedanism: An Historical Survey, by H. A. R. Gibb, is the most widely read introduction to Islam in English. Many Arab scholars, who have great respect for Sir Hamilton Gibb's scholarship, are a bit hesitant about giving the book unqualified approval because of its Western flavor: one young Arab who started to translate it into Arabic gave up when he found that the Mullahs who could not read English were very critical when they read his version. It is still the most readily available short introduction to Islam. A most interesting introduction to Islam is Kenneth Cragg's The Call of the Minaret. The first 170 pages are an exposition of Islam by a Western writer with scarcely a phrase to which a Muslim could take exception, and the rest of the book is a guide to Christian missionary work with Muslims, with which they have little sympathy. Those first 170 pages are one of the best introductions to Islam in English, a model of writing about a religion other than one's own.

Marshall G. S. Hodgson of the University of Chicago has prepared a three-volume syllabus with selected readings, Introduction to Islamic Civilization, which brings together a useful collection of readings, with seholarly introductions, covering the religious, social, and political aspects of Islam. Islam--the Straight Path, edited by Kenneth W. Morgan, was written by eleven Islamic scholars from six countries--scholars selected on the basis of the recommendations of religious leaders throughout the Islamic world--as an introduction to Islam from the point of view of the Muslims. It has now been translated into five languages for use by Muslims. The definitions in the glossary were written by Muslims.

The Encyclopaedia of Islam is out of print but a new edition is being published and will be available in a few years; in the meantime, the articles concerned specifically with religion and law in Islam have been published in the Shorter Encyclopaedia of Islam and provide a useful reference source. For the geographical background of Islam, showing the spread by centuries and giving useful statistics, there are two good atlases: Atlas of Islamic History, by Harry W. Hazard, and Historical Atlas of the Muslim Peoples, by Roelof Roolvink.

Detailed studies of aspects of Islamic history are the next step after reading the general introductions. For the early period, the studies by W. Montgomery Watt are standard, especially his Muhammad at Mecca. Gustave E. von Grunebaum is an Islamic scholar who seeks to observe Islam objectively, neither as a Westerner nor as an Islamic apologist; his Medieval Islam: A Study in Cultural Orientation is a perceptive, and at times provocative, analysis of the period of development following the initial expansion of Islam.

The book he edited on the Unity and Variety in Muslim Civilization is especially useful because of the papers on Iran, Spain, North Africa, Tropical Africa, and Turkey, as well as for the papers stressing the basic unity of Islam. His Muhammadan Festivals is the most convenient guide to the major holidays which play such an important part in all Muslim countries.

For Islam in modern times, Modern Trends in Islam, by H. A. R. Gibb, is a thoughtful survey by one of the most competent scholars in the field, giving the student the benefit of his extensive experience. Islam in Modern History, by Wilfred Cantwell Smith, is a study of what is happening to Islam in a time of rapid transition; it is a thoughtful, sometimes disturbing, book which should be read by anyone who is teaching about Islam. Its treatment of the major areas of the Islamic world is an aid to understanding the present diversity in Islam.

Among the many books dealing with Islam in specific areas, three are mentioned here because they are of more than geographic interest.

Leonard Binder's Religion and Politics in Pakistan is a study of the interplay of Islam and politics in modern Pakistan and as such is an aid to understanding Pakistan, but from the point of view of Islam it is a case study of the problem of creating an independent democratic state in harmony with the traditional law of Islam, a pressing problem throughout the Islamic world. The Shi'ite Religion, by Dwight M. Donaldson, is incidentally a study of religion in Iran and Iraq, but it is primarily a study of the Shi'as, whose widespread influence is often slighted in general studies of Islam.

The Religion of Java, by Clifford Geertz, does not even claim to speak for all of Indonesia, but it is useful to the student of Islam because it gives in rich detail a description of Islam in one village in the Far East. Geertz is an anthropologist, and this book is a good example of the valuable contributions anthropologists are making to the work of the historians and theologians.

The Religion of Java deserves careful reading, not only for what it tells about Islam in Java, but for its insights into the comparative problems raised by the study of religion as it is followed in distant parts of the world.

As with the other religions, books about Islam are not enough; there must be some study of the scriptures and religious writings if the perspective of a religion other than our own is to be understood. This is especially difficult in Islam for, although the Qur'an is the final authority and is constantly quoted in discussions with Muslims, Westerners have difficulty reading translated versions with sympathetic understanding. One useful way to approach the study of the Qur'an is, after having read about Islam in some of the sources recommended above, to make a detailed study of the

Second Surah, looking for the Qur'anic basis for the Fundamentals and Consequences of Islamic faith. The translation most frequently recommended by Islamic scholars who know English is Mohammed Marmaduke Pickthall's The Meaning of the Glorious Koran.

It has the advantage of being available in an inexpensive paperback edition. Pickthall's translation is largely dependent upon The Holy Qur'an, translated by Maulana Muhammad Ali, but since Ali is an Ahmadiyyah, and many of his notes express the unorthodox ideas of the Ahmadiyyahs, his translation is not often recommended by Sunni Muslims. Sunnis have been known to say, however, that if the reader will be on his guard when reading the explanatory notes, the translation by Ali is one of the best.

The third translation which is now widely recommended as superior is The Koran Interpreted, by A. J. Arberry. Arberry agrees with the orthodox Muslim that the Qur'an is untranslatable, that "the rhetoric and rhythm of the Arabic of the Koran are so characteristic, so powerful, so highly emotive, that any version whatsoever is bound in the nature of things to be but a poor copy of the glittering splendour of the original" (p. 24). In his version, he sought to "imitate, however imperfectly, those rhetorical and rhythmical patterns which are the glory and the sublimity of the Koran" (p. 25). Anyone who is seeking to understand the Qur'an in English would do well to compare the three translations.

For other Islamic literature, the most useful guide is Reynold A. Nicholson's A Literary History of the Arabs. Arthur Jeffery edited a useful anthology, Islam: Muhammad and His Religion, bringing together selections carefully chosen in consultation with devout Muslims to introduce important Islamic writings to Western readers.

Art is a special problem in Islam, for representation of any forms which might be suggestive of idolatry is forbidden. A Handbook of Muhammadan Art, by M. S. Dimand, is an excellent introduction to Islamic art. Painting in Islam: A Study of the Place of Pictorial Art in Muslim Culture, by Thomas W. Arnold, is a full discussion of the Muslim attitude toward portraying the living form.

THE RELIGIONS OF CHINA

Without stopping to argue whether or not Confucianism or Taoism are religions, or even offering a definition of religion, it can be urged that an understanding of the history of China requires a good background in Confucian, Taoist, and Buddhist thought. We have discussed Buddhism in China above, but it is also included in some of the books mentioned here.

Religion in China, by E. R and K. Hughes, is a quick introduction in the Hutchinson University Library series, giving a general sketch of the religious background of Chinese history. Karl Ludvig Reichelt's Religion in Chinese Garment, while also a small book, gives much more detail, covering animism, Confucianism, Taoism, Buddhism, and Islam in China, all in concise, introductory presentations. Religion in Chinese Society, by C. K. Yang, is a recent study of religion in the family, in economic and political life, as a moral force, as an institution, and in relation to Communism. For the contemporary picture, Wing-tsit Chan's Religious Trends in Modern China is indispensable; in addition to the two chapters on Buddhism, mentioned above, it discusses Confucianism, Islam, and the religion of the masses and of the intellectuals.

Chinese Thought from Confucius to Mao Tse-tung, by H. G. Creel, is a widely used introduction which covers some of the religious background. For the philosophy of China, Fung Yu-lan's Short History of Chinese Philosophy, a condensation of his two volume History of Chinese Philosophy, gives a clear discussion of Confucian, Neo-Confucian, Taoist, and Buddhist philosophy for the Western student who is trying to find his way. It is clear, without being oversimplified. And, again, de Bary's Sources of Chinese Tradition provides a wide range of readings, with introductions, for filling in the background of the religions of China.

Special studies with relevance for understanding Confucianism and Taoism include Arthur Waley's An Introduction to the Study of Chinese Painting and Laurence Sickman and Alexander Soper's The Art and Architecture of China, for to an unusual degree the understanding of the arts is necessary for an understanding of the religions of China. Arthur Waley's Translations from the Chinese, an anthology of Chinese poetry, adds another dimension to the understanding of Confucian, Taoist, and Buddhist thought in Chinese culture. Of more specialized interest are some of the essays in Studies in Chinese Thought, edited by Arthur Wright, especially the articles by Derke Bodde on Harmony and Conflict in Chinese Philosophy, by W. Theodore de Bary on A Reappraisal of Neo-Confucianism, by David S. Nivison on The Problem of "Knowledge" and "Action" in Chinese Thought Since Wang Yang-Ming, and by Schuyler Cammann on Types of Symbols in Chinese Art.

Although the chief religious trends in China have been Buddhism, Confucianism, and Taoism, some attention should be given to the influence of Motse, the radical critic of Confucius. The general writings mention him, but for a fuller treatment the best sources are two books by Y. P. Mei: Motse, Rival of Confucius, a biography and systematic discussion of his thought, and The Works of Motse.

CONFUCIANISM

The dates usually accepted for Confucius are 551-479 B. C. He was a wise man who spent his life as a teacher who tried to reform the government of his time. He insisted that he was not an innovator, but only sought to return to the wisdom of the ancients and his interpretation of that wisdom is given in the Analects. He taught the way of the true gentleman, respect for family ties, the importance of ritual and music in developing moral character. For centuries, a knowledge of Confucian teachings was required for advancement in government service in China. Mencius was his first great disciple.

Confucius and the Chinese Way, by H. G. Creel, is the most widely used biography of Confucius, written with understanding and admiration. For a short, brilliant interpretation of Mencius, the disciple of Confucius, see Waley's Three Ways of Thought in Ancient China. Arthur Waley has done a masterly translation of The Analects of Confucius with a more than adequate introduction and notes. A thorough knowledge of the Analects is a prerequisite for an understanding of Chinese religion, philosophy, and culture. There is also a translation of the Analects by James R. Ware, The Sayings of Confucius, available in paperback, and he has translated The Sayings of Mencius. Both the Analects and Mencius are translated by E. R. Hughes in Chinese Philosophy in Classical Times, an Everyman edition which has the advantage of including the writings of Taoism, of Mohism, and other writings Hughes found useful in his courses in Chinese thought, together with his introductory notes.

TAOISM

Taoism is based on the Tao Te Ching, dating from about the sixth century B. C. and attributed to an imaginary Lao-tse. Tao cannot be translated satisfactorily but can be understood in the context of the Tao Te Ching; it is interpreted to mean: the Way, course, method, order, norm, right conduct, reason, providence, the moral order, the physical order. It is like water, seeking the lowest place, yet penetrating the hardest substance. It is the way to be followed by those who achieve without striving; it is unassertive, inconspicuous, lowly, incomplete. Taoism teaches the way of harmony with nature, and has been the inspiration for much of the landscape painting of China. In its organized, cultic form, Taoism deteriorated in later years into a form of magic, seeking good fortune and long life, but even today the Tao Te Ching is an important element in Chinese and Japanese thought, especially in relation to Zen.

One of the best introductions to the Tao Te Ching, as well as the translation preferred by many, is found in Arthur Waley's The Way and Its Power. This is not an easy religious writing to master, but it is one of the most haunting, provocative, and rewarding of the writings of the religions of Asia. No one translation will exhaust its possibilities and for the Westerner who cannot read Chinese it is desirable to compare as many translations as possible. Many years ago, Paul Carus, aided by an unknown young Japanese scholar, D. T. Suzuki, published a translation called The Canon of Reason and Virtue, choosing that title as their interpretation of the meaning of Tao Te Ching. R. H. Blakney has a translation, published by Mentor; and Witter Bynner published a poetic translation, which is at times a graceful interpretation, called The Way of Life According to Laotzu.

For Chuang Tzu, one of the early disciples of Taoism, there is an excellent introduction in Waley's Three Ways of Thought in Ancient China, and the writings of Chuang Tzu are found in Hughes's Chinese Philosophy in Classical Times and in a recent reissue of Chuang Tzu, Taoist Philosopher and Chinese Mystic, by Herbert A. Giles. The writings of Chuang Tzu are a help in understanding the Tao Te Ching. The Parting of the Way: Lao Tzu and the Chinese Movement, by Holmes Welch, is an informative interpretation of Taoism, especially useful since the latter half of the book treats of the later developments in Taoism.

CONCLUSION

Those whose interest in the religions of Asia has been aroused to the point that they want to consider some of the comparative problems raised by the study of religions other than one's own will find thoughtful and searching discussions in two books recently published: World Religions and World

Community, by Robert Lawson Slater, and The Meaning and End of Religion, by Wilfred Cantwell Smith. Slater discusses problems of unity and diversity and of the developing of a "science" of religions, with applications to major Asian religions. Smith traces the use of the word "religion" in the West and argues that much of the difficulty in communication between religious groups is due to ambiguities arising from lack of discrimination in the use of the adjective "religious" and the noun "religion." It is a thoughtful book in which Smith reflects on the problems raised by the study of the religious thought and practices of the people of Asia, problems of historical method, of literary criticism, of language, of social organization, and of the values and standards by which men guide their lives.

10

THE JAIN AGAM LITERATURE

BACKGROUND

Lord Mahavir's preaching was orally complied by his disciples into many texts. This knowledge was orally transferred from acharyas (gurus) to the disciples over the course of about one thousand years. In olden times, monks strictly followed the five great vows of Jainism. Even religious scriptures were considered possessions and therefore knowledge of the religion was never documented. Also, during the course of time many learned acharyas (elder monks) complied commentaries on the various subjects of the Jain religion.

Around 500 A.D., which was one thousand years after Lord Mahavir's nirvana (death), Jain acharyas realized that it was extremely difficult to keep memorizing the entire Jain literature complied by the many scholars of the past and present. In fact, significant knowledge was already lost and the rest was polluted with modifications and errors. Hence, they decided to document the Jain literature as known to them. In this time period two major sects, namely Digambar and Swetambar, were already in existence. A thousand years later (1500 A.D.), the Swetambar sect divided into three subsects known as Swetambar Murtipujak, Sthanakvasi, and Terapanthi. Differences exist among these sects in their acceptance of the validity of the documented Jain scriptures and literature.

LITERATURE

Jain literature is classified into two major categories:

- *Agam Literature:* This consists of original scriptures complied by Gandharas and Srut-kevalis. They are written in the Prakrit language.
- *Non-agam Literature:* This consists of commentary and explanation of Agam literature and independent works, complied by elder monks, nuns, and scholars. They are written in many languages such as Prakrit, Sanskrit, Old Marathi, Gujarati, Hindi, Kannad, Tamil, German, and English.

Agam literature is also divided into two groups:

- *Ang-agams or Ang-pravista-agams:* These texts contain the direct preaching of Lord Mahavir. They were complied by Ganadharas.
- *Ang-bahya-agams (outside of Ang-agams):* These texts are expansions of Ang-agams. They were complied by Srut-kevalis.

Agam Literature: Lord Mahavir's preaching was methodically compiled by his followers into many texts. These texts are collectively known as Agams, the sacred books of the Jain religion.

Hence, the Jain religion does not have one sacred book like the Bible or Koran, but it has many books complied by many followers.

Ang-agams: Lord Mahavir's immediate disciples were known as Ganadharas. All Ganadharas possessed perfect knowledge (keval-jnan).

They orally complied the direct preaching of Lord Mahavir into twelve main texts (sutras). These texts are known as Ang-agams. Hence the Ang-agams are the oldest religious scriptures and the back bone of Jain literature.

The twelfth Ang-agam is called Drastivad. The Drastivad consists of fourteen Purva texts, also known as Purvas or Purva-agams. Among Ang-agams, Purvas were the oldest sacred texts. All Jain sects believe that knowledge of the Purvas (Drastivad) were gradually lost starting two hundred years after Lord Mahavir's nirvan (death). However, the subject matter of the Purvas has been referenced by other Jain scriptures and literature.

The Digambar Jain sect also believes that the remaining eleven Ang-agams were gradually lost. All Swetambar Jains believe that the proper meaning and the original intent of the eleven Ang-agams survived and were properly documented by elder monks one thousand years after Lord Mahavir's nirvan.

Sect	Number of Ang-agams Accepted	Present Status
Digambar	11	All are lost
Swetambar Murtipujak	11	Available
Swetambar Sthanakvasi	11	Available
Swetambar Terapanthi	11	Available

Ang-bahya-agams: Monks who had knowledge of a minimum of ten Purvas were known as Srut-kevlis. The Srut-kevlis wrote many texts (sutras) expanding the subject matter defined in the Ang-agams. Collectively these texts are called Ang-bahya-agams meaning outside of Ang-agams.

Sects	Number of Ang-bahya-agams Accepted	Present Status
Digambar	14	All are Lost
Swetambar Murtipujak	34	Available
Swetambar Sthanakvasi	21	Available
Swetambar Terapanthi	21	Available

The different Jain sects accept different numbers of Ang-bahya texts.

However the Digambar sect believes that they were also gradually lost starting about two hundred years after Lord Mahavir's Nirvan.

Classification of Ang-bahya-agams: The Swetambar sect has divided Ang-bahya-agams into the following categories:

- *Upang-agams:* The scriptures which provide further explanation of Ang-agams are called Upang-agams. There are 12 Upang-agams accepted by all Swetamber sects.
- *Chhed-sutras:* The subject matter described in Chhed-sutras is only for monks and nuns and not for lay people. It relates to the conduct and behavior of monks and nuns. It also explains how they can repent for their sins and mistakes. The Swetambar Murtipujak sect accepts 6 Chhed-sutra texts but the Sthanakvasi and Terapanthi sects accept only 4 texts.
- *Mool-sutras:* The scriptures which are essential for monks and nuns to study in the earlier stages of their monkhood are called Mool-sutras. The Swetambar Murtipujak sect accepts 4 Mool-sutras texts but the Sthanakvasi and Terapanthi sects accept only 3 texts.
- *Chulika-sutras or Sutras:* The scriptures which enhance or decorate the Ang-agams are known as Chulika-sutras or Sutras. There are 2 Chulika-sutras accepted by all Swetamber sects.
- *Prakirna-agams:* The scriptures which describe independent or miscellaneous subjects of the Jain religion are known as Prakirna-sutra. The Swetambar Murtipujak sect accepts 10 Prakirna-agams texts but none are accepted by the Sthanakvasi and Terapanthi sects.

Classification Summary:

agams	Swetambar Murtipujak Sect	Sthanakvasi Terapanthi Sects
Upang-agams	12	12
Chhed-sutra-agams	6	4
Mool-sutra-agams	4	3
Chulika-sutra-agams	2	2
Prakirna-agams	10	none
Total Ang-bahya-agams	34	21

Digambar Jain Literature: The Digambar sect believes that there were 25 Agam-sutras (11 Ang-agams + 14 Ang-bahya-agams) complied from the original preaching of Lord Mahavir. However, they were gradually lost starting about two hundred years after Lord Mahavir's nirvana. Hence the existing Agam-sutras (which are accepted by the Swetambar sects) are not accepted by them as authentic scriptures.

In the absence of authentic scriptures, Digambars use the following literature as the basis for their religious practice. These scriptures were written by great Acharyas (scholars) from 100 to 800 A.D. and are based on the original Agam Sutras.

- Two Main Texts:
  - Shatkhand-agam
  - Kasay-pahud
- Four Anuyogas:
  - Pratham-anuyoga (Dharma-kath-anuyoga)-Religious Stories
  - Charn-anuyoga-Conduct
  - Karan-anuyoga (Ganit-anuyoga)-Description of the Universe
  - Dravy-anuyoga-Philosophy

Shatkhand-agam: This Digambar scripture is also known as Maha-kammapayadi-pahuda or Maha-karma-prabhrut. It was written by two Acharyas; Pushpadant and Bhutabali around 160 A.D.

The second Purva-agam named Agraya-niya was used as the basis for this scripture. The scripture contains six volumes. Acharya Virsen wrote two commentary texts, known as Dhaval-tika on the first five volumes and Maha-dhaval-tika on the sixth volume of this scripture, around 780 A.D.

Kashay-pahud (Kashay Prabhrut): This scripture was written by Acharya Gunadhara. The fifth Purva-agam named Jnan-pravad was used as a basis for this scripture. Acharya Virsen and his disciple, Jinsen, wrote a commentary text known as Jaya-dhaval-tika around 780 A.D.

Four Anuyogas:

1. Pratham-anuyoga (Dharma-kath-anuyoga)-Religious Stories

   This anuyoga consists of the following texts which contain religious stories, art, literature, history, poetry, and like literature.

Name	Author	Time
Padma-puran	Ravisen	650 A.D.
Harivamsa-puran	Jinsen II	783 A.D.
Adi-puran	Jinsen II	783 A.D.
Uttar-puran	Gunabhadra	879 A.D.

2. Charn-anuyoga-Conduct

   This anuyoga consists of the following texts which contain principles of observances, conduct, behavior, and like literature.

Mulachar	Vattaura	600 A.D.
Trivarnachar	Vattaura	600 A.D.
Ratna-karanda-shravak-achar	Samantabhadra	600 A.D.

3. Karan-anuyoga (Ganit-anuyog)-Description of the Universe

   This anuyoga consists of the following texts which contain geography, mathematics, astronomy, astrology, and like literature.

Surya-prajnapti	Unknown	
Chandra-prajnapti	Unknown	
Jaya-dhaval-tika	Virsen/Jinsen	780 A.D.
Gommat-sar	Nemichandra Siddhant Chakravarti	1000 A.D.

4. Dravy-anuyog-Philosophy:

   This anuyoga consists of the following texts which contain philosophical doctrine, theories, Tattvajnan, and like literature.

Niyamasar	Kunda-kunda	100 A.D.
Panchastikaya	Kunda-kunda	100 A.D.
Pravachanasar	Kunda-kunda	100 A.D.
Samaya-sara	Kunda-kunda	100 A.D.
Tattvartha-sutra	Umaswami	200 A.D.
commentary by	Samantabhadra	600 A.D.
commentary by	Pujyapad	700 A.D.
commentary by	Akalank	750 A.D.
commentary by	Vidyanand	800 A.D.
Aptamimamsa	Samantabhadra	600 A.D.
commentary by	Akalank	750 A.D.
commentary by	Vidyanand	800 A.D.

SUMMARY

The Jain literature which was complied by Ganadharas and Srut-kevlis is known as Agam literature. These texts are the holy scriptures of the Jain religion. The Agam Sutras show great reverence for all forms of life and strict codes of vegetarianism, asceticism, nonviolence, and opposition to war. The existing Agam Sutras are accepted as the authentic preaching of Lord Mahavir by the Swetambar sects, but the Digambar sect does not accept them as authentic. Digambars follow two main texts (Shatkhand Agam and Kasay Pahud) and four Anuyogs (consisting of more than 20 texts) written by great Acharyas (scholars) from 100 to 800 A.D.

All other Jain literature is known as Non-agam literature.

Category Digambar	**Accepted by Swetambar Murtipujak**	**Sthanakvasi Terapanthi**	
Ang-agams	11	11	11
Ang-bahya-agams	14	34	21
Total Agams	25	45	32

Classification of Ang-bahya-agams of Swetamber Sects:

Upang-agams	12	12
Chhed-sutra-agams	6	4
Mool-sutra-agams	4	3
Chulika-sutra-agams	2	2
Prakirna-agams	10	none
Total Ang-bahya-agams	34	21

Details of Jain Agams:

Ang-agams: Ang-agams are the oldest religious scriptures and the back bone of Jain literature.

1. Acharang Sutra(Aayarang): This agam describes the conduct and behavior of ascetic life and the description of the penance of Lord Mahavir. This is the oldest agam from a linguistic point of view.
2. Sutrakratang Sutra (Suyagdang): This agam describes nonviolence, Jain metaphysics, and the refutation of other religious theories such as Kriyavada, Akriyavada, Ajnanavada, and Vinayavada.

3. Sthananga Sutra (Thanang): This agam defines and catalogues the main substances of the Jain religion (defines Jain metaphysics).
4. Samavayanga Sutra: This agam defines and catalogues the main substances of the Jain religion from a different perspective than the Sthananga Sutra.
5. Vhakhya Prajnapti or Bhagavati Sutra (Viyah Pannati): This agam explains the subtle knowledge of soul, matter, and other related subjects. 36000 questions and answers are presented in discussion form. It is the largest of the eleven Ang-agams.
6. Jnata Dharma Kathanga Sutra (Nayadhammakahao): This agam explains Jain principles through examples and stories. This text is very useful in understanding the mode of Lord Mahavir's religious preaching.
7. Upasaka Dashanga Sutra (Uvasagdasao): This agam explains the code of conduct of the ten lay followers (Shravaks) of Lord Mahavir. This agam is very useful for understanding the code and conduct of ordinary people (Shravaka Dharma) in the Jain religion.
8. Antah Kradashanga Sutra (Anatagaddasao): This agam tells the stories of ten sacred monks attaining liberation (Moksha) by destroying their karmas.
9. Anuttaroupa Patika Dashanga Sutra (Anuttarov Vaiya Dasao): This agam contains the stories of an additional ten sacred monks who attained the top-most heaven, known as Anuttara heaven.
10. Prashna Vyakrana Sutra (Panha Vagarnai): This agam describes the five great vows (mahavratas) and the five worst sins defined in the Jain religion.
11. Vipaka Sutra (Vivagsuyam): This agâm explains the results of good and bad karmas through several stories.

- Upang-agams: The scriptures which provides further explanation of Ang-agams are called Upang-agams.

1. Aupa Patika Sutra (Ovavaiya): This agam describes the splendid procession (view) of King Konika when he visited Lord Mahavir. It also explains how a person can attain heaven in the next life.
2. Raja Prashniya Sutra (Raya Pasen Ijja): This agam describes the story of Monk Keshi. Monk Keshi was the Ganadhara of Lord Parshvanath. He removed the doubts of King Pradeshi regarding the existence and attributes of the soul. Monk Keshi made the king a follower of the Jain religion. After his death, the king was born as a deva in heaven. He appeared from heaven to shower Lord Mahavir with unprecedented pomp and splendor. The thirty-two dramas (plays) described in this agam throw light upon the ancient dramatic art of India.
3. Jivabhigama Sutra: This agam describes the universe and the subtle description of all living beings (souls) of the universe. It gives very important information to the scholars of biology and botany.
4. Prajnapana Sutra (Pannavana): This agam describes the form and attributes of souls from a different perspective.
5. Surya Prajnapti Sutra (Surya Pannti): This agam describes the Sun, the planets and the associated mathematics regarding their motion.
6. Chandra Prajnapti Sutra: This agam describes the Moon, the planets and the associated, mathematics regarding their motion. Both of these upangas, the Chandra Prajnapti and Surya Prajnapati, sutras are very important in understanding the astrology of olden times.
7. Jambudveepa Prajnapti Sutra: This agam provides a description of Jambudveepa. Jambudeepa is a place explained in Jain geography. It also provides information on ancient kings.
8. Nirayarvali Sutra: This agam describes the story of ten princes. All ten princes fought with King Chetaka

of Vaishali in cooperation with king Konika. King Chetaka was the son of the 10 princes' step-mother. In the end all ten princes went to hell after dying in war.

9. Kalpa Vatansika Sutra (Kappavadamsiao): This agam describes the story of King Konika's children. They did not fight with King Chetaka in the war. They renounced the world and became monks. After their death, they went to heaven.
10. Pushpika Sutra (Puspiao): This agam describes the previous lives of certain devas (angels) who worshiped Lord Mahavir.
11. Pushpa Chulika Sutra: This agam describes stories similar to those in the Pushpika.
12. Vrashnidasha Sutra (Vanhidasao): This agam explains how Lord Neminath convinced ten kings in the Vrashni region to follow the Jain religion.

- Chhed Sutra Aagams: The subject matter described in the Chhed-sutras is for monks and nuns and not for lay people. It relates to the conduct and behavior of monks and nuns. It also explains how they can repent for their sins and mistakes.

1. Nisheetha Sutra (Nisiha): This agam explains the procedure of repentance (Prayashchitta) in the form of punishment for the monks and nuns who have conducted themselves badly.
2. Vrahat Kalpa Sutra: This agam explains which of the ten kinds of repentance (Prayashchittas) is appropriate for a particular wrong-doing by monks and nuns. It also defines in clear terms what is acceptable conduct for monks and nuns and what is not.
3. Vyavahara Sutra: * This agam describes the system of confession for monks and nuns who fall from proper conduct. It explains the qualifications of the listening monk or nun and with what sort of feeling the confession should be made. It also explains what sort

of repentance (Prayashchitta) the monk should perform. There are several other indication of the limits of ascetic life.

4. Dasha Shruta Skandha Sutra (Achardasha): There are ten chapters in this Sutra. It contains the following information:
    1. 20 places of Asamadhi
    2. 21 powerful faults bringing weakness in conauct
    3. 33 Ashatanas of Guru
    4. 8 Sampadas of Acharyas and their kinds
    5. 10 places of Chitta Samadhi
    6. 11 Pratimas of Sravaka
    7. Bhiksu Pratimas
    8. KALPASUTRA-recited during the Paryushanas
    9. 30 places of Maha Mohaniya karma bandhana
    10. 9 Nida nas (Niyane)
5. Panch Kalpa Sutra: * This sutra explains the daily rituals the monks and nuns have to perform. Only scattered chapters of this agam are now available. However, the commentaries (Bhashya and Churni) written about this agam by some elder monks are available.
6. Mahanisheetha Sutra: This agam explains the process of confession and repentance (Prayashchitta) for monks and nuns. It explains the magnitude of pain one has to suffer if he or she breaks the fourth vow (chastity). It also describes and explains the conduct of good and bad monks.

- Mool-sutras: The scriptures which are essential for monks and nuns to study in the early stages of their ascetic life are called Mool-sutras.

1. Avashyaka Sutra: The daily rituals or routines which it is necessary to perform during the day and night

for the purification of soul are called Avashyaka. A description of the six routines (Avashyakas) are explained in this agam. The six routines are; Samayika, Chaturvinshatistava, Vandanaka, Pratikramana, Kayotsarga, and Pratyakhyana.

2. Dasha Vaikalika Sutra: This agam briefly describes and explains the conduct of ascetic life.
3. Uttaradhyayana Sutra: This agam has the same place in Jain literature as the Dhammapada in Buddhism and the Geeta in the Hindu religion. It contains preaching regarding religious principles and practices, and many stories, dialogues, and examples based on such principles and practices.
4. Ogha Niryukti or Pinda Niryukti Sutra: * This agam explains certain rules and procedures for monks with respect to travelling, staying, accepting food and other necessities from lay people.

- Chulika-sutras or Sutras: The scriptures which enhance or decorate the Ang-agams are known as Chulika-sutras or Sutras.

1. Nandi Sutra: This agam contains an elaborate description of Tirthankaras, Ganadharas, and five types of Knowledge (Jnan); Mati, Shrut, Avadhi, Manaparyay, and Keval-Jnan.
2. Anuyogadvara Sutra: This agam provides the description of many rights regarding the mode of preaching.

- Prakirna-agams: The scriptures which describe independent or miscellaneous subjects of the Jain religion are known as Prakirna-sutra.

1. Chatuh Sharana: * This agam contains prayers to the four benevolent beings:
   1. Lord Arihant-God in the form of human being
   2. Lord Siddha-God in the form of pure consciousness

3. Sadhu-All monks
4. Dharma-Religion

2. Aatur Pratyakhyana (Aayur-Pachakhana): * This agam explains differences in the death of children, youths, adults, and old people. It also describes the types of vows a wise person should take during various states of illness and how he should beg the pardon of all living beings in the universe.
3. Bhakti Parijna (Bhatta-parinna): * This agam describes the process of fasting and how one should strive to feel at the time of death.
4. Sanstaraka (Santharag): * This agam describes the process of dying by one's own desire (Santhara) and its glory.
5. Tandulavaitalika: * This agam describes the state of pregnancy and provides knowledge about the human body.
6. Chandra-Vedhyaka: * This agam describes the method of concentrated meditation (Dhyana) that one should observe through the description of Radhavedha.
7. Devendra-Stava: * This agam describes the names, positions, and residences of Devas (angels) who live in heaven. It also provides a description of the moon, sun, planets, and stars.
8. Ganita Vidya: * This agam describes palmistry and how it is used to predict the future (Nimitta).
9. Mahapratyakhyana: * This agam explains how to completely give up the worst sins and how to repent these sins.
10. Veerastava: * This agam is considered lost. However, it appears from literature referencing this agam that it contained prayers of Lord Mahavir.

Note: * These 13 Agams are not recognized by the Sthanakvasi and Terapanthi Jain sects

11

Buddhism Vs Jainism

INTRODUCTION

Mahavira was a senior contemporary of Gautama Buddha, the founder of Buddhism. The Buddhist texts refer to Mahavira as an enlightened being. However there seems to be no personal contact or communication between the two when they were alive. Interestingly, no rivalry seemed to have existed between Buddhism and Jainism in the early days of Buddhism, definitely not so much as the rivalry between them and the Ajivakas sect, with whom the Buddha himself often indulged in prolonged debates and discussions. However the very fact that the Buddha denounced extreme asceticism as the means to salvation suggests that there was no scope for any reconciliation between the two.

Both Buddhism and Jainism deny the existence of God or the First Cause which is responsible for the entire creation. But both acknowledge the presence of gods, who are higher than human beings in status but subject to change and evolution and also plane of higher beings, called Jinas or Kevalins by Jains and Bodhisattvas by Buddhists. The Bodhisattvas take interest in the welfare of the world and work for its liberation, but the Kevalins are rather indifferent to our prayers and problems and remain unaffected.

They also differ on the question of the status and evolution of individual beings. According to Jainism, after liberation, the Jiva or soul continues to remain as an individual soul, but in the highest state of purity and enlightenment. According to Buddhism, there is no soul but the individuality or character of an individual which after nirvana passes into some kind of indescribable nothingness that cannot be speculated upon.

The followers of Jainism acknowledge the presence of soul in every animate and inanimate object of the universe, including the elements of the universe, such as the earth, the water, wind, fire and air. Buddhists on the other hand believe that some vague kind of individuality do exist in the plants and animals, but they do not find any such individuality in the inanimate things. The concept of a world filled with innumerable individual souls or clusters of souls, or souls lying hidden in the rocks and mountains, the rivers and lakes, the stars and planets is simply untenable in Buddhism.

Both Buddhism and Jainism acknowledge the universality of karma and its effect on the individual beings. But in Jainism the karma is not a mere effect or result of ones actions, but a real substance that flows into each individual body or jiva as it indulges in various actions. This karmic substance which is a kind of fine matter or energy field, remains with it until it is got rid of through good conduct and self purification.

Though both Buddhism and Jainism originated and developed as distinct religions in the same geographical area comprising the present day Bihar and adjoining states, Buddhism crossed the frontiers of Indian subcontinent and went to far away lands like Nepal, China, far eastern countries, central Asia, Sri Lanka and Japan, while Jainism remained mostly confined to the land of its origin.

Strangely over a period of time, Buddhism disappeared from the Indian soil, despite of making several compromises with Hinduism, and having almost been absorbed into Hinduism as a sect, while Jainism survived in India, with its teachings intact, mostly untouched by the overwhelming philosophy and practices of Hinduism, at the same time imparting to the latter some of its noblest ideas.

REACTION AND REBILLION

During the Axial Age, enlightened thinkers, throughout the known world, were developing new explanations of existence, and man's place within the order of the universe. In India, the Upanishads redefined the Aryan religious tradition. Led by ksatriya ascetics, this new development rebelled against the ritual superiority of the brahman class proliferated during the Vedic period. This movement gradually led to an integral transformation of Hindu thought. But, while these new thinkers quietly transmuted the Aryan belief system, two other luminaries, not only challenged the ritualism of the former tradition, but openly rejected the rigidity of class distinction, forming new religions.

Similar to the seekers, who reformed Hinduistic thought, the individuals responsible for the growth of these new religions came from the ksatryia caste that sought a release from the brahman's domination of ritual. Also significant, in this quest for change, were the members of the vaishya caste. With the collapse of tribalism, India experienced great material and economic growth from which this class, which included an increasing number of merchants, craftsmen, and professional, benefited. Many of the vaishya, therefore, resented the privileges afforded the upper two castes, which invariably prepared them for religious ferment.

Most prominent of the two individuals seeking answers to the orthodox Vedism, and the injustice of the caste system was Siddhartha Gautama(c. 563 BC-483 BC) who founded the religion known as Buddhism. Although this tradition significantly diminished in the land of its birth, it remained a powerful force in the rest of the world. Central to Buddhist thought are the Four Noble Truths: that all life is suffering (dukkha); the cause of suffering is desire; escape from dukkha can be attained by ending desire; the path to the cessation of desire can be achieved through the Noble Eight-Fold Path comprised by right views, motives, speech, conduct, livelihood, effort, thought and meditation.

Although Buddhism became more important because of its spread outside of India, Jainism, at least within the confines of the subcontinent, gathered equal support. Western scholars frequently list Vardhamana Mahavira (c. 540 BC-468 BC), as the founder of Jainism. According to Jain legend, however, Mahavira was the last in line of twenty-four Tirthankaras, or those who had successfully crossed the river of suffering and attained enlightenment.

Like Siddhartha Gautama, Mahavira came from the ksatriya caste, and eventually abandoned his family and earthly possessions to become a wandering ascetic in search of spiritual enlightenment. After an extended period of meditation, Mahavira attained full enlightenment and became a kevalin (completed soul), and a jina (conqueror). Mahavira continued his teachings for a number of years accompanied by a band of naked monks. Purportedly he died at the age of seventy-two as a result of starvation.

The codification of Jain religious doctrines did not occur until nearly two hundred years after Mahavira's death, but contained many of his teachings. According to Mahavira, all living things are divided into five categories and are delineated by the number of senses they posses. The highest class, which have five senses include men, gods, and animals with higher intelligence. The second class, with four senses (touch, smell, taste, and sight), include most larger insects. The third classification, supposedly devoid of sight, contains smaller insects such as fleas and ants. Included in the second group, with only touch and taste, are worms, some shellfish, and leeches. The final class of one sensed creatures, not only includes plants, but such inanimate objects such as minerals, fire, and water. In this respect, then, everything in nature contains karmic matter, and karma is the cause of bondage. Thusly, all Jains are instructed to respect all things unconditionally, and to practice ahimsa, or nonviolence, towards all things. Salvation, or enlightenment, according to Jain principles, can only be attained by freeing one's soul from karmic matter to reach a level of purity.

Jainism is older than Buddhism. Vardhaman Mahavira, the last Tirthankara of the Jainas was the contemporary of Gautam Buddha. The sects organised by the two leaders flourished for centuries together, before and after the Christian era. Although there were differences in the conduct of their monks in as much as the Jaina saints remained naked and the Buddhist monks wore cloths, there were closer resemblances between the two.

This book on Jaino-Buddhist religion places stress on the common factors on the religious life of the Jaina and Buddhists. On comparing the literature of both, the writer has come to the conclusion that coming in close association each sect has either borrowed from the other or both have derived material from common source. The work is an analytical account of Jainism and Buddhism. It is full of references. The author has exploited all the relevant material in discussing the subject. He has tried to show similarities between old Jainism and old Buddhism and prove that both were one and same at their base; that the old Buddhism was nothing but old Jainism and that Gautama Buddha must have preached the same philosophy that was preached by old Jainism.

He has shown that the nature of Nirvana and its path as found in Buddhist Pali books are not different from the nature of Nirvana and its path as given in old Jaina works. He has also thrown light on their concept of Karma and Ahimsa and shown reasons why the two sects are so alike. As no records of factual words of the teachers of both these sects are preserved and the speeches placed in their mouths are only the summaries of what they had said, he has attempted to collaborate the oldest records in the main outlines by the Pauranic tradition and other sources. He has tried to trace the influences of these sects upon Jewish and Christian religions also.

Linguist Background

While often employing concepts shared with Hinduism and Buddhism, the result of a common cultural and linguistic background, the Jain tradition must be regarded as an independent pheromenon. It is an integral part of South Asian religious belief and practice, but it is not a Hindu sect or Buddhist heresy, as earlier scholars believed.

The name Jainism derives from the Sanskrit verb ji, "to conquer." It refers to the ascetic battle that it is believed Jain renunciants (monks and nuns) must fight against the passions and bodily senses to gain omniscience and purity of soul or enlightenment. The most illustrious of those few individuals who have achieved enlightenment are called Jina (literally, "Conqueror"), and the tradition's monastic and lay adherents are called Jain ("Follower of the Conquerors"), or Jaina. This term came to replace a more ancient designation, Nirgrantha ("Bondless"), originally applied to renunciants only.

Jainism has been confined largely to India, although the recent migration of Indians to other, predominantly English-speaking countries has spread its practice to many Commonwealth nations and to the United States. Precise statistics are not available, but it is estimated that there are roughly four million Jains in India and 100,000 elsewhere.

Early History (7th century BCE-c. 5th century CE)

Jainism originated in the 7th-5th century BCE in the Ganges basin of eastern India, the scene of intense religious speculation and activity at that time. Buddhism also appeared in this region, as did other belief systems that renounced the world and opposed the ritualistic Brahmanic schools whose prestige derived from their claim of purity and their ability to perform the traditional rituals and sacrifices and to interpret their meaning. These new religious perspectives promoted asceticism, the abandonment of ritual, domestic and social action, and the attainment of gnosis (illumination) in an attempt to win, through one's own efforts, freedom from repeated rebirth.

Rishabhanatha and the other Twenty-three Tirthankaras

The first Jain figure for whom there is reasonable historical evidence is Parshvanatha (or Parshva), a renunciant teacher who may have lived in the 7th century BCE and founded a community based upon the abandonment of worldly concerns. Jain tradition regards him as the 23rd Tirthankara (literally, "Ford-maker," i.e., one who leads the way across the stream of rebirths to salvation) of the current age (kalpa). The 24th and last Tirthankara of this age was Vardhamana, who is known by the epithet Mahavira ("Great Hero") and is believed to have been the last teacher of "right" knowledge, faith, and practice. Although traditionally dated to 599-527 BCE, Mahavira must be regarded as a close contemporary of the Buddha (traditionally believed to have lived in 563-483 BCE but who probably flourished about a century later). The legendary accounts of Mahavira's life preserved by the Jain scriptures provides the basis for his biography and enable some conclusions to be formulated about the nature of the early community he founded.

Mahavira, like the Buddha, was the son of a chieftain of the Kshatriya (warrior) class. At age 30 he renounced his princely status to take up the ascetic life. Although he was accompanied for a time by the eventual founder of the Ajivika sect, Goshala Maskariputra, Mahavira spent the next 12 1/2 years following a path of solitary and intense asceticism. He then converted 11 disciples (called ganadharas), all of whom were originally Brahmans. Two of these disciples, Indrabhuti Gautama and Sudharman, both of whom survived Mahavira, are regarded as the founders of the historical Jain monastic community, and a third, Jambu, is believed to be the last person of the current age to gain enlightenment. Mahavira is believed to have died at Pavapuri, near modern Patna.

The community appears to have grown quickly. According to Jain tradition, it numbered 14,000 monks and 36,000 nuns at the time of Mahavira's death. From the beginning the community was subject to schisms over technicalities of doctrine, however, these were easily resolved. The only schism to have a lasting effect concerned a dispute over proper monastic practice, with the Shvetambara ("White-robed") sect arguing that monks and nuns should wear white robes and the Digambaras ("Sky-clad," i.e., naked) claiming that a true monk (but not a nun) should be naked. This controversy gave rise to a further dispute as to whether or not a soul can attain liberation from a female body (a possibility the Digambaras deny).

This sectarian division, still existent today, probably took time to assume formal shape. Its exact origins remain unclear, in part because the stories describing the origins of the schism were designed to justify each sect's authority and denigrate the other. These accounts were written centuries after the fact and are valueless as genuine historical testimony. The consolidation of the Shvetambara-Digambara division was probably the result of a series of councils held to codify and preserve the Jain scriptures, which had existed as oral tradition long after Mahavira's death. Of the councils recorded in Jain history, the last one, held at Valabhi in Saurashtra (in modern Gujarat) in either 453 or 456 CE, without Digambara participation, codified the Shvetambara canon that is still in use. The Digambara monastic community denounced the codification, and the schism between the two communities became irrevocable.

During this period, Jainism spread westward to Ujjain, where it apparently enjoyed royal patronage. Later, in the 1st century BCE, according to tradition, a monk named Kalakacarya apparently overthrew King Gardabhilla of Ujjain and orchestrated his replacement with the Shahi kings (who were probably of Scythian or Persian origin). During the reign of the Gupta dynasty (320-c. 600 CE), a time of Hindu self-assertion, the bulk of the Jain community migrated to central and western India, becoming stronger there than it had been in its original home in the Ganges basin.

Early Medieval Developments (500-1100)

There is archaeological evidence of the presence of Jain monks in southern India from before the Common era, and the Digambara sect has had a significant presence in what is now the state of Karnataka for almost 2,000 years. The early medieval period was the time of Digambara Jainism's greatest flowering. Enjoying success in modern-day Karnataka and in neighbouring Tamil Nadu state, the Digambaras gained the patronage of prominent monarchs of three major dynasties in the early medieval period-the Gangas in Karnataka (3rd-11th century); the Rashtrakutas, whose kingdom was just north of the Ganga realm (8th-12th century); and the Hoysalas in Karnataka (11th-14th century). Digambara monks are reputed to have engineered the succession of the Ganga and the Hoysala dynasties, thus stabilizing uncertain political situations and guaranteeing Jain political protection and support.

The Digambaras' involvement in politics allowed Jainism to prosper in Karnataka and the Deccan. Many political and aristocratic figures had Jain monks as spiritual teachers and advisers. Epigraphical evidence reveals an elaborate patronage system through which kings, queens, state ministers, and military generals endowed the Jain community with tax revenues and with direct grants for the construction and upkeep of temples. Most famously, in the 10th century the Ganga general Chamundaraya oversaw the creation of a colossal statue of Bahubali (locally called Gommateshvara; son of Rishabhanatha, the first Tirthankara) at Shravana Belgola.

During this period Digambara writers produced numerous philosophical treatises, commentaries, and poems, which were written in Prakrit, Kannada, and Sanskrit. A number of kings provided patronage for this literary activity, and some wrote various works of literature themselves. The monk Jinasena, for example, wrote Sanskrit philosophical treatises and poetry with the support of the Rashtrakuta king Amoghavarsha I. An author in Kannada and Sanskrit, Amoghavarsha apparently renounced his throne and became a disciple of Jinasena in the early 9th century.

The Shvetambaras in the north were less prominently embroiled in dynastic politics than their southern counterparts, though there is evidence of such activity in Gujarat and Rajasthan. They supported the accession of kings such as Vanaraja in the 8th century and Kumarapala, whose accession was masterminded by Hemacandra, the great Shvetambara scholar and minister of state, in the 12th century. The Shvetambaras were no less productive than their Digambara contemporaries in the amount and variety of literature they produced during this period.

While Mahavira had rejected the claims of the caste system that privileged Brahman authority on the basis of innate purity, a formalized caste system nonetheless gradually appeared among the Digambara laity in the south. This hierarchy was depicted and sanctioned by Jinasena in his Adipurana, a legendary biography of the Tirthankara Rishabhanatha and his two sons Bahubali and Bharata. The hierarchy differed from the Hindu system in that the Kshatriyas were assigned a place of prominence over the Brahmans and in its connection of purity, at least theoretically, with a moral rather than a ritual source. In addition, Jinasena did not see the caste system as an inherent part of the universe, as did Hindu theologians and lawgivers.

Late Medieval-early Modern Developments (1100-1800)

In the period of their greatest influence (6th-late 12th century), Jain monks of both sects, perhaps influenced by intense lay patronage, turned from living as wandering ascetics to permanent residence in temples or monasteries. A legacy of this transformation is the contemporary Digambara practice of the bhattaraka, through which a cleric takes monastic initiation but, rather than assuming a life of naked ascetic wandering, becomes an orange-robed administrator and guardian of holy places and temples. Some medieval Jain writers saw this compromise with ancient scriptural requirements as both a cause of and evidence for the religion's inexorable decline. However, Jainism's marginalization in India can best be ascribed to sociopolitical factors.

The Shvetambara Jain community's eclipse was greatly accelerated by the successful invasion of western and northern India by Muslim forces in the 12th century. Although it faced persecution and the destruction of important shrines, the Jain community perhaps suffered most from the sudden shift of political control from indigenous to foreign hands and the loss of direct access to sources of power. While some Jain laymen and monks served Muslim rulers as political advisers or teachers-including Hiravijaya, who taught the Moghul emperor Akbar-the Shvetambara community was gradually compelled to redefine itself and today thrives as a mercantile group.

At roughly the same time, various Shvetambara monastic subsects (gaccha) appeared, forming on the basis of both regional and teacher associations. Some of the most important of these subsects still exist, such as the Kharatara Gaccha (founded 11th century) and the Tapa Gaccha (founded 13th century). The gacchas included lay followers, often differed markedly from one another over issues of lineage, ritual, and the sacred calendar, and claimed to represent the true Jainism. According to tradition, their leading teachers sought to reform lax monastic practice and participated in the conversion of Hindu Rajput clans in western India that subsequently became Shvetambara Jain caste groups.

Although most gacchas accepted the practice of image worship, the Lumpaka, or Lonka Gaccha, did not. Founded by the mid-15th-century layman Lonka Shah, the Lonka Gaccha denied the scriptural warranty of image worship and in the 17th century emerged as the non-image-worshiping Sthanakavasi sect. At the end of the 18th century, the Sthanakavasi underwent a schism when Acarya Bhikshu founded the Terapanthi ("Following the 13 Tenets") sect, which claims to have avoided heresy and laxity throughout its history by investing authority in a single teacher.

In the south, Digambara Jainism, for all its prominence in aristocratic circles, was attacked by Hindu devotional movements that arose in Tamil Nadu as early as the 6th century. One of the most vigorous of these Hindu movements was that of the Lingayats, or Virashaivas, which appeared in full force in the 12th century in northern Karnataka, a stronghold of Digambara Jainism. The Lingayats gained royal support, and many Jains themselves converted to the Lingayat religion in the ensuing centuries. With the advent of the Vijayanagar empire in the 14th century, the Digambara Jains lost much of their royal support and survived only in peripheral areas of the southwest and in pockets of the north.

As with the Shvetambaras, the Digambara laity were among the most strident critics of their community's deteriorating situation. The most significant Digambara reform movement occurred in the early 17th century, led by the layman and poet Banarsidas. This movement stressed the mystical elements of the Jain path and attacked what it saw as the emptiness of Digambara temple ritual and the profligacy of the community's clerical leaders.

RECENT HISTORY

By the middle of the 19th century, image-worshiping Shvetambara monks had virtually disappeared, and control of temples and ritual passed into the hands of quasi-monastic clerics known as yati. Monastic life, however, experienced a revival under the auspices of charismatic monks such as Atmaramji (1837-96), and the number of Shvetambara image-worshiping renunciants grew to approximately 1,500 monks and 4,500 nuns in the 20th century. The Tapa Gaccha is the largest subsect; the non-image-worshiping Shvetambara sects (the Sthanakavasis and Terapanthis) are smaller in number. The Digambara monastic community also experienced a revival of its ideals in the early 20th century with the ascendence of the great monk Acarya Shantisagar, from whom virtually all the 120 or so contemporary Digambara monks claim lineal descent.

In modern times the Shvetambara and Digambara communities in India have devoted much energy to preserving temples and publishing their religious texts. The Jains also have been involved in general welfare work, such as drought relief in Gujarat in the 1980s, support for Jain widows and the poor, and, as part of their philosophy of nonviolence and vegetarianism, maintaining shelters to save old animals from slaughter.

During the 20th century, Jainism evolved into a worldwide faith. As a result of age-old trading links, many Jains from western India settled in eastern African countries, most notably Kenya and Uganda. Political unrest in the 1960s compelled many of them to relocate to the United Kingdom, where the first Jain temple outside India was consecrated in Leicester, and then increasingly to the United States and Canada, where they successfully assumed their traditional mercantile and professional occupations.

A desire to preserve their religious identity has led expatriate Jains to form trans-sectarian organizations such as the Jain Samaj, founded in Europe in 1970, and the Federation of Jain Associations in North America, founded in 1981. English-language publications such as Jain Digest and Jain Spirit have presented Jain ideals, such as nonviolence, vegetarianism, and, most recently, environmentalism, to members of the Jain diaspora and the wider world.

IMPORTANT FIGURES OF JAIN LEGEND

The Jains developed their own legendary history, the Deeds of the 63 Illustrious Men, which Western scholars call the Universal History. The most important figures in this history are the 24 Tirthankaras, perfected human beings who appear from time to time to preach and embody the faith.

Other important figures in the history are from the Hindu tradition, most notably Krishna-regarded by the Jains as a cousin of the 22nd Tirthankara, Arishtanemi-and the hero Rama, who is treated as a pious, nonviolent Jain. By incorporating yet redefining such important Hindu figures, the Jains were able to both remain part of and separate from the surrounding Hindu world.

DOCTRINES OF JAINISM

Even though Jain doctrine holds that no one can achieve liberation in this corrupt time, the Jain religious goal is the complete perfection and purification of the soul. This, they believe, occurs only when the soul is in a state of eternal liberation from corporeal bodies. Liberation of the soul is impeded by the accumulation of karmans, bits of material, generated by a person's actions, that attach themselves to the soul and consequently bind it to physical bodies through many births.

This has the effect of thwarting the full self-realization and freedom of the soul. As a result, Jain renunciants do not seek immediate enlightenment; instead, through disciplined and meritorious practice of nonviolence, they pursue a human rebirth that will bring them nearer to that state. To understand how the Jains address this problem, it is first necessary to consider the Jain conception of reality.

CONCLUSION

Buddhism over Jainism Hinduism offers little hope for salvation. Although salvation is possible in Hinduism, the margin for error is so small, that it is almost impossible to ever be released from the wheel and achieve moksha. With that in mind the hunt for a new religion begins. The two options laid before me are Jainism and Buddhism. Both religions will be compared and a the better of the two religion will prevail. Although both religions have many followers, it is necessary when confronting an issue as large and expansive as religion beliefs to go into grave detail when examining and comparing the available options.

Jainism and Buddhism both have many great aspects that make each religion a worthy candidate. Although both religions have great aspects, one religion is clearly the winner in my heart. For many factors that will be discussed later, Buddhism is my new choice for spiritualism. Hinduism offers little hope to it's followers. It is based on a rigid caste classification system of which people are born into.

The caste system offers little to no upward mobility and an even smaller amount of hope for the people to ascent through the caste system. Hinduism relies heavily upon it's traditions and rituals as a means of worship and salvation. These duties and places in the caste system are described in detail in the law of Manu. "The Law of Manu is more explicit concerning the duties of the four varna. It specifies particular occupations for each of the four social groups, which are seen as being divinely ordained.

For the growth of the worlds, (Brahman) created Brahmanas (Brahmins or priests), Kshatriyas (warriors), Vaishyas (traders) and Shudras (manual workers) from his face, arms, thighs, and feet respectively"(Hopfe, 84). These caste assignments are non-negotiable and are engraved in the fabric of Indian culture. If a person leads an exemplary life in their given section of the caste system, the best that person has to look forward to is to be re-incarnated into a higher section of the caste system. That very rarely happens, if ever. With that in mind the search for a new religion begins. Both of the religions have great qualities that make up a desirable religion. "Both Jainism and Buddhism rejected the sacrifice system taught in the Vedas. Both taught that one achieved release from life not by offering sacrifices to the gods or by any form of worship but through accomplishments in one's own life. Both rejected the Vedas as sacred scripture, and both taught that anyone of any caste who lived properly might find release."(Hopfe, 87) Both Jainism and Buddhism taught that all forms of life were sacred and were to be loved and preserved whenever possible (ahisma). This belief contradicted the ritualistic sacrifices to the gods of Hinduism.

The most important aspect in the transition from Hinduism to either Jainism or Buddhism is the belief that salvation and release is not achieved from ritualistic practices or other forms of worship, it is achieved through personal accomplishment and hard work and dedication. Anyone who lived a good moral life and who was focused and dedicated could achieve moksha, the release from re-incarnation, regardless of caste position. Jainism and Buddhism offer hope for members of the lower castes. This is a reason for the increased popularity and the easily spread word of Buddhism and Jainism. Both religions have great aspects. The foundations of practice of the two religions are very different. Jainism is is a religion born out of suffrage. "Jainism taught that one found release from life through asceticism. The more one denied pleasures and satisfactions to the body, the more likely that person was to achieve freedom from the endless cycle of birth and rebirth."(Hopfe, 87) Jainists believe the body is evil and to deny the body to the realm of pleasure is the primary means for salvation. This is the most important aspect of Jainism and consequently, the most prominent aspect of Jainism that led me to Buddhism.

The foundation for Jainism is extreme asceticism. To deny the body of all pleasures is looked upon as a means for salvation. Asceticism for me is not a means for salvation. It was tried by Siddhartha Gautama and did not yield any benefit. The trials of Gautama will be discussed later. My own conclusion is asceticism hurts the body without yielding any spiritual benefits. Without the right frame of mind, it can be seen as just a way of torturing the body. Asceticism is not a means of salvation. It is a slow and painful way to die. The perfect life for a Jain might be to do nothing all day long while depriving the body of all pleasure. "All living beings owe their present form of existence to their own Karma; timid, wicked, suffering latent misery, they err about (in the circle of births), subject to birth, old age and death."(Hopfe, 117) Jainists believe like most other South east Asian religions that karma is the source of re-incarnation. The way to increase a chance for moksha was to decrease the negative karma. Doing as little as possible, leads to little margin for error, which in turn leads to little negative karma. "Thus, the ideal life for a Jain might simply be to do as little as possible and thereby escape karma and be freed from life."(Hopfe, 117) Jainism has some great religious beliefs attributed to the religion.

Ahisma is very important in my mind. Another belief that is held dear to my heart is the belief that anyone can achieve salvation, regardless of class or caste. A universal salvation can be achieved. A negative side of Jainism is the practice of asceticism which is so deeply entrenched in the inner workings of Jainism that it is hard for me to look past the asceticism to the lighter aspects of the religion. Buddhism is the means for salvation for me. One reason in which Buddhism appeals to me more than Jainism is, Siddhartha Gautama tried asceticism. For all intents and purposes, he was practicing an early form of Jainism. "Gautama joined five other monks and with them began a life of severe asceticism that lasted six years. The ascetic measures Gautama took were as severe as any recorded in the history of religion. According to legend, he became something of a champion ascetic."(Hopfe, 128) Gautama tortured himself for six years. His body became very frail and brittle. His health was in jeopardy. According to legend, he was so frail, he went to take a drink from the river and due to his weakened physical state, passed out face down in the river. The cold water revived him and revived his state of awareness and from that point on, Gautama was no longer an ascetic. He tried it for six years and didn't find the path to enlightenment or a release from the wheel of birth and re-birth. After he put asceticism behind him, he meditated for a period of weeks under a Bo tree until he was enlightened. Jainism believes in asceticism as a means of salvation. It did not work for Gautama.

The simple fact that the asceticism associated with Jainism did not yield salvation for Gautama is enough for me to disagree with the whole notion of asceticism. "Shortly after his Awakening, the Buddha (the Awakened One) delivered his first sermon, in which he laid out the essential framework upon which all his later teachings were based. This framework consists of the Four Noble Truths, four fundamental principles of nature (Dhamma) that emerged from the Buddha's honest and penetrating assessment of the human condition and that serve to define the entire scope of Buddhist practice. These truths are not statements of belief. Rather, they are categories by which we can frame our direct experience in a way that is conducive to Awakening"

Buddha has given instructions of how to live a good life to his followers. He asks that these truths are not beliefs. Beliefs come and go. These truths are categories in which one can receive salvation. A pathway to be freed from the wheel. All Buddhists believe in the four noble truths. "The Four Noble Truths: The truth of Dukkha (suffering, unsatisfactoriness, discontent, stress); The truth of arising of Dukkha (the cause of this dissatisfaction is craving (tanha) for sensuality, for states of becoming, and states of no becoming); The truth of the cessation of Dukkha (the relinquishment of that craving); The truth of the path which leads to the cessation of Dukkha."(Lester,25) This is a great system of beliefs. Human beings are miserable and unsatisfactory due to stress and other suffering. The cause for this dissatisfaction is craving (Tanha). We as human beings can relinquish the craving. Buddha even gives us guidelines, a path, to lead us to the cessation of all dissatisfaction in life. The eightfold path. All Buddhists believe in the four noble truths and the eightfold path. Although fundamentally, both types of Buddhism are the same, there are differences in ways of salvation and rituals performed by the two schools of thought: Therevada (teaching of elders) also known as the lesser vehicle and Mahayana (The Great Vehicle). In the Greater vehicle, Mahayana, Buddhists not only look for salvation inward, but also get help to stop Dukkha.

The practice of Yoga is one example. One contrast from Therevada and Mahayana Buddhism is "In contrast to the teachings of early Buddhism and those of the Theravada school, the Mahayanists began to teach that the Buddha was really a compassionate, eternal, and almost divine begin who came to earth in the form of a man because he loved humankind and wished to be of assistance."(Hopfe,136) This belief that Buddha was more than a man, even a demi-god is, in my opinion, contrary to Buddha's early teachings. He taught that he was just a man. And his new religion is not anything more than a pathway to find enlightenment but that every man could find enlightenment just as he did. This belief of Gautama as more than a man is clearly contradictory to his earlier work. Theravada Buddhism is the religion of choice for this scenario. It is the older, more conservative Buddhism. It's teaching are very straightforward. Look for salvation though meditation. "The teaching of the Buddha according to this school is very plain. He asks us to 'abstain from all kinds of evil, to accumulate all that is good and to purify our mind'."(www.buddhanet.net/twoschs.htm) People must find enlightenment for themselves, without relying on anything else. That is the fundamental basis for Theravada Buddhism. "We admit that in different countries there are differences with regard to the life of Buddhist monks, popular Buddhist beliefs and practices, rites and ceremonies, customs and habits. These external forms and expressions should not be confused with the essential teachings of the Buddha."(Rahula,1138) Although the external forms and expressions of Mahayana Buddhism are acceptable, it might be easy for one to confuse the rituals with the religion. Hinduism offers the common people no hope of moksha. Asceticism as proven through Gautama's six year effort, does not lead to moksha. The divisions between Mahayana Buddhism and Theravada Buddhism are subtle but noticeable in my mind. The religion of choice for all of it's positive aspects and limited negative aspects is Theravada Buddhism. It is the more conservative Buddhism that is founded on obtaining salvation through meditation and personal experiences rather than relying on others and rituals to help you obtain salvation. This is the closest to Buddha's early teachings.

CYCLE OF BIRTH

'Cycle of Birth' is a significant concept of Buddhism and Jainism. Body and life are explicated in these religions but not the soul and God.

There are differences between the political concept and the religious concept. The political concept gives rules and regulations to discipline our life in this world alone, but the religious concept talks not only about the life in this world but also about life before one's birth and the life after one's death.

Since there is no doctrine for soul and God in Buddhism and Jainism, human beings are considered equal with the plants, animals and other living beings, since they also possess life and body.

According to Jainism and Buddhism one's birth is based on the activities of his previous birth and one's actions of the present birth would lead to the next birth. A man may be born in the next birth as a plant or an animal or a bird or a fish...... since all of these are equal having life and body alone.

But according to the doctrines which believe in God and soul, man is the crown of the creation of God, and he alone has soul and all other creatures were created for the welfare of the human beings, and according to one's actions his life after death will be either in heaven or hell.

In the first century A.D. the religions that were prevalent in India were Buddhism and Jainism. The problem that the people were facing at that time was the cycle of birth, as according to Buddhism and Jainism. They were thinking of the ways and means to get out of the cycle of birth and acquire liberation.

There are regions where people do not have belief in God. It is a Herculean task to make these people believe in God in those regions. Only after making them theists only can one tell them the good news that God became a man and bore the sufferings of human beings and obtained liberation for them. When this news was preached, naturally there would have been questions, asking whether God can give liberation from their rebirth. The answer to this question is seen in Early Indian Christian literature.

Hence in the Early Indian Christianity the doctrine of cycle of birth can be seen. However, it should be understood that explanation is given according to the theistic view alone and not according to the atheistic view, and that emancipation can be obtained through God alone. A key point that should be keenly observed here is that the people who were the converts from Buddhism and Jainism into the Six-fold religion were trying to obtrude their doctrine of cycle of birth into the Six-fold religion.

Hence, the concept of cycle of birth in Buddhism and Jainism is different from the concept of cycle of birth in the Six-fold religion. If we ask the Buddhists and the Jains, whether they are cognizant of the difference between soul and life? They cannot give a clear answer since they are not cognizant of the difference between soul and life. However in the Six-fold religion the doctrine about soul and life is found. Unless one knows the difference between soul and life, one cannot understand the difference between the place of cycle of birth in Jainism and Buddhism and the place of the same concept in the Six-fold religion.

In Christianity which developed outside India, this concept of Cycle of birth and the solution cannot noticed since this concept did not exist there.

BIBLIOGRAPHY

Abe, Masao: *A Zen Life: D.T. Suzuki Remembered,* New York, Weatherhill, 1986.

Balsys, Bodo: *Ahimsa: Buddhism and the Vegetarian Ideal,* New Delhi, Munshiram Manoharlal Publications, 2004.

Batchelor, Martine and Kerry Brown: *Buddhism and Ecology,* London, Cassell, 1992.

Bhattacharya, N.N.: *Jain Philosophy, Historical Outline,* New Delhi, Munshiram Manoharlal, 1976.

Bothra, P.: *Jain Theory of Perception,* Delhi, Motilal Banarsidass, 1976.

Chayat, Roko Sherry: *Subtle Sound: The Zen Teachings of Maurine Stuart.* Boston, Shambhala, 1996.

Cooper, David E. and Joy A. Palmer: *Spirit of the Environment: Religion, Value and Environmental Concern,* New York, Routledge, 1998.

Coward, Harold: *Visions of a New Earth: Religious Perspectives on Population, Consumption, and Ecology,* Albany, State University of New York Press, 2000.

Dator, James Allen: *Soka Gakkai, Builders of the Third Civilization American and Japanese Member,* Seattle, University of Washington Press, 1969.

Davies, Shann: *Tree of Life: Buddhism and the Protection of Nature,* Hong Kong, Buddhist Perception of Nature Project, 1987.

Dresser, Marianne: *Buddhist Women on the Edge: Contemporary Perspectives from the Western Frontier,* Berkeley, Publishers Group West, 1996.

Dundas, Paul: *The Jains,* New York, Routledge, 1992.

Dwivedi, O. P.: *World Religions and the Environment*, New Delhi, Gilanjal Publishing House, 1989.

Einarsen, John: *The Sacred Mountains of Asia,* Boston, Shambhala Press, 1995.

Eppsteiner, Fred: *The Path of Compassion: Writings on Socially Engaged Buddhism,* Berkeley, Parallax Press, 1988.

Fischer, Eberhard and Jyotindra Jain: *Art and Rituals: 2500 years of Jainism in India,* New Delhi, Sterling, 1977.

Foltz, Richard: *Worldviews, Religion, and the Environment.* Belmont, Thomson/Wadsworth, 2003.

Gopalan, S.: *Outlines of Jainism*, New Delhi, Wiley Eastern, 1973.

Gosling, David L.: *Religion and Ecology in India and Southeast Asia*, London, Routledge, 2001.

Halifax, Joan: *The Fruitful Darkness: Reconnecting with the Body of the Earth,* San Francisco, HarperSanFrancisco, 1993.

Ingram, Catherine: *In the Footsteps of Gandhi: Conversations with Spiritual Social Activists,* Berkeley, Parallax Press, 1990.

Jacobsen Knut A: *Prakrti in Samkhya-Yoga: Material Principle, Religious Experience, Ethical Implications*, New York, Peter Lang Publishing, 1999.

Jain, C. R.: *Fundamentals of Jainism*, Meerut, Veer Nirvan Bharti, 1974.

Jain, J. P.: *Religion and Culture of the Jains*, New Delhi, Bharatiya Jnanpith, 1975.

Jain, K.C.: *Lord Mahavira and his Times*, Delhi, Motilal Banarsidass, 1974.

Jaini, Padmanabh: *Gender and Salvation: Jaina Debates on the Spiritual Liberation of Women,* Berkeley, University of California Press, 1991.

James, Simon P.: *Zen Buddhism and Environmental Ethics*, Aldershot, Ashgate, 2004.

Johnston, William: *Christian Zen,* New York, Harper & Row, 1971.

Jones, Ken: *Beyond Optimism: A Buddhist Political Ecology,* Oxford, Jon Carpenter, 1993.

Khoroche, Peter: *Once the Buddha Was a Monkey: Arya Sura's Jatakamala,* Chicago, University of Chicago Press, 1989.

Lalwani. K.C.: *Kalpa Sutra of Badrabahu Svami,* Delhi, Motilal Banarsidass. 1979.

Lishk, S.S.: *Jaina Astronomy (Post-Vedic Indian Astronomy): A Challenge to Western Influences,* Delhi, Arihant International, 2000.

Lodrick, Deryck O.: *Sacred Cows, Sacred Places: Origins and Survivals of Animal Homes in India,* Berkeley, University of California Press, 1981.

Loori, John Daido: *Teachings of the Insentient: Zen and the Environment,* Mt. Tremper, Dharma Communications Press, 1999.

Macy, Joanna, and Molly Young Brown: *Coming Back to Life: Practices to Reconnect Our Lives, Our World,* Gabriola Island, New Society Publishers, 1998.

Mookerjee, S.: *The Jain Philosophy of Non-absolutism, a Critical Study of Anekantavada,* Delhi, Motilal Banarsidass, 1978.

Morgante, Amy: *Buddhist Perspectives on the Earth Charter,* Cambridge, Boston Research Center for the 21st Century, 1997.

Nhat Hanh, Thich: *A Joyful Path: Community Transformation and Peace,* Berkeley, Calif.: Parallax Press, 1994.

Nhat Hanh, Thich: *Love in Action: Writings on Nonviolent Social Change,* Berkeley, Parallax Press, 1993.

O'Reilley, Mary Rose: *The Barn at the End of the World: The Apprenticeship of a Quaker, Buddhist Shepherd,* Minneapolis, Milkweed Editions, 2000.

Payutto, Prayudh: *Buddhist Economics: A Middle Way for the Marketplace*, Bangkok, Buddhadhamma Foundation, 1994.

Roy, A.K.: *History of the Jains*, New Delhi, Gitanjali Publishing House, 1984.

Ryan, P. D.: *Buddhism and the Natural World: Toward a Meaningful Myth*, Birmingham, Windhorse Publications, 1998.

Sethia, Tara: *Ahimsa, Anekanta and Jainism*, Delhi, Motilal Banarsidass, 2004.

Singhvi, L. M.: *The Jain Declaration on Nature*, London, Office of Jaina High Commissioner for India, 1990.

Sotoshu Shumucho: *International Symposium: The Future of the Earth and Zen Buddhism*, Tokyo, Sotoshu Shumucho, 1991.

Spretnak, Charlene: *States of Grace: The Recovery of Meaning in the Postmodern Age*, San Francisco, Harper San Francisco, 1991.

Suzuki, Shunryu: *Zen Mind, Beginner's Mind*, New York, Weatherhill, 1970.

Taylor, J. L.: *Forest Monks and the Nation-State: An Anthropological and Historical Study in Northeastern Thailand*, Singapore, Institute of Southeast Asian Studies, 1993.

Titmuss, Christopher: *The Green Buddha*, Devon, Insights, 1995.

Tobias, Michael: *Life Force: The World of Jainism*, Berkeley, Asian Humanities Press, 1991.

Tucker, Mary Evelyn, and John A. Grim: *Worldviews and Ecology: Religion, Philosophy, and the Environment*, Maryknoll, Orbis, 1994.

Zaveri, J.S.: *Microcosmology: Atom in the Jain Philosophy and Modern Science*, India, Jain Vishva Bharati Institute, 1991.

INDEX

□□□